P9-DMB-308

WORLD INDUSTRY STUDIES 9

Transaction costs and trade between multinational corporations

A study of offshore oil production

WORLD INDUSTRY SERIES

Edited by Professor Inigo Walter,
Graduate School of Business Administration,
New York University

POLITICS VS ECONOMICS IN WORLD STEEL TRADE
Kent Jones

ELECTRONICS AND INDUSTRIAL POLICY
The case of computer controlled lathes
Staffan Jacobsson

THE WORLD MINING INDUSTRY
Investment strategy and public policy
Raymond F. Mikesell and John W. Whitney

GLOBAL CONSTRUCTION INDUSTRY
Edited by W. Paul Strassmann and Jill Wells

MICROELECTRONICS
An industry in transition
Richard N. Langlois, Thomas A. Pugel, Carmela S. Haklisch, Richard R. Nelson and William G. Egelhoff

TRANSACTION COSTS AND TRADE BETWEEN
MULTINATIONAL CORPORATIONS
A study of offshore oil production
C. Paul Hallwood

Transaction costs and trade between multinational corporations

A study of offshore oil production

C. Paul Hallwood

Boston
UNWIN HYMAN
London   Sydney   Wellington

© C. Paul Hallwood, 1990
This book is copyright under the Berne Convention. No reproduction
without permission. All rights reserved.

Unwin Hyman Inc.
955 Massachusetts Avenue, Cambridge, MA 02139, USA

Published by the Academic Division of
Unwin Hyman Ltd
15/17 Broadwick Street, London W1V 1FP, UK

Allen & Unwin (Australia) Ltd
8 Napier Street, North Sydney, NSW 2060, Australia

Allen & Unwin (New Zealand) Ltd
in association with the Port Nicholson Press Ltd
Compusales Building, 75 Ghuznee Street, Wellington 1, New Zealand

First published in 1990

Library of Congress Cataloging in Publication Data

Hallwood, Paul.
  Transaction costs and trade between multinational corporations:
A study of offshore oil production/C. Paul Hallwood.
    p.   cm.—(World industry studies 9)
Includes bibliographical references.
ISBN 0-04-445618-2
1. Offshore oil industry. 2. Transaction costs. I. Title.
II. Series.
HD9560.5.H24   1990   90-34800
338.2'7282—dc20   CIP

British Library Cataloguing in Publication Data

A CIP catalogue record for this book is available from the British Library.

Typeset in 10 on 11 point Times by Fotographics (Bedford) Ltd
and printed in Great Britain by
Billing & Sons Ltd, London & Worcester

Contents

List of tables

List of figures

Author's preface

The organization of economic activity in the oil industry is a fascinating subject, for a number of reasons: the oil industry is one of the largest industries in the world; oil is the single largest commodity (by value) in international trade; oil production and consumption are vital to the prosperity of many nations; the oil industry's political importance is enormous; and the organizational arrangements that are found within it are varied and complex. It is this latter subject – the organization of production in the oil industry, or, more specifically, the offshore oil industry – that engages the attention of this book. Organization in the oil industry has, of course, already attracted attention (e.g. Adelman, 1972; Jacoby, 1974; Mitchell, 1976; Penrose, 1968, 1971; and Teece, 1976). This attention, however, has primarily been focused on the subject of the organization of the channels through which crude oil and petroleum products are distributed from oil production forward through several stages (transportation, refining) into retailing. Little has appeared on the matter of the organization of production in oil exploration, development and production – known collectively as 'oil gathering' – and what has appeared is rather fragmentary and unrelated to a thorough theoretical basis.

One of the most striking features of the offshore (and onshore) oil-gathering industry is that the oil companies purchase and hire on a contract basis most of the intermediate inputs necessary in oil gathering – over 90 per cent of requirements according to the estimate made in Chapter 3. Another striking feature is that offshore oil supply firms are often themselves, like the oil companies which they supply, multi-national corporations; this is especially true in those sectors that are the most closely associated with specialist oil field technology, for example drilling and associated activities at the wellhead. What is observed then is a relatively small group of firms which dominate offshore oil gathering – as leaseblock owners and operators (the oil companies) and as providers of technical services and other oil industry-specific inputs (the supply companies). Moreover, these companies are found together in many offshore oil provinces around the world. In Chapter 4 a description of the global offshore oil supply industry is provided and Chapter 6 describes its features in one of the world's major offshore oil services bases. Later, in Chapter 5, we will draw upon the theory of the multinational corporation to explain why both buyers and sellers should have internationalized themselves into a kind of symbiotic relationship.

The preference of the oil companies for vertical disintegration has also to be explained (Chapter 3), for without this the offshore oil supply firms would not exist as independently owned entities. The reasons for this preference are to be found in the set of theories that have become known as the transaction cost paradigm (described in Chapters 1 and 2, and developed further in the light of the findings in this book in Chapter 12). The transaction cost paradigm has grown from the seminal work of Coase (1937) and has been extensively further developed, in particular by Williamson (1985) but also by many other contributors as cited in the text.

In agreement with Williamson (1985) and Alchian and Woodward (1988), in fact, there are really two main branches of the transaction cost paradigm. These are the rent appropriation (or holdup) branch, which is bound up with the problem of coping with monopoly power, opportunism and bounded rationality, and the measurement cost branch, which is concerned with the cost of operating organizational and exchange arrangements. It will be seen that both of these branches of the transaction cost paradigm are needed to explain the organizational arrangements that are found in the offshore oil-gathering industry. As a very rough description of the division of labour utilized in the text, the rent appropriation branch is drafted to explain the oil companies' preference for the market over 'inhouse' provision of intermediate inputs, i.e. vertical disintegration (Chapter 3), while measurement costs are used to explain the use by the oil companies of the particular market arrangement that they have chosen to use – the invited tender-bid auction (Chapters 7, 8, 9 and 10). This characterization is rather incomplete, however, as both of the main elements of the transaction cost paradigm are used in each case.

An objective of the book is to go at least a little of the way towards integrating the largely American literature on the transaction cost paradigm with the literature on the multinational corporation, which happens to have a large British component. Until quite recently (see Teece, 1985, 1986), American transaction cost theorists, when applying transaction costs to an understanding of the multinational corporation, largely ignored the British contribution (as a prime example see Williamson, 1981); while, on the British side, there was some frustration with what they saw as the extraordinarily opaque terminology used by the Americans (see Casson, 1987, p. 5). In fact, both 'traditions' have a lot to add to each other: there is no need for transaction cost theorists to 'discover' a transaction cost theory of the multinational corporation (although they may modify it) and the theory of the multinational corporation can benefit by taking on board some of the arguments of what is the more general theory of the firm. For example, it ought to be recognized that the theory of the multinational corporation appeals mainly to the rent appropriation branch of the transaction cost paradigm when discussing the internationalization of manufacturing production, while the newer theories concerned with multinational service companies relate more closely to the measurement cost branch. It is perhaps no accident, therefore, as the offshore oil supply firms provide a mixture of both services and manufactured inputs, that both rent appropriation and measurement costs need to be drafted in order to explain organization in this complex industry.

It is also true that the existing theory of the multinational corporation cannot (or at least has not attempted to) explain certain organizational features which are used by the international oil companies and multinational offshore oil supply firms – in particular, quasi-vertical integration and tapered integration (see Chapters 3 and 12). Nor has this literature gone into much (if any) detail on the choices that must be made between the different market organizational forms which may be used (e.g. fixed prices versus procurement through sealed-bid auction) and accompanying investments in exchange arrangements which companies may make to increase the efficacy of these arrangements (such as in market survcillance – Chapter 10). Yet, factors such as these do bear on the cost of using a market and, therefore, on a firm's choice of whether to internationalize production or, somewhat less adventurously, to employ an arm's-length market to service a foreign market.

Then again, the transaction cost literature has not paid a great deal of attention to some organizational arrangements used between multinational corporations. The invited tender-bid auction is one such arrangement which is used extensively by the oil companies. It provides a fine opportunity to develop a case study of transaction costs 'in action' as it were, and the example should be of interest to specialists in both industrial organization and the economics of the multinational corporation. Chapter 7 lays out the legal and practical background and the three chapters which follow it discuss the invited tender-bid auction's most interesting economic features. Chapter 8 shows how the invited tender-bid auction relates to the adjustment of the offshore oil supply industry in a given location in the long run and how resource quasi-rents are distributed between the oil companies and offshore oil supply companies in the short run. Measurement cost aspects of the invited tender-bid auction are considered in Chapter 9, where a model of the optimum number of invited tender-bidders is developed. Chapter 10 considers the role of buyers as market-makers.

Organization in the oil-gathering industry and the activities of the multinational offshore oil supply companies are also of great interest to host country governments – a matter given attention in Chapter 11. Such is the extent of the barriers to entry into the technological core of the offshore oil supply industry (barriers which are themselves rooted in the transaction costs of gathering appropriate technological, managerial and skill-related information) that indigenous host country companies have been unable to penetrate very far into it without some sort of government assistance. Even then, success has been very limited. An array of policies have been adopted by different host country governments. These extend from the British 'open door' policy, which originally aimed for the rapid development of British offshore oil and gas resources using the technology and organizational skills of the multinational offshore oil supply industry, through various degrees of protection for domestic industry – based on appeal to infant industry arguments – as practised by Norway and France, and more strictly in Latin America and China.

On a personal note, the contributions that the following people have made in one way or another to the writing of this book must be explicitly and gratefully recognized. In alphabetical order they are: Mark Casson, Barbara Creed, Stuart Daldry, Robert Elliott, Philip Hemmings, Alexander Kemp, Richard Langlois, John Leeth, Philip Murphy, Kathy Segerson, who gave very helpful advice on some of the quantitative elements in Chapters 8 and 10, and Hector Williams.

Most of the book was written while I was a member of the Economics Department at the University of Aberdeen, Scotland. The financial contributions of Aberdeen University's Advisory Committee on Research must be recognized, for these made possible the over 250 interviews with the oil companies and the offshore oil supply firms which provided much of the empirical information used here. At present I am Professor of Economics, University of Connecticut, USA.

Woodstock, CT.
March 1990

For Barbara and Sarah

1

Introduction

This book presents an industry case study in 'transaction cost economics'. Empirical, theoretical and policy-related matters are given detailed consideration. The presentation contains an economic appraisal of a major industry and it may be seen as an exploration in the economics of the multinational corporation. As we also discuss the economics of the invited tender-bid auction system, which the oil companies use to procure inputs from the offshore oil supply firms, some of the chapters are concerned with the economics of such auctions.

The international oil industry is, in fact, made up of two quite distinct groups of firms – the oil companies and the multinational offshore oil supply firms. The oil companies create 'pools' of demand in geographically widely spread offshore oil provinces and the offshore oil supply firms supply these markets, usually through affiliates which they establish for this purpose. Much of our discussion will concern itself with the nature of this particular globalized economic relationship – a relationship which we will describe as 'symbiotic'.

We will combine 'standard' microeconomic theory with transaction cost economics in a way which, we trust, will be illuminating. In fact, we will argue that these 'schools', if we may call them such, are not so nearly different as is sometimes imagined. However, there is the distinction that the transaction cost paradigm is primarily concerned with matters relating to the choice of organizational arrangements (or 'organizational form') at the level of the individual firm. This question has been largely, though by no means entirely, overlooked in 'traditional' microeconomics, or at least it has according to Oliver Williamson, a leading transaction cost theorist. Moreover, transaction cost economics, or the strand of it that we may characterize as the 'rent appropriation approach', bases itself upon some assumptions which differ from those made in neoclassical economics. These assumptions are concerned both with agents' cognizance of their environment as well as with their behavioural motivations – these will be spelled out shortly.

The transaction cost paradigm, concerned as it is with comparative institutional arrangements, originated in the seminal work of Coase (1937) and has been further developed, particularly, by Williamson (1971, 1975, 1981, 1985), Klein, Crawford and Alchian (1978) and Barzel (1982) and by many other writers cited later in the book. These have become so influential that they have now given rise to what has been described as the 'new institutional economics' (Langlois, 1986),[1] and they have so challenged the established structure–conduct–performance models of industrial organization as to begin to push them from the pages of undergraduate textbooks (see Clark and McGuinness, 1987, for example).

A good deal of theorizing on the economics of the multinational corporation also concerns itself with choice of institutional arrangement through which a firm may gather rent on firm-specific knowledge (see, for example, Buckley and Casson, 1976; Caves, 1982; Dunning, 1977; Hennart, 1982; Hymer, 1976; McManus, 1972; Rugman, 1982; Vernon, 1966). Indeed, Williamson (1981) and Casson (1987) have commented on the broad similarities between transaction cost economics and the economics of the multinational corporation. Later we will try to exploit these similarities in our discussion of the organization of the international offshore oil supply industry.

Transaction costs: a paradigm with two blades

In a seminal paper, Coase asked 'why [does] a firm emerge at all in a specialized exchange economy?' (1937, p. 390). In a few pages he gave an answer which has sparked off a line, or rather two lines, of reasoning, which have continued on and off for more than fifty years.

Coase's answer was that:

> the main reason why it is profitable to establish a firm would seem to be that there is a cost of using the price mechanism. The most obvious cost of 'organizing' production through the price mechanism is *that of discovering what the relevant prices are.* (p. 390, emphasis added)

And he described the main 'price discovery costs' as: '*the cost of negotiating and concluding a separate contract for each exchange transaction*' (p. 390–1, emphasis added).

But Coase did not specify exactly what these costs may be or what might influence their size, though he did note that 'in certain markets, e.g., produce exchanges, a technique is devised for minimizing these contract costs; but they are not eliminated' (p. 391). This latter observation on the cost of running a market is a most interesting point, suggesting as it does that cost-economizing motives lie behind the design of market organizational forms.

What is immediately important to us is to recognize that contract negotiation costs depend positively upon (a) the pay and number of personnel engaged in contract negotiation; and (b) expectations about the potential future behaviour of the contractual partner. Point (b) arises because either of the parties to a contract may, for good reasons, desire to constrain the future behaviour of the other party.[2]

This 'cost of negotiating contracts' answer to the question 'why firms, why markets?' has, in fact, led to two separate versions of the transaction cost paradigm: one that stresses 'measurement costs' and one stressing 'rent appropriation' (the latter has also been called the 'holdup' version – Alchian and Woodward, 1988). The measurement cost approach emphasizes the *incurred* cost of executing transactions, while the rent appropriation concept refers to costs which *might* have to be borne in the event of an unforeseen contingency – especially an 'unfriendly' act on the part of the contractual partner. There is a relationship between the two versions as, in an effort to anticipate contingencies, transactors may attempt to draw up more complete contracts – so incurring increased contract negotiation costs.

The measurement cost version is the more closely associated with Coase's original insights as it stresses factors which have to do with actually incurred costs of using the price mechanism, e.g. legal costs of drawing up contracts, the cost of inspecting or monitoring goods exchanged and the cost of determining (or discovering) prices. However, largely due to Williamson (1975, 1981, 1985), Klein, Crawford and Alchian (1978), Alchian and Woodward (1988) and, in the context of the multinational corporation, Buckley and Casson (1976), it is the 'rent appropriation' branch of the transaction cost paradigm which has dominated this literature for more than two decades. As Williamson has pointed out, the combination of a potential for opportunistic behaviour (i.e. 'self-interest seeking with guile') in the future and the existence of specific assets is likely to lead arm's-length transactors to engage in protracted and expensive contract negotiation. Integration of such imperfect markets within the firm is a means of avoiding such transaction costs.[3] Demsetz (1988) is critical of the idea that the cost of drawing up contracts can be crucial in the choice between firm and market. He argues that the extra cost of drawing up a contract when opportunism is thought to be present is unlikely to amount to much. It is in agreement with this view that here 'holdup' costs are viewed probabilistically as the cost incurred if a contract fails – rather than as the actual cost of negotiating a contract.

So, for both versions of the transaction cost paradigm, the firm may replace the market as a means of economizing, but not altogether avoiding, transaction costs although the nature of these transaction costs varies widely. Measurement costs are incurred with a probability of unity when the market is used, while rent appropriation cost at the point of drawing up a contract is probabilistic in nature. Thus, at the time of integration (of the market into the firm) a firm cannot be sure that an opportunistic potentiality would in fact have been realized. Moreover, rent appropriation, when it occurs, extracts quasi-rents that would otherwise be earned by the fixed factors and this is obviously a different sort of cost from the cost of drawing up a contract.

Motivational and methodological context

The methodological context employed here is straightforward: the case study is used as a 'test' of the predictions that may be derived from the transaction cost paradigm. In particular we will investigate whether the observed organizational features of the offshore oil-gathering industry are consistent with the constraints emphasized in the transaction cost paradigm.

A justification, if one is needed, for this case study is Oliver Williamson's call for more detail in the application of (transaction cost) theory 'if the study of economic organization is to progress' (Williamson, 1985, p. 105). He has also referred to Morishima calling for economic theory to be applied to actual mechanisms in the economy (p. 386) and Loasby (1986a) has written in similar vein.[4] This book presents such an application. Furthermore, we will find that we will be able to make a small contribution to the literature on the multinational corporation; in particular, to the case of the internationalization of production of intermediate inputs.

Before going further, a word about the methodology used is necessary. Williamson has written that 'There is no single correct unit of analysis for addressing issues of economic organization' (1985, p. 104), and he cites eight different types of micro-analytical study that have been used (including the 'case study'). He also points to the common methodology in these studies:

> direct measures of transaction costs are rarely attempted. Instead, the comparative institutional issue of interest is whether transactions, which differ in their attributes, are supported by governance [i.e. organizational] structures in conformity with the predictions of the theory. (1985, p. 105)

This will be the methodology used here. The attributes of transactions made in the business of oil gathering will be described and we will see if the governance structures in which the transactions occur conform with the predictions derived from transaction cost reasoning. Special attention will be paid to the matter of the transactional efficiency (i.e. minimization of transaction costs) of the markets between the transactors. Joskow (1988) also recognizes the importance of the case study as an empirical test of the transaction cost paradigm, arguing that data collection problems are particularly difficult in this branch of industrial organization.

The most obvious task is to explain the high degree of vertical disintegration that exists at a certain juncture in the vertical production chain between the technical stages of oil exploration at the one end and the petrol or 'gas' station at the other. The explanation will be shown to accord with the economics of governance structures as hypothesized in the transaction cost paradigm. This approach accords with other industry case studies which have found support for a transaction cost explanation of vertical organization in automobile components (Monteverde and Teece, 1982), bauxite–aluminium production (Perry, 1980; Stuckey, 1983), aeroplane components (Masten, 1984), 'inhouse' sales force employment (Anderson and Schmittlein, 1984), coal production–electricity generation (Joskow, 1985) and the American automobile industry (Langlois and Robertson, 1989). Levy (1985) has also found support for the transaction cost paradigm using a cross-section analysis of sixty-nine American manufacturing firms.

Some basic concepts used in the transaction cost paradigm

As we have already said, two broad strands of the transaction cost paradigm have been identified: the rent appropriation approach and the measurement cost approach. As it happens the first of these concepts is also one of the main planks upon which the modern theory of the multinational corporation stands and we will have occasion to draw upon both approaches in some depth.

In transaction cost economics it is asserted that vertical integration is largely due to contractual incompleteness (Williamson, 1971, p. 120, and 1975, p. 95, for example; Grossman and Hart, 1986; Hart, 1988): complete contingent claims contracting – in one giant haggle before production begins – is, in practice, impossible. It is impossible because all future contingencies (together with their associated probabilities) are unknowable. This is the 'nature of the universe' and, even if knowable, could not be coped with by the limitedly rational brain of the human being (even if computer assisted). Thus, *bounded rationality* is the first cognitive assumption upon which the two strands of the transaction cost paradigm rest themselves.[5] A related concept is that of *impacted knowledge*, where the knowledge that does exist is not known to all of the transactors. We will make use of both concepts in our industry case study.

Opportunism is the key behavioural assumption lying at the heart of the rent appropriation view, but it plays little or no role in the measurement cost approach. Opportunism is defined as 'self-interest seeking with guile' (Williamson, 1985, p. 30) where a transactor may *not* go into a transaction in all good faith. Relevant information (e.g. on the true length of time that one of the parties wishes to maintain a particular exchange relation) may be withheld or falsified. At the recontracting stage, one (or both) of the transactors may reveal the truth and haggle to drive price in the desired direction, so appropriating an increased share of the rent due to the reordering of resources brought about by a given transaction.

This opportunistic behaviour would not be of great importance, however, except for the existence of *asset specificity*. This is a 'state of nature'. A durable asset (human or non-human) with few alternative uses (i.e. low transfer earnings) may have been obtained by one of the parties to a transaction in order to facilitate that particular transaction (e.g. special skills learned, special machinery installed, or relocation to a specific site undertaken). The opportunistic party may, at a later recontracting stage, attempt to appropriate the quasi-rent due to this asset for himself. (Klein, Crawford and Alchian, 1978, have dwelt on this point.)

With asset specificity, an *ex ante* competitive environment (many potential buyers and sellers) may be reduced to an *ex post* small numbers bargaining situation – where monopoly, monopsony or bilateral monopoly prevail. Williamson calls this 'the fundamental transformation' and makes it the centrepiece of his 1985 opus. The existence of any of these anti-competitive elements is likely to compromise the efficacy of market exchange (for one of the transactors at least) and the market may be superseded by vertical integration or some organizational form intermediate between the market and hierarchy such as quasi-integration or the long-term contract. Or, posted price markets could be replaced with an auction market – as has been suggested by Demsetz (1968a) in his study of franchise bidding.

Transaction costs and governance structures

Thus the main question in transaction cost economics is 'What governs the limits of the firm?' Or, where should administered, hierarchical, resource allocation end and use of the market begin? In principle, the firm could be decomposed into the smallest possible unit, which might be a separable technological unit, or, conceivably, to the level of the individual worker. If this was to be so, all economic activity would be organized through markets and hierarchical organization would be at the minimum.

To repeat, the transaction cost theory of the choice of governance structure predicts that organizational form will be determined so as to minimize the cost of organization. Transaction costs are defined as the costs of organizing business (that is, the cost of making transactions). The *ex ante* costs of carrying out a market transaction includes finding a suitable transactor and informing it of the desire to transact, negotiation costs, the costs of drawing up contracts, policing costs, and contract renewal costs. But further substantial *ex post* costs may be incurred if opportunistic behaviour by one of the transactors occurs. These *ex post* costs include haggling costs, the costs of any disputes machinery that may be used and the loss of quasi-rent on transaction-specific assets that are appropriated by the opportunistic party.

An implication that has been drawn is that the market would always be used if perfect competition (including perfect knowledge) existed, because transaction costs are assumed to be zero in that model. Recently, however, this view has been challenged by Demsetz (1988), who points out that firms may continue to exist even when the cost of market transacting is zero. He distinguishes cost of using the market (transaction cost) and cost of organization within a firm. Perfect decentralization does not eliminate organization cost, as each worker still has to organize their own activities. Then, if economies of scale to management exist, workers may combine (in a firm) even though the cost of using the market is free of cost. Notwithstanding this point, the transaction costs of using the market can be expected to rise as market imperfections grow. Market imperfections derive from two sources: government imposition and market failure. The former includes taxes on arm's-length trades, tariffs, non-tariff barriers and uncertainty as to future government policy on these matters.

Market failures, however, are the real core of the dominant branch of the transaction cost paradigm. Transactors are posited to be characterized by bounded rationality and, as we have seen, bounded rationality rules out comprehensive *ex ante* contingent contracting. This would not matter if sequential recontracting was desirable. However, recontracting is undesirable if opportunism and asset specificity go hand in hand. Asset specificity is the cause of the 'small numbers' bargaining problem as one or both of the transactors commit assets that are specific to a given transaction. That is, a transactor becomes locked into a transaction. Such a transactor fears that the quasi-rent on the specific assets will be appropriated by an opportunistic trading partner. Williamson argued that, when the transaction costs of using the (imperfect) market become greater than the costs of governance that is internal to the firm, the firm will replace the market as an organizational form for that class of transactions. Solutions to organizational failures within the corporation also favour the internalization of markets. One such development is that of transfer pricing between subsidiaries. This helps to economize on the amount of information that needs to flow (expensively) within the corporation in order for rational resource allocation to be accomplished.

The most important implication of all of this is that, when market imperfections are slight and the costs of 'inhouse' governance are significant, transactions will be organized through the market.

As will be discussed at greater length in Chapter 2, the measurement cost approach is somewhat different as it relies upon costs of measuring component parts of a transaction and/or enforcing the terms of the contract. One such component is quality. Few goods or services are entirely (or reliably) homogeneous. Because of this, transactors are aware that they might be able to appropriate for themselves more value from a given transaction than otherwise by incurring measurement costs. To use Barzel's (1982) example, buyers may sort amongst a barrel of oranges to find the ones of highest quality. Sellers too will be willing to incur sorting costs if they can sell the higher-quality oranges at a premium high enough at least to cover the sorting cost. Thus, Cheung (1983) has argued that, if sorting costs are low within the firm compared with transactions effected through a market, the comparative advantage will mitigate in favour of 'inhouse' production (i.e. the market will be superseded). However, if sorting costs are low, market transactions are favoured and the firm will be decomposed. In general, standardized goods/services have low sorting costs so they will be exchanged through markets. But non-standardized goods/services, with higher sorting costs, will be produced, and exchanged, within the firm.

In the following chapters we will find that both strands of the transaction cost paradigm need to be drawn upon to explain the organization of the offshore oil supply industry. In particular, we will see how the oil companies use the invited tender-bid auction as a means of both economizing on measurement costs and coping with potential opportunistic behaviour.

The chapters

In Chapter 2 we review at greater length the extant literature on the matter of transaction costs and choice of organizational form by transactors. The objective is both to broaden and to deepen the somewhat brief outline of the essentials of the transaction cost paradigm that we have laid out above. We will also assess the relevance of the auction theory literature to the choice of organizational form in general and in the offshore oil-gathering business in particular. It will be argued that this literature is complementary to that on transaction costs and is highly relevant to understanding the organizational forms found in this industry.

Chapter 3 has two main objectives: first, to measure the extent of vertical integration by the oil companies into the provision of inputs that they need for oil exploration, development and production; and, secondly, to establish whether the finding that the extent of vertical integration is very limited is consistent with the predictions that may be derived from the transaction cost paradigm.

Data on the extent of vertical integration were gathered for the study through a questionnaire distributed to all oil companies in the North Sea oil service base in Aberdeen, Scotland – Britain's main supply base and the largest in Europe. It was answered in face-to-face interviews by ten companies out of a total of twenty-three located in the city in 1984 – a time when this service base had reached maturity and before the steep fall in oil prices in December 1985 led to retrenchment. An 'external procurement index' (the ratio of volume of input purchased to volume used) was devised to measure the extent of vertical integration in thirteen subsectors of the offshore oil-gathering industry. The overall (weighted average) external procurement index turned out to be very high at 91.1 per cent, implying that only 8.9 per cent of input was procured 'inhouse'. This is a good deal lower than the degree of vertical integration in other industries (compare with the findings in MacDonald 1985). It is also much lower than the extent of integration by the oil companies forward from oil production through the various stages into petroleum products retailing.

It is also pointed out in Chapter 3 that in some offshore oil supply industry subsectors seller concentration is high. But the oil companies have not used this as a reason for internalizing these markets. Rather, the oil companies have adopted a market price-setting arrangement which negates the potential monopoly power that might otherwise reside with suppliers in these subsectors. Through the invited tender-bid auction the oil companies are able to create rivalry in price-setting between their suppliers.

As the oil companies rely heavily upon independent suppliers and many of these are themselves multinational corporations, Chapter 4 describes the main features of the international offshore oil supply industry. It is shown that the international offshore oil supply firms are global in their vision and in the distribution of their operations; in particular they follow the oil companies to the many offshore oil provinces located around the world.

Examination of the oil companies' strong preferences for vertical disintegration from production of the inputs provided by the offshore oil supply industry could be taken as the *raison d'être* of Chapters 5–11. But this is not narrowly interpreted as a matter concerning only the oil companies. This is because we will of necessity (due to the symbiotic relationship) have to examine the economics of the offshore oil supply industry in a good deal more detail. The globalization of the offshore oil supply industry is an important topic in its own right. This matter is taken up in Chapter 5, where the transaction cost paradigm is used further to illuminate the subject of choice of organizational form in the globalized offshore oil industry.

One of the arguments developed in Chapter 5 is that, while the literature on the multinational corporation has, of course, already embraced the transaction cost paradigm (see Casson, 1987; Rugman, 1981; or Williamson, 1981, for example), it does so in a way that does not entirely correctly emphasize the reasons for the internationalization of the leading offshore oil supply firms. The thrust of this literature is that companies 'go multinational' in order to internalize markets that are subjected to market failure characteristics. However, it is emphasized in Chapter 5 that these firms have 'gone multinational' in order to enhance the efficacy of the market between themselves and the oil companies rather than to replace a transactionally inefficient market relationship (actual or potential). The argument rests on the measurement cost advantages which (multinational) firms have created for themselves vis-à-vis potential host country rivals.

In Chapter 6, the predictions of the transaction cost paradigm are compared with the observed organizational structure of the offshore oil supply industry as found in the Aberdeen service base. A 241 firm sample survey of this industry was undertaken in Aberdeen, also in the summer of 1984, with a questionnaire answered in face-to-face interviews. This sample survey provided the data set. The relevant predictions which follow from the transaction cost paradigm are stated in Chapter 6 in the form of eight propositions, and these are compared with the data set. In each case the predictive value of the transaction cost paradigm is well supported by the observed organizational structure of the offshore oil supply industry in its major North Sea oil supply base.

We have already alluded to the central importance of the invited tender-bid auction arrangement – which has been adopted by the oil companies on a worldwide scale – to the efficacy of the transactional relationship between themselves and their suppliers. This price-formation arrangement is scrutinized in some detail in Chapters 7–9.

Chapter 7 sets out the legal and customary practices that are employed by the oil industry to effect exchange between the oil companies and the offshore oil supply firms. These practices are of interest because they represent an actual institutionalized market arrangement. The observed practices are used subsequently to frame assumptions for the models set out in Chapters 8 and 9.

In Chapter 7 the various stages of the price-bidding system used to effect nearly all non-trivial exchanges in the oil industry are described: pre-selection, pre-qualification, invitation to bid, replies by bidders and contract award. It is pointed out that the invited tender-bid system has certain peculiarities: first, prices are never published, even after an auction is over, and, secondly, the oil companies are at all times ultra-restrictive of price information flow between themselves and the offshore oil supply industry. Such an informationally restricted price-formation system might be expected to be inefficient, yet, as Chapter 8 shows, this is not necessarily the case.

Chapter 8 begins the theoretical modelling of the transactional relationship between the oil companies and their offshore oil supply industry suppliers. Supply-firm optimal bid-price and buyer probabilities of finding the lowest potential bid-price are each modelled. From these models the factors governing the distribution of natural resource rent between the oil companies and offshore oil supply firms can be appreciated, as can the dynamics of the long-run adjustment of the supply industry.

In Chapter 9 we develop a model of the optimum number of invited tender-bidders, or, simultaneously, the optimal investment in transaction costs. This model is presented because the transactional characteristics of the invited tender-bid auction as employed by the oil companies are described in it. It is also an example of the importance of measurement costs to institutional organization.

The presentation of this model is followed, in Chapter 10, by a discussion of the factors which drive the oil companies to select the invited tender-bid auction market arrangement, rather than some alternative such as search-shopping, as the preferred means of acquiring inputs from their suppliers. Related to this we develop the concept of market *surveillance* and show how it relates to transaction cost considerations. The subject of subcontracting is also briefly discussed.

Chapter 11 assesses the problems that host country indigenous enterprises face in penetrating into the core of the globalized offshore oil supply industry. This assessment, within the context of the transaction cost paradigm, enriches somewhat the more traditional discussion of 'barriers to entry' and further emphasizes the difficulties of establishing a local presence in one of the world's most globalized of industries. Policies of several host country governments towards the offshore oil supply industry are discussed at greater or lesser length and the differences between them are stressed. Successive British governments have adopted the least protectionist of policies towards the indigenous offshore oil supply industry and they have emphasized the speedy development of British offshore oil and gas resources under the leadership of the multinational offshore supplies corporations. Most other governments, however, have appealed in one way or another to the infant industry argument for protection and have given indigenous enterprise more or less shelter from international competition. In Europe, the Norwegians and, especially, the French have been protectionist minded. Latin American countries have adopted the most thoroughly protectionist stance in favour of indigenous enterprise but they have continued to operate within the orbit of the international oil industry. Only recently China has joined this orbit.

Finally, Chapter 12 draws much of the earlier discussion together in order to reconsider the importance of asset specificity to the choice of organizational form. Williamson (1985) has laid great emphasis on asset specificity as *the* major argument in the choice of organizational form. However, it is concluded in Chapter 12 that this is an overly one-dimensional view, as both product idiosyncrasy and the dynamic development of production processes need also to be emphasized as arguments in the choice of organizational form. Product idiosyncrasy is one determinant of the measurement cost of using a market and, for given high levels of asset specificity, idiosyncratic goods are more likely to be procured through a (auction) market while standardized goods are produced 'inhouse' or procured through fixed-price markets.

Attention turns first to a deeper consideration of the concept of measurement costs and its relevance to the choice of governance structures. Some attention is also given to the matter of *market* organizational forms (as opposed to the firm *versus* market consideration). In pursuing this we will have occasion to consider some aspects of the literature on auction theory.

Notes

1 Langlois has discussed the origins of the new institutional economics. He wrote: 'The skein of ideas I will be concerned with comprises . . . a number of identifiable strands. Principal among these, in my view, would be the evolutionary theory of Nelson and Winter . . . and other work influenced by Joseph Schumpeter . . .; the modern Austrian school (Kirzner) . . ., especially as influenced by the work of F. A. Hayek . . .; the transaction cost economics of Oliver Williamson . . .; and certain aspects of the property rights literature inspired by Ronald Coase . . . There are other affinities and sources of influence, notably Herbert Simon . . . and the behaviouralist school' (1986, p. 1).

2 In fact, one of Coase's principal arguments was that desired behaviour in the future
   was a factor in contract design. His example is of the wage contract. An employer–
   employee authority relationship comes into existence because, at the time of purchase
   (contract signing), the buyer may not know in advance exactly what work it wishes
   the employee to perform. Coase wrote that: 'A firm is likely therefore to emerge in
   those cases where a very short term contract would be unsatisfactory' for then, under
   the wage contract, desired behaviour can be directed by the employer.

3 The statement quoted in note 2 in fact does not establish that Coase clearly saw the
   implication of his argument for a holdup version of the transaction cost paradigm. He
   went on to argue that '[Desired future behaviour] is obviously of more importance in
   the case of services – labour – than in the case of buying commodities. In the case of
   commodities the main items can be stated in advance and the details which will be
   decided later will be of minor significance' (1937, p. 392). This latter point would seem
   to deny the holdup version's case for vertical integration.

4 Loasby (1986a) lamented the dominance of abstract economic theory as follows: 'the
   opportunity costs for the science of economics of this revealed preference of its most
   eminent theorists are beginning to be recognised: the concentration . . . on
   equilibrium states at the expense of adjustment processes, and the assumed
   irrelevance of institutions have simply excluded a whole range of questions' (p. 156).

5 Williamson recognizes his debt to Simon (1957), who was the first systematically to
   develop the idea of bounded rationality.

2

Measurement costs, auctions and the process of price formation

In Chapter 1 it was pointed out that there are two aspects to the transaction cost paradigm – those of rent appropriation and of measurement costs – and the essentials of the former were set out. As both versions of the transaction cost paradigm will be used to explain governance in the offshore oil-gathering business, in the first three sections of this chapter attention is focused on measurement costs.

However, while it is true that the transaction cost paradigm has, in the last two decades, made great strides in developing a theory of institutional choice, it has not fully embraced some issues which have been raised in the literature on auction theory – for example, different types of flexible price *markets* may allocate 'surpluses' (producers' and consumers') between transactors in different proportions. As the choice to be made between *market* organizational forms is also relevant to the explanation of governance arrangements in the offshore oil-gathering industry, some attention will be paid to it in this chapter.

Thus, in the section on the process of price formation and the sections that follow it, the issue of the choice of organizational form is extended to incorporate some relevant aspects of auction theory. The main argument is that the transaction cost literature, while exploring the question of firm *versus* market, has given less attention (though by no means none – see the papers by Demsetz, 1968a; Goldberg, 1977; and Williamson, 1976) to the matter of choice between different market (flexible or otherwise) organizational forms.

Certainly, Barzel (1982) considers the use of *market-accompanying* arrangements such as trade marks and product warranties as a means of reducing market-related transaction costs. Also Casson (1982b, Chapter 9) has developed a theory which could be extended to model the choices which may be made between market organizational forms that are different in their measurement cost characteristics. However, it is the auction literature that has, perhaps, done most to develop a theory of the determinants of choice between different types of flexible price markets. Under certain assumptions there is a revenue equivalence between different types of (auction) market,[1] so there is no reason for a transactor to prefer one market over another. However, risk aversion may affect a transactor's choice between market types, as may also a market's price convergence (to equilibrium) characteristics. Even so, the auction literature has not as yet completed a general theory of choice of market organizational form, for it has only begun to develop a theory of the auction with positive transaction costs.[2] It is left to Chapter 9 to discuss the subject of an oil company's measurement cost optimization problem within their chosen market organizational form. There we make a modest contribution to the theory of the first-price sealed-bid auction with positive measurement costs.

The contribution of Demsetz (1968a) also must not be overlooked because he pointed to the circumstances in which an auction market might be preferable to a posted price market. When posted prices might also be monopoly prices, a procurement auction may be a beneficial replacement. So, it will also be pointed out later in this chapter, commitment to an auction by one of the transactors is a means of diffusing potential opportunistic – rent-appropriating – behaviour by the other party to the transaction. Thus, a high transaction cost (measurement or rent appropriation cost), fixed-price market may be efficiently replaced by an auction market arrangement rather than by internalization within the firm. However, within the more limited immediate context, it is argued that it is the use of an auction – the invited tender-bid auction (a variety of first-price sealed-bid auction) – by the oil companies that largely diffuses suppliers' potential for rent appropriation even though, in some subsectors, supplier concentration is high.

Attention turns first to a discussion of measurement costs.

Measurement costs and the transaction cost paradigm

Taking off from Coase's seminal ideas, several authors have contributed further to the development of the measurement cost theory of the choice of organizational form. These include Barzel (1982), Casson (1982a), Cheung (1983), McManus (1972, 1975), and Ouchi (1980).

These authors point to the importance of measurement costs in the choice of organizational form by economic agents and they identify the factors that lead to the existence of positive measurement costs. Ouchi (1980) states that 'a transaction cost is any activity which is engaged in to satisfy each party to an exchange that the value given and received is in accord with his or her expectations' (p. 130). Amongst these factors may be listed the cost of evaluating or monitoring the quantity or quality of a good or service exchanged. For instance, there is the cost of weighing quantities or inspecting goods prior to purchase. McManus (1975) points out that, as transactors may 'cheat' in an exchange, use of the price mechanism is not without cost: 'measurement costs will be incurred in order to *enforce* a bargain' (p. 337) – 'The enforcement cost associated with a price constraint on behaviour is the expenditure of resources for the measurement of the activity for which one is paying' (McManus, 1975, p. 337). Similarly, Ouchi (1980) writes: 'Transactions costs arise principally when it is difficult to determine the value of the goods or service' (p. 130).

Barzel (1982) argues that 'virtually no commodity offered for sale is free from the cost of measuring its attributes' (p. 28). His analysis differs from McManus's in that 'costly transfers of wealth' need arise not from 'cheating' but from random variation in a product's/service's attributes around expected values (i.e. of quality or quantity).[3] Cheung (1983) put forward several reasons to explain how the substitution of the market by the firm can serve to reduce measurement costs. First, the firm economizes on the number of transactions requiring prices to be affixed to them. Secondly, information costs of 'knowing a product' are reduced when a 'final' product is purchased: 'It simply costs too much to learn about everything in every commodity' (p. 7). Thirdly, if it is very expensive to define in advance exactly what is wanted, an employment contract may come to replace market exchange (piece work).[4] Finally, drafting in an idea from team theory (Alchian and Demsetz, 1972), the cost of separating the contributions to total product of individual workers may be prohibitive, so direction by authority (within the firm) may replace payment by results through the market (this is the case where the incentive–reward mechanism of the market fails to operate). Ouchi also stresses this point.

Casson (1982a) includes measurement cost amongst transaction costs and says that the former arises 'from the need to monitor for product quality' (p. 25). Recognition of the importance of measurement costs to the choice of organizational form by Casson is particularly interesting because, together with Buckley, he originated what we may now call the 'rent appropriation' version of the theory of the multinational corporation (Buckley and Casson, 1976). In that theory, arm's-length markets are imperfect and subject to rent appropriation problems – owing to the possible existence of opportunism, bilateral monopoly, lack of suitable contingent claims or futures contracts – while impacted knowledge may also reduce the efficacy of market exchange.

What is especially significant about Casson's (1982a) paper is that it recognizes that the measurement cost and rent appropriation versions of the transaction cost paradigm are relevant in explaining the existence of multinational corporations. This is precisely the thesis developed in the following chapters, where the organization of the internationalized offshore oil supply industry and its interrelationship with the international oil companies is explained using both versions of the transaction cost paradigm.

Product idiosyncrasy and the cost of affixing prices

It is a part of the transaction cost paradigm that positive measurement costs arise in order to enforce a bargain. And it is the existence of ignorance on the part of either the potential buyers and/or sellers as to the true value of a given item to be exchanged that lies at the root of the problem. As has already been pointed out, random variations and/or fear of cheating are reasons enough to incur measurement costs even for the simplest of goods. Product idiosyncrasy further increases the need for and cost of measurement.

Product idiosyncrasy ('multi-attribute' or 'variable multi-attribute' goods or services) has the effect of complicating the process of selection and so raising measurement costs. With standardized goods, or, more precisely, if buyers regard the goods to be standardized, a buyer's measurement costs will be zero. Barzel (1982) points out that it is in sellers' interests to sort a multi-attribute commodity (e.g. oranges which vary in size, colour, taste and juiciness) into standardized 'baskets' in order to eliminate 'multiple-sorting' and so minimize the buyers' gross purchase prices. Barzel argues that competition leads sellers to sort and buyers to avoid direct sorting costs (some sorting costs will be incident upon the buyer if passed on by the seller). To be more explicit: if items for sale are not sorted by sellers then buyers, in seeking value, will sort for themselves. Any item put up for sale may well be inspected more than once and, as sorting costs are positive, gross price paid by a buyer (but not received by the seller) will be increased. It is clearly in a seller's interests to sort to the point where it is not worthwhile the buyer sorting any more: this is because efficient sorting by the seller will remove the incentive for double, triple, etc., sorting by buyers and so reduce the gross price paid and raise sales.

However, sorting by sellers is not always feasible. This would be the case when a good or service is made to order, because no items will be brought into existence until an order has been placed and only one unit may be produced. Then it is the buyer who sorts between potential suppliers prior to purchase and it is the buyer who incurs *direct* sorting costs in the process of choosing a suitable supplier. This, in fact, is the case with the oil companies when they make purchases from the offshore oil supply industry. We will show later why such a circumstance has arisen, and how the oil companies cope with the problems of minimizing sorting costs through their use of the invited tender-bid auction. The selection by the oil companies of such an organizational form (the market) is then to be understood in terms of (measurement) transaction cost minimization. This type of auction also has advantages for the oil companies as buyers in reducing the possibility of rent appropriation by monopolistic or (potentially) collusive suppliers.

There is also a type of measurement cost which has not been much emphasized in the transaction cost literature, yet it can be of importance and it was referred to by Coase when he mentioned the cost of running produce exchanges (Coase, 1937, p. 391). This is *the cost of affixing prices* to the quantities to be exchanged. Clearly prices are agreed upon before an exchange takes place, or at least this is nearly always the case. Examples of the cost of affixing prices to quantities are fees paid to market-makers such as an auctioneers and brokers, and dealers are usually compensated by a bid-offer spread (Demsetz, 1968b). Another example of the cost of stating prices is that it can be expensive simply to perform the necessary actuarial or cost accountancy calculations needed to name a price. This would be true when it is necessary to employ the services of an estimator, quantity surveyor or cost accountant to size up a job or to give a valuation.

These estimation costs will be more significant (have a larger bearing on the final price) for goods that are exchanged only once (or infrequently), as the full cost of price estimation will have to be recovered on that single transaction. Or, the cost of price estimates made for 'hoped for' exchanges (e.g. as when competitively bidding for a contract) which turn out *not* to take place may be loaded onto a subsequent exchange which does take place. (Goldberg, 1977, and French and McCormick, 1984, also make this point.)

Clearly, average price-estimation costs decline if a firm sells many units of a standardized good. This is an advantage of standardization. Non-standardized goods or services suffer from a smaller number of exchanges – maybe only one. A variable multi-attribute good may be represented as a matrix of what may be regarded as different goods, each one of which requiring to have a price (at expense) affixed to it. For example, many goods and services used in the oil-gathering business are variable multi-attribute: oil rigs come in many specifications, as do geological and geophysical engineering services. And an item of a given specification may be exchanged only once, or it may be exchanged a few times but under varying market conditions so that the seller would anyway want to reassess price.

Optimum expenditure on measurement costs

Coase provided a clear and often-quoted definition of the rule for optimum expenditure on measurement costs:

> a firm will tend to expand until the costs of organizing an extra transaction within the firm become equal to the costs of carrying out the same transaction by means of an exchange on the open market . . . (1937, p. 395)

This is a general statement implying that optimization occurs where marginal costs and benefits of market exchange are equal. McManus (1975) builds an explicitly deterministic model where expenditure on measurement costs is optimized. He notes that optimization can be set in a probabilistic model. Casson (1982b) correctly asserts that risk neutrality is needed if an optimization condition such as the above is to be true; after all, the use of a market compared with inhouse production may have different uncertainty characteristics. Indeed, risk neutrality is a pretty well universal assumption in the measurement cost literature. This assumption is restrictive but it does not really reduce the generality of the arguments: by employing it, it is shown that the firm and other organizational forms can come into existence without needing to invoke risk aversion – as was done by another influential author who provided a (rival) theory of why firms exist in market economies (Knight, 1957). Indeed, Mead (1978) argues that in the downstream petroleum industry (from crude oil production to marketing) risk aversion is a factor in the oil companies' propensity to practise vertical integration and that capital costs are reduced as a result.

Measurement error

Since marginal measurement costs can be assumed to remain positive at the point of optimum expenditure on measurement, the marginal benefit of extra expenditure on measurement will also be positive. As Barzel (1982) put it: 'errors of measurement are too costly to eliminate entirely' (p. 48). Also Stigler (1961) showed that in a posted-price search model the existence of positive search costs would truncate a buyer's search, on average, before the lowest posted price was revealed. These observations lead to the argument that suppliers will be under competitive pressure to find means of compensating buyers for measurement errors which may be made (e.g. buying an item that does not work properly, or, more generally, when price paid is greater than value received).

This competition to reduce the negative consequences – for buyers – of the measurement errors explains the existence, according to Barzel, of product warranties (guarantees), brand names (trade marks) and share contracts (e.g. royalty agreements). The existence of high measurement costs also explains suppression of information – to discourage measurement (e.g. the de Beers' diamond auctions) and vertical integration (especially when it is measurement cost-efficient to use 'quantity of inputs' as a proxy measure for 'value of output').

With a brand name a buyer can avoid costly measurement if he/she, from past experience of consuming the good/service or on the basis of a creditable reputation, is willing to take it on trust that the next purchase will be up to the standards of the previous purchases. Barzel (1982) and Casson (1982a) independently had similar insights into the importance of brand naming. Casson relates the concept directly to the theory of the multinational corporation, explaining the proliferation of multinational hotels (e.g. Hilton, Sheraton). In his view multinational hotels have one important competitive advantage over local rivals: the measurement cost saving to international travellers due to an inter-nationally standardized brand name. Thus, 'the buyer's knowledge of the seller's personal characteristics acts as a surrogate for knowledge of product quality. Typically this confidence is built up by the successful repetition of trades' (Casson, 1982a, p. 41).

The important factor here is that the 'repetition of trades' at one location gives the brand name company a (measurement cost) competitive advantage over potential rivals at other locations – assuming that the customers are themselves geographically mobile, which is the case in the international hotel business. Brand naming may be taken as a barrier to entry not only for potential new rivals in the industry, but also for *existing* rivals located in the new location of the brand name supplier.

These observations are of relevance to some organizational issues in the international offshore oil supply industry, which are discussed further in Chapter 5, and they also help to explain the difficulties which host country firms often have in creating their own presence in the internationally mobile core of that industry (Chapter 11).

As far as vertical integration and measurement costs are concerned, Cheung (1983) is explicit: as measurement costs rise, as a consequence of attempting to reduce measurement error, the incentive for vertical integration will increase. For example, Cheung argues that, when the quality or value of a worker's output is difficult to assess, an employment contract is likely to predominate. But when the worker's output is easily assessed (i.e. at low measurement cost), piece work arrangements are likely to predominate and these activities will be decomposed (i.e. dis-integrated) from the firm. Barzel (1982) made essentially the same point.

We will see that the oil companies and offshore oil supply firms seem to incur high measurement costs because of the peculiarities of the exchanges that occur between them: the products/services exchanged are often idiosyncratic, and the cost of affixing prices may also be high. Moreover, potential bilateral monopoly problems exist in some sub-markets of the offshore oil supply industry. Yet, despite these high measurement costs, the oil companies are highly vertically *dis*integrated from the offshore oil supply industry. Why should this be so, and could it be a counter-example to the Barzel–Cheung arguments on the measurement cost/vertical integration relationship? In fact, not. Once we take account of the peculiarities of the international oil-gathering business, backward integration into all facets of oil exploration, development and production would be very costly to organize.

Process of price formation

In many of the papers cited earlier it was assumed, implicitly or explicitly, both that suppliers determine prices and that prices are fixed prices. Yet, it is an obvious extension of the measurement cost literature to appeal to measurement cost economizing to endogenize the choice of price-formation process. This has been done to some extent by Demsetz (1968a), Goldberg (1977) and Williamson (1976), who considered the comparative merits of the auction versus negotiated prices accompanied with the expense of subsequent (public utility) regulation. But a complete answer has not yet been found. Indeed, Shubick (1970) has identified an even broader group of methods of allocating resources, several of them lying outside of the price system – such as voting, allocation by dictatorship, force, fraud and chance. Presumably, the choice between these could be endogenized and measurement costs would be *one* of the determining variables.

Restricting ourselves to the market allocation process, there is the matter of which party to an exchange determines the choice of the institutional arrangements through which an exchange takes place. To illustrate, it is the seller who determines that admission tickets to the American Super Bowl or the English FA Cup Final are sold at fixed prices rather than, say, through some auction-type arrangement; it is the oil companies, as buyers, that have independently chosen to use the invited tender-bid auction to procure intermediate good inputs; and it is the United States Treasury, as borrower, which has decided to use the discriminate sealed-bid auction through which to sell Treasury Bills. In all three of these cases the parties on the other side of the market are passive in the choice of the specific market organizational forms.

Secondly, choices have to be made between the many types of market arrangements that exist or could be brought into existence, including: suppliers determine fixed selling prices; buyers set fixed offer prices; face-to-face negotiation; 'haggling' (a brief 'negotiation'), and a rich variety of competitive auction arrangements.

What the auction literature has to say about price formation

In their reviews of the auction theory literature, McAfee and McMillan (1987) and Milgrom (1989) recognize that the study of auctions provides one way of approaching the question of price formation. It is asked why auctions are used rather than some other market organizational form such as posted pricing. McAfee and McMillan provide two complementary answers: (a) irrevocable commitment to an auction has advantages in the price-determination process; and (b) the auction is a means of finding prices for goods that lack standardized values – although the term 'standardized value' is not defined.

Taking the first of these. In most auctions there is one seller and only a few buyers, so perfect competition does not exist. Indeed, in a monopoly–monopsony or oligopsony situation the price outcome is often indeterminate – an observation developed by Milgrom (1989) to suggest that a seller (or, more generally, the agent choosing the market organizational form) can expect to obtain a better price in an auction than in face-to-face negotiation. By committing itself to the rules of an auction, the seller can induce the buyers to act competitively: bidding up to its own individual private valuation is the only means of obtaining the item being sold. So long as the bidders are convinced that the seller will not renege after the auction is complete – e.g. by entering into further negotiations over price with the highest bidder – they know that they must compete in this way. The rules of the auction induce competition. Schelling (1956, 1960) is the standard reference for this argument on the importance of commitment by one party inducing desirable behaviour in the other parties.

With regard to the second reason for choosing the auction – the absence of standardized values – the answers given in the auction literature are at best incomplete, for this literature does not identify the elements that determine why some goods are sold at fixed prices and others through an auction. Indeed, in Milgrom's (1989) review of auction theory it is readily admitted that 'the circumstances . . . that make one or other trading institution most appropriate . . . [have] received less attention from researchers [and only] informed guesses are possible' (p. 18). Thus, we may ask, what determines the 'standard value' of any good or service?

It is surely the case that no good has a standard value in the sense that its price is fixed for all time, or somehow or other determined without reference to markets. Indeed, that part of the body of economics now known as microeconomics was also known as 'value theory'. And the value of any exchange is determined through the process of interaction in the market. Only in a static world – one where the supply and demand functions are frozen in position over time – would relative values never change. Certainly, in history, certain precious metals have been used as standards of value, but that role was made possible by a monetary authority's willingness to buy and sell the standard of value at predetermined monetary prices. It might be argued that the posted (i.e. fixed) pricing of many goods by sellers (or buyers in some cases) is similar in that the seller agrees to sell at a predetermined fixed price. But this would be a wrong analogy because it begs the question of how the seller came to determine that particular fixed price or, indeed, why the seller chose to sell through a fixed-price market rather than through some other *market* organizational form.

Thus, in a world where the values of all goods have to be discovered – or determined – by some means, we can ask what determines the choice of 'discovery process'. Or, what determines the choice of *market* organizational form.

There would seem to be four broad classes of reasons on which to base a rational choice of *market* organizational form:

(1)   measurement cost economizing;
(2)   rent appropriation cost economizing;
(3)   price advantage; and
(4)   price convergence.

First, as already discussed at some length earlier in this chapter, since different organizational forms are likely to have different measurement costs, for reasons of measurement cost economizing one organizational form may be preferred to another. The measurement cost literature establishes that measurement cost economizing may be crucial in the choice between *firm* and *market* and in the selection of certain market-accompanying devices (e.g. trade marks and warranties). If markets differ in their measurement cost characteristics, then it is reasonable to expect that measurement cost will be a factor in the choice between market organizational forms. For example, the owner of an antique chair may choose to sell it at an advertised fixed price; or to a dealer at a negotiated (or haggled) price; or through an auction. If the expected prices do not differ, then the choice between them will be based upon the relative measurement costs – the fees charged by the advertiser or the auctioneer and the other costs associated with the time and effort sunk into the transaction.

Secondly, the choice of price-determination process may be made for rent appropriation economizing reasons. This particular argument was developed in Chapter 1 and the gist of it is straightforward enough: internalization of exchange and the use of transfer prices (which may not be related to any market price) are preferred when it is thought to be to a transactor's advantage in avoiding rent appropriation. This may be the case when asset specificity is combined with a potential for opportunism.

Thirdly, one market may be chosen rather than another because it is thought that a more advantageous price will be obtained in it. The main thrust of the auction literature is the pursuit of questions concerned with the allocation of surpluses (consumers' and/or producers') between the transactors. It has been established in this literature that under certain standard assumptions, there is an equivalence of auctions (Myerson, 1981; Riley and Samuelson, 1981). In other words, under these assumptions, it does not matter which auction type a transactor chooses, the price outcome will be the same. But this strong conclusion is shown to be untrue if one or more of the standard assumptions is changed (see McAfee and McMillan, 1987, for a discussion of this).

The fourth possible factor that may determine the choice of organizational form is the rapidity at which exchange prices reach the market-clearing level. Risk-averse transactors will prefer organizational forms that yield lower, rather than higher, variances of market prices around the equilibrium level. Much of the literature on the microstructure of securities markets concerns itself with the analysis of the price-determination characteristics of these markets (see Cohen, Maier, Schwartz and Whitcomb, 1986). The experimental approach to economics has also made a contribution to this line of investigation (see, especially, Smith, 1976).

Price advantage and choice of auction
The standard assumptions of auction theory referred to earlier are, according to McAfee and McMillan (1987), zero transaction costs, risk neutrality, payments equal to the bid, and bidders symmetric in their possession of information (i.e. they know their own private valuations of the item to be bid for). The revenue equivalence of auctions breaks down if these assumptions are altered.

Consider first the introduction of risk aversion. Suppose that bidders are risk averse in the reward that they gain from winning an auction – profits in the case of winning a procurement contract. It turns out that the sealed-bid auction is the most favourable for the seller when the bidders are risk averse (Maskin and Riley, 1984; Milgrom and Weber,

1982). The reason is that, in the sealed-bid auction, by reducing information flow on the other bidders' valuations, uncertainty is introduced for each bidder, which would not be present in an ascending open outcry auction where each bidder reveals his/her valuation during the bidding process. Now, with risk aversion in the sealed-bid procurement auction, a bidder can trade lower profit for greater certainty and does so by reducing the tender-bid price. The buyer, of course, gains from this through all-around price reductions.

In a procurement auction the buyer may also increase a bidder's uncertainty as to the outcome of the auction by preventing it from knowing how many rivals there are bidding for the contract. Again, bidders are induced to reduce bid-prices and trade lower profits for increased certainty of outcome.

Non-publication or broadcasting of price-bids during and after a procurement auction may also be to a buyer's advantage when collusion is possible between the bidders. A feature of the offshore oil-gathering industry in an oil service base is that the same group of bidders compete with each other time and again. In a repeated oligopoly, game collusion between the bidders can be maintained over time if retaliation will be provoked when one of the bidders breaks the collusive agreement. But how can the collusive bidders be sure that one of the bidders has broken the agreement? It is relatively easy to deduce this if prices are published, but much more difficult if bid-price information is unobservable. Thus, a sealed-bid auction may be used to spoil collusion (Alchian, 1977; Isaac and Walker, 1985; Robinson, 1985; Stigler, 1964).

Price convergence and choice of auction
The fourth class of reasons upon which to base a choice of market organizational forms is the rate of price convergence to the equilibrium price. The experimental approach to the economics of institutions has thrown up an interesting observation: that some market organizational forms converge to the market-clearing equilibrium price faster than others (Smith, 1976). Fast convergence of price may be a reason for choosing one market type over another. This would be the case when the transactors wish to make decisions on the basis of equilibrium prices, especially when transactors are risk averse. Greater variability of price around the equilibrium value increases the variability of consumers' and producers' surpluses and only risk-neutral transactors would be indifferent to price variability around the expected equilibrium value (Edwards and Hallwood, 1980). Risk-averse transactors will prefer, *ceteris paribus*, the market arrangement that most quickly stabilizes price on the equilibrium value.

Indeed, the 'quality' of a market is often judged according to its depth, breadth and resilience. A deep and broad market has a large number of transactors willing to trade near the current market price and it is resilient if buy/sell orders pour in when prices move slightly; the opposite would be true in a thin market. In a resilient market, however, price variability will tend to be low. It is the desirability of this characteristic – especially to risk-averse transactors – that induces market-makers in commodity and security markets to create standardized contracts which attract large numbers of transactors. Moreover, the existence of residual price variability (i.e. fluctuating equilibrium prices) has led to the development of futures and options markets so that transactors can hedge their positions. Risk aversion, as well as transaction costs, must also be recognized as a factor in the choice of organizational arrangement.[6]

Conclusions

It is going to be argued in the next chapter that the oil companies are constrained – for reasons of high measurement costs – from backward integration into the inhouse provision of inputs into offshore oil exploration, development and production. They are then faced with the problem of choosing a suitable market type through which to procure the necessary inputs from arm's-length suppliers. Following from the discussion of this chapter we may expect that the oil companies will be concerned with the comparative measurement cost, rent appropriation cost, price advantage and price convergence characteristics of the market types over which their choice may range. In fact – as already mentioned – most inputs are acquired at prices determined in a competitive auction, and the choice of this would appear to rest on its ability to defuse the potential in some subsectors of the offshore oil supply industry for rent appropriation by oligopolistic suppliers. Moreover, as was pointed out earlier, when collusive behaviour is possible, a transactor may bind itself to the rules of an auction and so induce the other party to bid up to own-valuation (all, that is, except the winning bidder in most cases). Of course, if there is only one bidder, and that bidder knows that this is the case, it can still bid a price equivalent to the monopoly price that would anyway have been set in a posted-price market. However, even a monopolist may be induced to sell at a price below the monopoly price if it can be prevented from knowing that it is the only bidder. In fact, the oil companies will sometimes attempt to achieve just this. On occasion they will invite only one bidder for a contract, not reveal this, and operate the full rules of the auction. On other occasions, in subsectors where a single supplier is widely known to have a large technological lead (e.g. wireline services), an oil company will invite the leading company and another supplier with a lesser technology to bid and award the contract to the latter company. The oil companies see this as a means of 'creating competition': the technological monopolist is encouraged not to monopoly-price and the contract winner is given scope to improve its own technology through on-the-job practice.

The invited tender-bid auction run by the oil companies incurs measurement costs (defined in Chapter 9 as tender-bid assembly costs and tender-bid assessment costs). We will enquire into the measurement cost economizing characteristics of this auction. Finally, the price convergence (to equilibrium price) features of this market is shown to be complicated, as we need to consider not only convergence but also the definition of 'equilibrium price'. The latter changes with time as the supply industry expands or contracts in response to changes in the level of expected economic rents.

Notes

1   The English, Dutch, first-price sealed-bid and second-price sealed-bid auctions.
2   The literature on the theory of the auction is extensive. See the literature reviews by Engelbrecht-Wiggans (1980), McAfee and McMillan (1987) and Stark and Rothkopf (1979).
3   'Product information is defined as information on the levels of the attributes per unit of the commodity and on the actual amount contained in the nominal quantity. Measurements of these magnitudes are subject to error' (Barzel, 1982, p. 28).
4   Cheung's work on organizational form and piece work is an interesting extension of Coase's ideas on the nature of the employment contract.
5   Stigler commented on this with respect to the procurement auction: 'The system of sealed bids, publicly opened with full identification of each bidder's price and specifications, is the ideal instrument for the detection of price cutting . collusion will always be more effective against buyers who report correctly and fully the prices tendered to them' (1964, p. 48).
6   In financial markets such as the New York Stock Exchange and other exchanges a main objective of market design is to maximize the liquidity of the traded financial instruments (Sofianos, 1988). The components of liquidity are low transaction cost (as measured by the cost of a round trip, which depends mainly on the size of the bid-offer spread), continuity of trading through time, and trading at prices near the 'true price' (where the 'true price' may be loosely defined as the price that would be determined if all potential transactors were active, were fully informed and were rational). Compromises have, in practice, had to be made between these components. For example, when buy/sell orders do not flow at a high rate and/or evenly over time, it may not be desirable to adjust prices on a minute-by-minute basis. Thus, the London gold fixing is a discontinuous, twice-daily, event – prices being set in an auction when sufficient interest has accumulated. Even where trading normally occurs at high rates through time, such as on many stock exchanges, special institutional arrangements have to be made because market supply of and demand for a given company's shares are not balanced near the 'true price' at every instant of time. Thus, the market-maker performs more than an auctioneering function. A dealer function is also performed in order to stabilize short-term, minute-by-minute price swings: a dealer buys for or sells from its own portfolio as it 'leans against the market' and evens out price over

time. By adjusting the level and, perhaps, width of the bid-offer spread, a dealer earns profits from this activity and also prevents its own portfolio from becoming either too large or too small. However, it is also realized that when the 'true price' becomes very unpredictable (e.g. as was the case during the day of the stock market crashes of October 1987) a market-maker may prefer to withdraw from the price-making function. Such actions, especially if widespread, threaten asset liquidity and the credibility of the exchange. As exchanges are themselves, in a sense, in competition with one another for the rents to be had from market-making, the exchange's organizers have devised rules (backed up by penalties) that require market-makers to provide market continuity even when they would prefer to withdraw from doing so.

3

Vertical disintegration

This chapter discusses the issue of why the oil companies have chosen *not* to integrate vertically, at least to any great extent, into the provision of intermediate inputs supplied by the offshore oil supply industry. The reasons will be found to be consistent with the predictions derived from the transaction cost paradigm. The oil companies, certainly the so-called 'majors' such as BP, Shell and Exxon, display similar features of vertical structure which may be characterized as vertical integration through the stages of production forward from crude oil production into refining and retail marketing. However, even the giant oil companies – which are amongst the largest companies in the world – do not produce 'inhouse' much of the inputs necessary for oil exploration, development and production. That is, they tend to 'buy in' most of the services and equipment needed to discover and to gather crude oil and natural gas. As a result, an entire industry has sprung up which is geared to servicing the needs of the oil companies for intermediate inputs. This is the offshore oil supply industry (OOSI).

The oil companies and the many thousands of firms in the offshore oil supply industry coordinate their activities through market relationships. While several types of market relationship are used, the bulk of the intermediate inputs (certainly those costing more than just a few thousand pounds sterling) are acquired by the oil companies through an arrangement known as the invited tender-bid auction system. Only a fraction of inputs are acquired from suppliers at posted prices.

We begin with a discussion of vertical disintegration by the oil companies from the activities performed in the offshore oil supply industry. The chapter is divided into three sections. In the first section we measure the extent to which the oil companies are disengaged from the offshore oil supply industry. Backward vertical integration into the offshore oil supply industry is slight: the oil companies provide inhouse less than 10 per cent of the volume of inputs required.

The second section discusses the reasons why the oil companies have chosen the market over vertical integration. The efficacy of the offshore oil supply firms in meeting the needs of the oil companies is assessed against a set of eleven factors, which are used to predict whether vertical integration or market organizational arrangements are likely to be chosen.

The third section of the chapter shows that the oil companies perceive many (but not all) of the markets which they use as being, for the main part, competitive, relatively inexpensive to monitor and geographically responsive to their relocational needs and as yielding an acceptable rate of technological advance. It is also pointed out that the oil companies perceive certain constraints on their choice of organizational form which bias it in favour of the market.

Before proceeding to a discussion of these matters it is necessary to provide a brief description of the main subsectors of the offshore oil supply industry. This industry has many subsectors (listed in Table 3.2 below) and is technologically complex. Indeed, the industry's broad scope and complexity are two reasons that have discouraged the oil companies from vertically integrating into it.

Subsectors of the offshore oil supply industry
Figure 3.1 lays out the relative time-frame of the several stages of offshore production of hydrocarbons. As can be seen, the exploration phase usually lasts between two and four years and is particularly intensive in the use of technical services such as geological and geophysical engineering. In this stage, exploratory wells are drilled which may strike commercial oil reservoirs, in which case the development phase is entered into. In this phase, heavy equipment and large constructions will be installed. The development phase can last between three and five years and is followed by the production phase. Depending upon reserves and optimal rates of flow, the production phase can last up to fifty years and usually lasts at least ten years. In this last stage virtually all of the service inputs used in the earlier stages are again drawn upon, as data analysis remains as an important input and additional wells are sunk.

Thus, the offshore oil-gathering industry combines physical inputs, such as structures (platforms and rigs), tools, equipment, machinery and raw materials, together with manpower to undertake oil exploration, development and production activities. Much of the manpower is in the form of highly skilled and technically advanced consultancy services.

To facilitate discussion later in the book a brief description of the physical and service inputs into offshore oil will be given, beginning with exploration equipment.

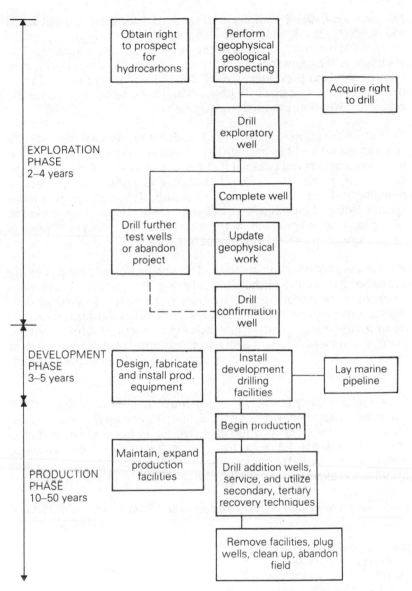

Figure 3.1 *A relative time-frame for offshore production of hydrocarbons*
Source: McDermott Inc.

Oil field exploration equipment (Standard Industrial Classification 35331, 35332, 35335, and 35336).[1] The rotary drilling rig is the primary exploration tool manufactured by the oil field machinery industry. The complete drilling package includes mast, rotary table, draw works, mud pumps, blow out preventer, swivel clutches and power units. Larger drilling rigs are equipped with derricks and hoisting equipment for the repair of down-hole production equipment.

Production machinery (SIC 35333 and 35615) is required once a commercial oil well has been drilled. Casings are set in cement in the hole with a sucker rod pump at its bottom and various types of above-surface equipment are installed including Christmas tree valves, a pumping jack unit or a submersible pump. Table 3.1 gives a more specific listing of the major types of equipment and machinery used in oil exploration and production, together with their shares in shipments by the American oil field equipment industry.

Production structures construction. The production platform is easily the largest item used in offshore oil gathering. The platform construction company employs (perhaps on a subcontract basis) the design engineers, site surveyors and project managers, and undertakes platform fabrication using a large range of materials including structural steel, tubulars, plates and cement. The platform will carry topside fabrications such as housing modules, a helideck, flare structures and an offshore loading system.

Mud supply and engineering. Drilling 'mud' (a mixture of clays, water and chemicals) is pumped down the drill string and up the annulus (i.e. the annular space between the drill string and the well bore) during drilling in order to lubricate the system, carry away rock cuttings, maintain the required pressure at the bit-end and provide an aid to rock-formation evaluation. The application of drilling mud is the specialized

Table 3.1   *Oil field machinery and product shipments: 1982 (USA)*

	% of shipments
Rotary oil field drilling machinery	40
Other oil field machinery	8
Oil field production equipment	32
Portable drilling rigs	6
Oil field derrick and surveying machinery	8
Oil field machinery not specified elsewhere	6
TOTAL VALUE OF SHIPMENTS (US$ billions)	9.487

Source: Department of Commerce, 1985.

function of the mud engineer, who is responsible for determining the correct mixtures and amounts of mud to be used in each case. The mud contractor will provide the mud and this requires the purchase, mixing and storage of the required materials.

Geophysical services are a hybrid application of physical and geological principles to determine the oil-bearing potential of rocks. A major investigatory tool is the seismic survey, whereby the refraction of sound-waves (created by an explosion) through underlying rock strata are read by specialized electronic equipment. The geophysicist's job is to collect the data, process and interpret them. *Geological services* are used to assess the nature of the earth's crust, especially in sedimentary basins. Information complementary to the seismic survey is added by the geologists: rock samples and fossil remains are analysed by the application of physical, chemical and palaeontological principles.

Drilling services are performed by a drilling contractor, who undertakes to provide the equipment and manpower needed to drill a well on behalf of an oil company. Types of holes drilled are wildcats, appraisal wells and production wells. The drilling contractor selects the equipment to be used (e.g. suitable drill bits and drilling fluids) and performs the necessary operations. Directional drilling (i.e. away from the vertical) is an operation requiring specialized skills and the use of 'fishing' tools (varieties of the latter are also used when the drill string breaks in the hole and recovery has to be effected).

Well-site geology (drilling control and mud logging services). A 'well-sitting' geologist is present while drilling is under way. By mud logging the geologist is able to determine, by examining rock cuttings brought to the surface in the mud, whether hydrocarbons are present or are likely to be so in the geological formations. Drilling control is used in the drilling process: data on the rate of penetration and torque are collected and these too are used in the determination of geological formations.

Core analysis and laboratory-based services. Cylindrical rock cores are obtained when a core barrel with an annular bit is withdrawn during drilling. It is analysed for geological features away from the drill site. Palaeontology and even more specialized palynology principles are used to determine features (such as density and fluid saturation of the rocks) that indicate the likely presence of hydrocarbons.

Electrical logging services. A log is a tabular or graphic description of drilling conditions or sub-surface features prepared during the drilling of a well or its subsequent evaluation. The electrical log information is obtained by dropping electrical logging equipment on a wire down the drill hole and collecting data while it is slowly drawn back to the surface. Acoustic and radioactive logs are also sometimes used with the same objective of supplementing geological information.

Wireline services are performed by lowering and retrieving special tools from the bore hole in order, for example, to perforate the casing and allow hydrocarbons to flow into the well, to cut the casing when necessary, and to perform production logging.

Well-testing services are undertaken when oil-bearing strata have been reached. The objective is to determine the quantity/quality of oil available and the best ways to promote its flow to the surface. Various tests are used: the drill stem test, the bottom-hole pressure test, the pressure value and temperature test and the formation fluid test. Apart from the tests themselves, the testing service agent will provide the necessary tools and equipment.

Workover services. The processes whereby a completed production well is subsequently re-entered and necessary cleaning, repair and maintenance work done.

Reservoir engineering consultancy. The reservoir engineer deals with the characteristics of an entire oil/gas reservoir rather than with a single well. It is the engineering consultancy that determines how a reservoir will be exploited. Mathematical models of the reservoir are constructed in order to calculate potential oil and gas reserves as well as the optimum development programme (e.g. well spacing, optimal production rates and potential for secondary recovery).

Production engineering consultancy is involved with the operation of an entire oil field. The production engineer will attend to matters such as artificial lift (pumping, water, gas or steam injection) and well stimulation (swabbing, fracturing and acidation).

Just what proportion of these subsector activities are performed inhouse by the oil companies is discussed in the following sections.

Measurement of the degree of vertical integration

In the literature on industrial organization, measurement difficulties have tended to hold back empirical investigation of vertical integration. This is not so much because good measures could not be invented but that such measures required the use of data that were not readily available from published sources. This measurement difficulty has been overcome here with the use of a detailed questionnaire answered by a sample of oil companies.

One, once popular, measure of vertical integration is the ratio of a firm's value-added to the value of its sales (Adelman, 1955). However, this measure is flawed: it is not invariant to a firm's place in an industry's vertical hierarchy (with a firm at the primary stage having a higher index ratio than firms at the secondary or tertiary stages, even though each firm is in fact integrated to the same extent); is not invariant to whether a firm is integrating forwards or backwards (with backward integration raising the index of vertical integration by more than an equal amount of forward integration); and the index changes if input costs change relative to output prices.

Accordingly, 'physical' measures of vertical integration have been found to be superior to value-added measures. The measure used here is, for each intermediate input, the ratio of inhouse physical production to total physical usage. A weighted average is calculated because more than one intermediate input is used. This weighted ratio lies between zero and unity, with a low value showing a low degree of backward vertical integration. We may call this ratio *the external procurement index*.[2]

The principal advantages of the external procurement index are: comparability between companies; additivity across companies (so as to yield industry averages); and non-distortion in the face of sales-price or input-cost changes. The main disadvantage of the external procurement index is that physical input–output data at the firm level are not generally available and this is probably why it was not until MacDonald (1985) that this type of measure was employed.

An important first step, therefore, in the study of backward vertical integration by oil companies into the production of inputs required for offshore oil gathering is to collect firm-specific data on input usage. This involves the design of an appropriate questionnaire followed by a series of interviews based upon it with oil company personnel.

A questionnaire was sent to all twenty-three oil companies with offices located in the city of Aberdeen, Scotland, in the summer of 1984 – a year which pre-dated the collapse of oil prices in December 1985 and the subsequent retrenchment that that event provoked. The questionnaire had two main objectives: to ascertain statistical information on vertical integration at the level of the individual oil company; and, secondly, to discover if the observed degree of vertical integration was consistent with the propositions advanced by transaction cost economics.

The resultant findings are believed to be quite general, as questioning of senior oil company personnel revealed that the Aberdeen oil service base was by no means exceptional in its industrial organization practices. This is also confirmed in the next chapter where the global organization of the offshore oil supply industry is analysed in detail.

Altogether nine oil companies assisted the study.[3] All of the questionnaires were completed in interviews between the author and senior procurement and/or production department personnel employed by the oil companies. The results, in summary form, are displayed in Table 3.2.

The left-hand column of Table 3.2 divides the intermediate inputs required by the oil companies into thirteen subcategories. The items numbered 3, 12 and 13 are intermediate products and all other items

Table 3.2   *Number of companies providing services, equipment and products inhouse: sample of nine North Sea oil companies*[a]

Subsector	Percentage of input provided inhouse					
	0%	1–20%	21–40%	41–60%	61–80%	81%+
1. Geophysical and geological surveying and consultancy services	3			1[b]		
2. Drilling services	5	3		1		
3. Mud supply	8					
4. Well-site geology, drilling control and mud logging services	6	1		2		
5. Core analysis and laboratory-based services	7	1				1
6. Electrical logging services	8	1				
7. Wireline services	8					1
8. Well-testing services	7	1		1		
9. Workover services	6	2	1			
10. Reservoir engineering consultancy	0	1[b]				6
11. Production engineering consultancy	0			1	1[c]	5
12. Production structures construction	2	4				1
13. Tools and other equipment manufacture	8	1				

Source: Questionnaire.

[a]   Firms sometimes failed to provide information.
[b]   All of this is supplied by the regional headquarters.
[c]   One half of this inhouse provision in Aberdeen and the rest by regional headquarters.

are intermediate services. The right-hand side of Table 3.2 records the proportion of input requirements provided inhouse by the questionnaire respondents. For example, eight oil companies had zero inhouse provision of item 3, drilling mud.[4]

Table 3.2 shows that inhouse provision is limited in its scope across the thirteen subsectors. The main findings are, first, that only two subsectors can be characterized as largely or entirely inhouse functions.[5] These are reservoir engineering consultancy (10), and production engineering consultancy (11). In subsector 10, the low Aberdeen inhouse provision by one oil company is boosted by intra-company transfers from the regional headquarters in England. In subsector 11, five companies have 100 per cent inhouse provision while in the other two cases this inhouse provision is also boosted by non-market transfers from the regional headquarters.

Secondly, in the majority of subsectors inputs are acquired from arm's-length suppliers. In four subsectors (3, 6, 7 and 13), eight oil companies had zero inhouse provision. To these can be added a further two subsectors (5 and 8) where seven oil companies had zero inhouse provision. Moreover, while inhouse provision is more prevalent in another five subsectors, it is still low in relation to the oil companies' usage of these inputs.

The data in Table 3.2 are presented as unweighted (for company size) averages in Table 3.3. The entry against each subsector shows inhouse provision by the nine oil companies as a percentage of their collective

Table 3.3   *Total inhouse provision of inputs: unweighted averages,[a] industry basis (nine oil majors) Aberdeen, 1984*

Subsector	% inhouse provision
1	12
2	9
3	0
4	12
5	15
6	1
7	11
8	7
9	6
10	79–87
11	81–88
12	20
13	1

Source: Questionnaire.
[a] Inhouse provision at mid-point of ranges listed at the top of the columns in Table 3.2, except when 81% + is indicated where the middle and upper end-points (100%) are recorded.

use of each input. It can again be seen that inhouse provision in subsectors 10 and 11 is high, while all the other subsectors display low inhouse provision, at most 20 per cent and usually 12 per cent or less.

While Tables 3.2 and 3.3 do give an indication of the limited extent of vertical integration in the sampled oil companies, the numerical value of the industry's external procurement index cannot be calculated unless weights are applied to the thirteen subsectors so as to allow for proportionate differences in contributions to the cost of finding and gathering oil. The weights, p_i, should be equal to the proportionate distribution of cost incurred in drilling and equipping offshore oil wells across each subsector, i. Thus,

$$\text{external procurement index} = 1 - \sum_{i=1}^{13} S_i \cdot p_i, \qquad (3.1)$$

where S_i is the percentage of inhouse procurement averaged across the oil companies in subsector i. Table 3.3 shows the unweighted averages of S_i, $i = 1 \ldots 13$ for the oil companies. It is acceptable to use an unweighted average because, as Table 3.4 shows, the oil companies display similar degrees of inhouse procurement over the thirteen subsectors.

Table 3.4 *Inhouse provision of services: unweighted averages, company basis, Aberdeen, 1984*

Company number	% inhouse provision		Approximate number of OOSI firms from which purchases are made, p.a.
	Subsectors 10 and 11	All other sectors together	
1	0[a]	9[b]	100
2	n.a.	n.a.	150+
3	81–100	14	n.a.
4	81–100	3	n.a.
5	0[a]	0	70
6	high [cd]	8	n.a.
7	81–100	low[c]	n.a.
8	90	low[c]	500
9	81–100[d]	13	600–1,000
10	81–100	18	1,500–2,000

Source: Questionnaire.
n.a.   Not answered
[a]   Not yet at stage where inputs 10 and 11 are used.
[b]   Drilling services 100% inhouse, all other subsectors 0 per cent.
[c]   Some firms gave qualitative information.
[d]   Some in regional headquarters.

The share of each subsector in oil company costs has been calculated by Data Resources Inc. (Standard and Poor's, 1986) and is shown in Table 3.5. Combining this information with that in Table 3.3, the above equation yields an external procurement index of 91.1 per cent.

This is a very high degree of vertical disintegration: the oil companies provide inhouse somewhat less than 10 per cent of their needs for the intermediate products and services used in oil gathering. It turns out that the two subsectors that show a high degree of inhouse provision (10 and 11) account for less than 4 per cent of total costs.

The existence of this low degree of vertical integration is confirmed by data on shipments in 1977 by manufacturers of oil field machinery and equipment (Department of Commerce, 1981).[6] In the USA only 7 per cent of sales of oil field machinery and equipment are to non-manufacturers in the same ownership group, which was the one category that could include oil companies. The predominant means of marketing oil field machinery and equipment is by direct (arm's-length) sales to the oil companies (57 per cent of the total) through sales offices located close to the oil companies' operating bases, rather than through channels such as wholesale and retail outlets. As will be discussed in Chapter 4, this method of marketing also predominates outside of the USA.

Other studies have provided measures of vertical integration in the oil industry from the stages *forward* from crude oil production through to petroleum products retailing. It is possible, therefore, to compare the degree of *backward* integration from crude oil production into the offshore oil supply industry (as measured by the external procurement

Table 3.5 *Subsector shares in oil companies' costs*

Subsector[a]	% share
1	1.2
2	43.5
3	7.9
4	1.7
5	3.1
6	1.2
7	1.2
8	1.3
9	5.3
10	1.8
11	1.8
12	6.9
13	22.9

Source: Standard and Poor's, 1986.
[a] Subsector numbers taken from Table 3.2.

index) with the degree of forward integration from that same stage. Adelman (1955) measured forward integration at 31 per cent for the year 1955. Teece (1976) has pointed out that American oil refining companies are vertically integrated into ownership of crude oil reserves, pipelines, marketing, and research and development to a high degree. The *raison d'être* of his book was to explain this phenomenon. More recently, MacDonald (1985) calculated vertical integration in the petroleum industry (excluding backward integration into the offshore oil supply industry) at 44 per cent.

The main point here is that, while the oil companies display (relatively) high degrees of *forward* integration from crude oil production, and this has been shown to be consistent with the predictions of transactions cost economics (Teece, 1976), reasons need to be found as to why they largely avoid *backward* vertical integration from this stage.[7] Or, put another way, just why in the oil-gathering business do the oil companies 'aim to own as little as possible'? Is this also consistent with the transaction cost explanation of choice of governance structures?

Examination of vertical disintegration in the oil industry

As the oil companies have demonstrated a strong preference for the market over inhouse provision of most of the intermediate inputs that they use in oil exploration, development and production, it is appropriate to examine their view of the economic efficiency of the markets that they use. In this section, attention is concentrated upon the structural characteristics of these markets both as a matter of fact and as seen by the oil companies. A good deal of use will be made here of the answers that were given in the questionnaire referred to earlier. In Chapter 4 the structure and dynamics of the offshore oil supply industry will be examined in still more depth and the issues raised here will be further illuminated.

What we now seek is a relatively comprehensive listing of the factors that relate to the vertical integration/disintegration decision in a practical context. Fortunately, Porter (1980) has examined 'the economic and administrative consequences of vertical integration, in order to help the manager determine the appropriate degree of vertical integration in a strategic context and to guide decisions to vertically integrate or disintegrate' (p. 301). It is against the background of Porter's categorizations that we have constructed a list of factors relating to the backward vertical integration decision by oil companies. This list clarifies the discussion in Chapters 1 and 2 of the transaction cost paradigm and it will throw light on its predictive value in the context of the offshore oil supply industry.

The presumption upon which this study is based is that the oil companies are responsive to economic factors and that these economic factors are responsible for their choice of governance structure. The main questions with which we are confronted then are: (a) why are the oil companies vertically integrated into the provision of some inputs?; and (b) why do they rely upon the market for the provision of most inputs?

Eleven factors are relevant to an assessment of the efficiency of the markets (relative to inhouse provision) used by the oil companies to procure intermediate inputs. These relate both to the competitiveness of the markets themselves as well as to particular constraints faced by the oil companies. These constraints could be important because it is conceivable that a market is not competitive yet an oil company is constrained to use it. The eleven factors are:

(1) volume of throughput relative to efficient scale;
(2) economies of combined operation;
(3) economies of internal control and coordination;
(4) economies of information through vertical integration;
(5) economies of stable relationships;
(6) vertical integration as a lead into technology;
(7) vertical integration to assure supply;
(8) vertical integration to offset suppliers' bargaining power;
(9) vertical integration and fixed costs;
(10) vertical integration and company flexibility;
(11) vertical integration as an exit barrier.

In each of the eleven items listed in Table 3.6 (one for each of these factors), a predicted outcome is stated which gives the main reason for preferring use of the market to backward vertical integration. These predictions will be compared with the oil companies' perceptions of the structural characteristics of the markets and of the constraints under which they operate as revealed in the completed questionnaires. The eleven items in Table 3.6 are grouped into four categories:

● the *perceived efficiency* of the offshore oil supply markets (items 1–6);
● *internal constraints* on choice of governance structure (items 7–9);
● *economies of scale* (item 10); and
● *market monitoring costs* (item 11).

First, we briefly consider perceived market efficiency. As will be discussed in the next section, the oil companies were found to perceive

Table 3.6 *Factors bearing on the decision to integrate vertically*

Market Efficiency

(1) *Economies of combined operation*

Short lines of communication have cost advantages for buyers.
- If offshore oil supply firms (OOSFs) locate close to oil companies, then low communication costs will result.

PREDICTED OUTCOME
Use independent suppliers if located in the vicinity.

(2) *Economies of internal control and organization*

If suppliers cannot be relied upon, then inhouse provision may prevent occasional disruption and reduced cash flows.
- Independent suppliers must meet the standards demanded by the oil companies. If they do not, then, with well-informed buyers, loss of reputation will be disastrous.

PREDICTED OUTCOME
Use independent suppliers if they can be relied upon.

(3) *Economies of stable relationships*

Major questions:
- Do the oil companies have 'stable' relationships with their suppliers?
- Does it matter to the oil companies if they change suppliers? *Considerations:*

    (i)   switching costs;
    (ii) absence of superior proprietary technology (standardized technology favours use of the market);
    (iii) similarity of quality among suppliers.

PREDICTED OUTCOME
Low switching costs enhance use of the market.

(4) *Vertical integration as a lead into technology*

Are other channels of technological advance and transfer open?

PREDICTED OUTCOME
Adequate external sources enhance use of the market with or without tapered integration.

(5) *Vertical integration to assure supply*

Have the oil companies in any locations had problems in obtaining supplies of inputs?

Table 3.6 *Contd.*

PREDICTED OUTCOME
Use the market if OOSFs are locationally responsive.

(6) *Vertical integration to offset bargaining power*

What is the structure of bargaining power between the oil companies and the OOSF?

Answers relate to:
  (i) concentration among sellers;
  (ii) availability of technology through the market;
  (iii) strategy used by the oil companies to reduce bargaining power residing with the OOSFs.

PREDICTED OUTCOME
Use the market if suppliers' bargining power is restricted.

Constraints on choice of governance structure

(7) *Vertical integration and fixed costs*

Potential costs of vertical integration:
● high fixed costs may result in large losses if expected cash flows do not appear. Use of the market has the advantage of raising the proportion of variable costs.

PREDICTED OUTCOME
When future cash flows are uncertain, favour using the market.

(8) *Vertical integration and oil company flexibility*

● Especially relevant if technical change is occurring: oil companies do not want to foreclose sources of technical advance;
● Latent danger of rising inhouse costs relative to OOSF supply prices.

PREDICTED OUTCOME
Desire for flexibility favours use of the market.

(9) *Vertical integration as an exit barrier*

● In the oil industry, exit from a locality is certain and not necessarily distant in time;
● Ownership of fixed assets raises exit costs.

Examples of exit barriers:
* redundancy payments;
* penalty clauses on leases;
* labour resettlement costs;
* retraining costs;
* sagging employee productivity when intention to exit is made known.

Table 3.6   *Contd.*

PREDICTED OUTCOME
Certainty of exit favours creation of low exit barriers and use of the market.

Economies of scale

(10)   *Volume of throughput and efficient scale*

● Volume of throughput may at no time reach efficient scale.
● Efficient scale may be reached but for only a short duration.

These problems can lead to:
* inability to sell surplus output because of confidentiality problems of supplying one's competitors;
* undesirability of operating with excess capacity;
* costs of shifting inhouse capacity between locations.

PREDICTED OUTCOME
Use independent suppliers when throughput is not sustained at efficient scale.

Market monitoring costs

(11)   *Economies of information through vertical control*

Monitoring the market might be expensive relative to internal control.

PREDICTED OUTCOME
Low market monitoring costs favour use of the market.

the markets between themselves and their suppliers in the offshore oil supply industry in the Aberdeen location as locationally responsive (items 1, 2 and 5 in Table 3.6), competitive (items 3 and 6), relatively inexpensive to monitor (item 11) and yielding an acceptable rate of technological advance (item 4). Market failure then is not seen as being an important problem (except in subsectors 10 and 11 – listed in Table 3.2). Furthermore, the existence of the offshore oil supply firms has the extra advantage of enabling the oil companies to divest certain fixed costs. This reduces the latter's risks of entry into new, unproven, oil provinces and also reduces their barriers to exit.

Items 7, 8 and 9 in Table 3.6 are constraints that would be imposed upon an oil company if it were to carry a relatively high proportion of fixed costs into a new oil province. A high proportion of fixed costs in total costs raises risk when cash flows are unpredictable (item 7) (Mitchell, 1976) and they may constitute an exit barrier by raising exit costs (item 9). Yet exit is certain if commercial oil wells are not discovered and even if they are discovered exit is still a foreseeable event. Item 10 also relates to the flexibility constraint. As offshore oil supply markets do exist, vertical integration may foreclose tapping into cost and/or technological advantages that may be procured through them. Thus, given the perceived transaction cost disadvantages of carrying a high proportion of fixed costs, *ceteris paribus*, an oil company can be predicted to choose vertical decomposition rather than inhouse provision of intermediate inputs. This would be so even if the transaction costs of using the market are positive.

Finally, item 10 in Table 3.6 relates to the relationship between vertical integration and economies of scale. Achievement of scale economies in a given department of an integrated company has been identified as the main reason for vertical disintegration (Stigler, 1951). But this view has been challenged by Kay (1983) and Langlois (1988), who questioned whether achievement of scale economies has to be accompanied by transfer of ownership. Thus, contrary to received wisdom, it is unclear what relationship scale economies bear to vertical decomposition. However, what is more certain is that inhouse provision of intermediate inputs that does not reach efficient scale builds in production cost disadvantages. The advantage of the market here is that it can aggregate the demands of individual oil companies and so reduce costs. The prediction of item 10 in Table 3.6 is use the independent suppliers when throughput is not sustained at efficient scale. As we shall see, this is the circumstance that the oil companies, even in a major offshore oil industry location such as Aberdeen, find themselves in.

The existence of a competitive offshore oil supply industry in a single far-flung – from its American home-base – location such as Aberdeen is somewhat remarkable. Its existence is possible only because the offshore oil supply industry is itself, like the oil companies, organized on a global scale. What is being observed are groups of multinational corporations acting as buyers and sellers organizing offshore oil gathering on a global scale, with the sellers following the buyers from one location to another and seeking no other external markets as an element in their location decisions.

Are the offshore oil supply markets competitive?

In the transaction cost paradigm the fundamental reason for vertical integration is the absence of perfectly competitive markets. In the real world, however, 'perfectly competitive' cannot mean 'without transaction costs' (i.e. prices being formed by the unpaid Walrasian auctioneer) and is unlikely to mean 'atomistic competition'. All markets display positive transaction costs and at least some seller concentration.

The existence of an approximately efficient market ('efficiency' meaning price equal to marginal cost) is an inducement to vertical disintegration, especially if inhouse governance would be expensive. Here, the efficiency of the relevant offshore oil supply markets can be judged with reference to seven factors:

(1) locational factors;
(2) extent of choice between rivals;
(3) switching costs;
(4) standardization of inputs;
(5) organization of technical change;
(6) personnel relocation costs;
(7) continuity of market relationships.

These will be discussed in turn.

Locational factors

Table 3.7 shows the importance of the locational factor for the oil companies that responded to the relevant question in the questionnaire. In seven of the thirteen subsectors into which the offshore oil supply industry has been divided, close proximity of suppliers to buyers is considered to be 'very important'. These seven subsectors are all either directly operational in character (drilling services, mud supply, wireline services, and workover services), or are closely connected with well data collection (well-site geology, drilling control, mud logging services, electrical logging services and well-testing services). It was *not* thought necessary that firms engaged in data analysis (included in subsectors 1

Table 3.7   *Importance of service companies to be located in close proximity to oil companies' operational offices (% of respondents)*

Subsector	Little	Importance Some	Great	No. of respondents
1	80	20	0	5
2	12	0	88	8
3	12	0	88	8
4	17	33	50	6
5	29	57	14	7
6	0	14	86	7
7	0	22	78	9
8	0	29	71	7
9	0	20	80	5
10	86	14	0	7
11	43	43	14	7
12	83	17	0	6
13	50	33	14	6

Source: Questionnaire.

and 10), tools manufacture or structures construction should be located in close geographic proximity to the purchaser.

Necessity of close proximity can often be a reason for common ownership (Williamson, 1985). This is because close proximity can lead to a small numbers problem and problems of quasi-rent appropriation (Klein, Crawford and Alchian, 1978). Yet this does not seem to be a factor in the offshore oil supply industry. The supply firms are responsive in that they place fixed assets in new locations. However, these decisions are also responsive to the number of oil company purchasers that they serve. For example, if an oil company strikes out on its own into a new area (such as Burmah Oil did into Pakistan in the late 1970s), it must greatly increase the use of inhouse provision. This is necessary because the offshore oil supply firms are reluctant to devote fixed assets and risk a small numbers problem supplying a single buyer. The conditions for the creation of an approximately competitive market are not present and market failure is all too likely. The need for close proximity is not a sufficient condition for vertical integration: absence of alternative market outlets as well as low supplier switching costs are also required.

When asked, the oil companies stated that they were satisfied that the service companies had been sufficiently mobile in establishing supply bases to service their input requirements. This cannot be surprising given that over 1,000 offshore oil supply firms had, by 1984, established themselves in the Aberdeen area of north-east Scotland. Moreover, data on the global offshore oil supply industry suggest that the supply firms had been responsive in relocating to viable new oil provinces as they have been sequentially and severally developed.

The oil companies were asked why they thought the supply firms had been so accommodating in responding to their locational needs. Attractive price markups (something approaching monopoly prices) were *not* seen as an important relocation inducement. Rather, the prospect of growing, broad and stable markets was viewed by the oil companies as the most important factor. Again, we observe the oil companies as perceiving the market as being relatively efficient.

Wide choice between rival suppliers
A fundamental proposition in the theory of industrial organization is that the greater is the number of competitors the closer will price be to average production cost. Bain (1970) has called this 'Mason's hypothesis'. Mason (1939) had argued that a firm's profit performance was determined, *ceteris paribus*, by the structure of the market in which it operated. Examination of Table 3.8 shows that many competitors had established themselves in several offshore oil supply industry subsectors in the Aberdeen area.[8] Nor, as the contestable markets hypothesis

suggests, should the list of rival suppliers be strictly limited to just those with offices located in Scotland, for potential rivals exist elsewhere. Indeed, the oil companies indicated that they believed that 'outside' supply firms could be 'quite easily found in the medium term'. This is an artefact of the globalization of the offshore oil supply industry to be discussed in the next chapter.

Table 3.8 *Number of competitors located in Scotland: various offshore oil supply industry subsectors, mid-1980s*

Subsector		No. of firms
Exploration		
Seismic contractors	7	Seismic equipment suppliers 4
Rig builders	4	Rig equipment suppliers 55
Drilling contractors	19	Drilling equipment suppliers 54
	Drilling consumables suppliers 32	
Platforms		
Suppliers of valves and fittings	60	Piping suppliers 31
	Suppliers of drill packages 13	
Platform services		
Installation/positioning	14	Hookup services 81
	Catering services 16	
Drilling		
Drilling contractors	26	Bit suppliers 14
Mud suppliers	38	Down-hole contractors 58
Directional drilling services	16	Wellhead/BOP suppliers 18
	Derrick/drillfloor equipment suppliers 29	
Sub-sea technology		
Completion engineering	8	Wellhead/template suppliers 7
Installation services	5	Diving equipment suppliers 49
Well completion contractors	5	RCV/ROV builders/operators 31
	Inspection/maintenance contractors 37	
Pipelines/loading		
Pipeline engineering consultants 24		Coating companies 11
	Trenching contractors 3	
Specialized vessels		
Designers/builders	6	AHT supply vessel operators 13
DSV operators	16	MSV operators 10
Electronics		
	CAD/CAM systems designers/suppliers 13	
	Drilling monitoring/control systems 10	
	Well analysis systems suppliers 10	

Source: Noroil Contacts, Summer 1984.

Switching costs

The existence of a large number of competitive firms may not provide a competitive environment if, once having chosen a particular supplier, the buyer becomes 'locked in', perhaps owing to the installation of capital equipment specific to a particular supplier's inputs. The reference here is to what Williamson has called 'the small numbers problem'. This could be generated in the way described even from an initially large pool of competitors. The existence of supply-firm specificity could give rise to high switching costs and would be incurred when the input-user had to install, for example, new capital equipment when changing to a new supplier.

The oil companies were probed on the matter of switching costs, with nine of them providing answers. Only two oil companies answered that switching costs were of no particular importance and one acknowledged that, while they did exist, they were not an obstacle to changing suppliers whenever the need arose.

No definite variation in response across the thirteen subsectors showed itself. However, one oil company stated that loss of access to specialized skills was a factor that contributed a switching cost in geophysical and geological surveying and consultancy services, core analysis and reservoir engineering consultancy. In drilling and drilling-related work (subsectors 2, 7, 9 and 11), lack of familiarity of new contractors with equipment, materials or methods of procedure could also be a switching cost factor – indeed, it was the most frequently cited switching cost across the thirteen subsectors. Only two oil companies cited loss of access to patented technology and/or loss of access to special skills. No company thought that the cost of drawing up new contracts constituted a switching cost. One important response was that new supply firms might face a learning curve, with costs falling as familiarity increased, but that this learning curve was relatively flat, as the oil majors themselves tend to use similar inputs in similar ways.

The generally low level of switching costs can also be judged from answers to another question: all of the nine oil companies that responded answered that they did, from time to time, change suppliers, even though the incumbent supplier was performing satisfactorily. This was usually because another supplier had offered to do the same work more cheaply. (Such an offer could arise when an extant contract had run its course and a new invited tender-bidding contest was arranged.)

Monteverde and Teece (1982) pointed out that quasi-vertical integration will be prevalent when bargaining power is asymmetric, and they measure this, following Klein, Crawford and Alchian (1978), by the relative sizes of appropriable quasi-rents. Asymmetric bargaining power itself arises when one firm has low switching costs between suppliers (or customers) and the other firm has invested in capital assets specific to the contractual relationship between the firms. The example they give is where an auto-assembler (the downstream firm) has low switching costs and it can obtain intermediate inputs from many sources, while the upstream parts supplier has invested in equipment specific to a single downstream customer. The downstream firm is in a position to appropriate the quasi-rent earned on this equipment (where the quasi-rent is the difference between the value of the equipment in its current (best) use and in the next-best use – which might be its scrap value). However, the asymmetry in the bargaining power is not necessarily to the advantage of the downstream firm, for the risk of quasi-rent appropriation will lead the upstream firms to underinvest in the specialized equipment. This is a case of market failure and can be corrected by quasi-vertical integration: the downstream firm owning and providing the upstream firm with the necessary capital equipment.[9]

Several examples of quasi-integration were found to exist between the oil companies and their suppliers. The oil companies often provided contractors working on offshore rigs or platforms with drilling equipment, lifting gear, kitchens and wireline and logging equipment. The appropriable quasi-rents hypothesis seems to be a good explanation of why this should be so. For example, if a crane operating company had also to provide the lifting equipment it might fear that the quasi-rent would be appropriated – the specialized offshore lifting gear perhaps having no readily found alternative use with another oil company in the locality. With the threat of underinvestment in, or a lack of rivalry (owing to small numbers) between, suppliers of lifting services, the solution is for an oil company to own the capital assets (the cranes) and for the 'crane' companies to supply the specialized personnel.

The fact that much of the equipment used in the offshore oil supply industry is *not* provided by the oil companies reflects an absence of appropriable quasi-rents. Both the suppliers and the buyers enjoy a relatively large number of competitive outlets or sources respectively. This, again, is an artefact of the globalization of the offshore oil supply industry: competition removes quasi-rents and the (widespread) absence of appropriable quasi-rents enables the oil companies to decompose from ownership of the capital assets required in oil gathering.

Standardization of inputs

Standardization of inputs is a factor contributing to low switching cost and, therefore, the enhancement of competitive market conditions in the offshore oil supply industry. A general feature of the industry is that, while patented and trade marked items do exist (the latter in abundance), close substitutes can nearly always be found. This is hardly surprising given that oil recovery is an old-established industry with a relatively standardized technology, particularly in the production phase and, also, to a high degree in the exploration and development phases. When asked for examples of 'non-substitutable' or 'substitutable only at high cost' inputs, the oil companies were able to respond with only a few examples: certain down-hole services supplied by a particular supplier (Schlumberger), incoloy weld overlay, an automatic latching device, a tool for drill stem tests, a milling tool and some completion equipment. Of course, offshore oil recovery is a more recent development than is land recovery and its development has required technological advancement on several fronts. Here the problem encountered by the oil companies is not so much that they might face monopolistic or collusive suppliers, rather that cost-efficient devices or methods may not exist at all.

Organization of technical change
Despite the rigours of oil gathering in the deep and rough northern North Sea waters, it is arguable that no entirely new technologies have been developed for this purpose. Rather, while technological change has progressed on a broad front, it has been a process of adaptation and modification of existing technologies, rather than new creation. Some examples are:

- Submergent equipment for rough seas
- Weld overlay
- 22/25% high chrome tubing
- Well positioning by satellite
- Dynamic position drilling
- Deep-water mooring systems
- Some diving equipment
- 'J' curve deep-water pipe-laying equipment
- Tension leg platforms
- Hyperbaric welding systems
- Fluorescent spectrometer
- Offshore lifting equipment
- Electrical submersible pumps
- Down-hole heat resistant pumps

Whatever the truth of this view it is clear that technological advance has been required as a means both of cutting costs and even of making possible oil production in the deep-water North Sea environment. For the oil companies, especially the large integrated companies, technological development could be encouraged through a combination of three channels: expenditure on independent internal research and development programmes; by working jointly with supply firms; and being prepared to pay market prices sufficiently high to reward suppliers for their own independent research and development expenditures. Questioning of the oil companies revealed that, while all three channels have been used over the last ten years or so, one in particular dominates.

Eight out of ten respondents to the questionnaire said that they had shared in the development of some technological advances. Importantly, little of this had been accomplished entirely inhouse, and most of it had been developed in association with supply companies. This is surprising given that the transaction cost literature uniformly views R&D expenditures as a reason for vertical integration. It is not clear how much of each particular technological advancement can be apportioned between the oil company and its supplier, but this is somewhat beside the point. The most important lesson to be drawn from this experience is that a satisfactory rate of technical advance had been achieved through a market relationship (all the oil companies said that they were satisfied in this respect). The reward for the supply firm is not necessarily increased cash flows from the job in hand; rather, it may take the form of promoting its relationship with the 'partner' oil company as well as enhancing its reputation in the industry and providing it with new knowledge that it may sell to other operators. The reward for the oil company is a cost-efficient solution to an immediate exploration, development or production problem.

Internal relocation costs
The transaction cost paradigm points to the need to compare the costs of using the market with the cost of operating an alternative internal organization. It has been argued that the cost of using the market between the oil majors and the offshore oil supply firms is relatively low. This point is sustained both by the competitive structure of some supply subsectors and by the use of the particular price-determination arrangement that the oil companies have chosen to use. The cost of using the market, according to the theory, is then compared with the cost, or potential cost, of vertical integration.

Ownership of resource inputs, including skilled technical personnel on employee contracts, implies a need to amortize these fixed costs by frequent use on company business. Failure to amortize fixed costs by repeated use will raise average costs and cut profits. However, repeated use at a sufficiently high level cannot be guaranteed by an oil company in a given location. This is most likely to be the case with an oil company still in the exploration phase, and also for companies with relatively small-scale development or production needs. We are dealing here with item 10 in Table 3.6. It turned out that the problem is not that the volume of throughput may at no time reach efficient scale, rather that efficient scale may be reached but only for short duration. An oil company then faces the problem of what to do with its surplus capacity as its inhouse needs decline. (In fact, inhouse needs fluctuate over time as an oil company passes through successive levels of use-need at separate wells or in aggregation at separate leaseblocks.) Amortization of fixed costs could still be accomplished by moving personnel and equipment between oil provinces as needs arose. But this approach to the amortization problem will incur certain organizational costs (i.e. exit barriers, item 9 in Table 3.6), which mitigate against its use and so constitute another argument in favour of vertical decomposition on the part of the oil companies.

Direct evidence of oil companies' internal organization costs does not exist. In order to gauge whether they are important or not the operators were asked about the problems they had experienced when moving (or planning to move) personnel from one part of the world to another. Eight oil companies provided answers and only two of these had experienced no problems at all (as seen by the respondents in Aberdeen). Of the latter, one was a very recent arrival to the North Sea oil province and the other was vertically decomposed to such a great extent that the manager saw his establishment as little more than a 'drilling office'. The other oil companies all replied that high mobility cost (for example, higher wages and removal expenses) was a factor that arose in the relocation of company personnel. Three oil companies also referred directly to organizational difficulties in arranging for the geographical relocation of personnel, especially in the identification of appropriate staff and/or job outlets. All eight companies pointed to employee dissatisfaction either pre- or post-move. This factor could also affect costs through lowering employee morale.

Another means of using excess capacity is for an oil company to sell it on the market. But this raises the matter of the opportunistic use of the knowledge that may be gained. Provision of inputs, especially in subsectors 10 and 11, may yield the supplier incidental knowledge about a well's geology. That such knowledge is valuable is obvious and has been established statistically by Mead (1986). He showed that winning bidders for offshore leaseblocks adjacent to a tract that they currently worked bid higher prices than winning bidders that did not own an adjacent leaseblock. The presumption must be that the owners of adjacent tracts had superior knowledge about the new leaseblock's geology and were able to make a more exact appraisal of whether commercial oil/gas would be found. Accordingly, one oil company would not wish to hire the services of another oil company for fear of giving away valuable knowledge to a potential rival.

This explanation is also relevant to the explanation of why subsectors

10 and 11 are highly integrated while the other subsectors are not. It is in reservoir engineering and production engineering consultancy that most incidental knowledge transfer can take place. Knowledge of the geology, geophysics and oil reserves of an entire oil reservoir is disproportionately more valuable than is knowledge of a single oil well. For example, such knowledge is highly useful to oil companies that may bid for an adjacent leaseblock concession. While the oil companies are willing to risk such incidental transfers in the other subsectors, they are simply not in the case of these two subsectors.

Continuity of market relationships
If we divide the offshore oil supply firms into two types, those that are organized on a global scale and those that provide 'locationally determined' inputs, then the continuity of market relationships with the oil companies occurs at two levels: the global and the local. Both levels display the necessary continuity characteristic, that is, commercial relationships with the oil companies are established on a continuous basis. The providers of locationally determined inputs (which are somewhat peripheral to the 'core' of the oil industry, for example: service boats, products supplied from the heavy 'metal bashing' industries and services such as banking, insurance and hotels) respond to the commercial opportunities provided by the arrival of the oil companies on their doorstep. Their responsiveness to these market opportunities is evidenced by the arrival of hundreds of such companies in the Aberdeen service base concurrent with (or soon after) the arrival of the oil companies themselves.

The continuity of the market relationships between the oil companies and the offshore oil supply firms that constitute the technological 'core' of the offshore oil supply industry (i.e. the thirteen subsectors listed in Table 3.2) is rather different from that with the providers of locationally determined inputs. Thus, while the latter are dependent upon the local market, firms in the 'core' supply the needs of the oil companies on a global scale. That is, the core offshore oil supply firms are themselves multinational corporations and they establish facilities so as to create a globalized market relationship with the oil companies. This and related matters are the subject of the next chapter.

Conclusions

This chapter has appraised the governance structures chosen by the oil companies and substantial support has been found for the transaction cost paradigm. The choice of market rather than inhouse governance mode is consistent with the oil companies' perceptions concerning the competitiveness of the markets that exist between themselves and the firms in the offshore oil supply industry. In eleven of thirteen subsectors, market failure was not perceived by the oil companies as being anything like a problem, while in the two subsectors where market failures might occur (due to opportunism) the inhouse governance mode was chosen. These findings were shown to be consistent across all nine oil companies that gave sufficiently full answers to the questionnaire designed for this study. The transaction cost literature also predicts that market failures may be precluded by quasi-vertical integration and this intermediate organizational form has been used by the oil companies in a manner predictable within the transaction cost paradigm.

Notes

1 The Standard Industrial Classification groups similar economic activities into industries. There are ten industries in the broadest, one-digit classification (e.g. 0: agriculture, forestry and fishing; 5: construction). Successive decomposition of broad industry groups into composite, less broad groups produces classifications at the two-, three-, four- and five-digit levels.

2 Forward vertical integration (which is not the primary concern here) would be measured by the ratio of intra-company transfers to a firm's total sales. MacDonald (1985) defined the total (forward) vertical integration index (TVI) as 'the share of all industry shipments that are directed to establishments owned by the seller' (p. 382). The external procurement index used here is the mirror image: as a measure of backward vertical integration by oil companies into the procurement of the intermediate goods and services needed for oil gathering.

3 There were in fact ten respondents, but one of them was reluctant to provide quantitative information. The ten respondents were Amoco, Burmah Oil, Chevron, Conoco, Marathon Oil, Occidental, Superior Oil, Total and Union Oil. For reasons of confidentiality, data are presented in aggregate form and companies are not identified in the text.

4 In each row the number of respondents sums to less than nine because the interviewees sometimes could not provide the necessary information.

5 Only seven of the nine respondents are recorded as performing these two tasks inhouse because in two cases the companies had not yet reached the oil production stage.

6 SIC 3533: oil field machinery and equipment, defined as establishments primarily engaged in manufacturing machinery and equipment for use in oil and gas fields or for drilling water wells.

7 Teece (1976) did comment on backward vertical integration by oil refiners but this amounted to only two pages in an entire book and used only secondary information.

8 The number of competitors may be large even though concentration ratios may be high. For example, fourteen suppliers of drill bits had located offices in Scotland, while the four-firm concentration ratio (i.e. the share in total sales of the four largest suppliers) is as high as 90 per cent.

9 Blois (1972) had earlier argued that quasi-vertical integration was a means of reducing excessive costs that might be incurred through full vertical integration.

4

The offshore oil
supply industry

On the other side of the market from the oil companies are the offshore oil supply firms. The nature of ownership and economic relationships between these two groups of firms and the internationalization[1] of the offshore oil supply industry itself will be discussed in this and the next chapter.

Here we describe the main ownership and locational features of the internationalized offshore oil supply industry. To set the scene, five of these features may be described as follows:

- the widespread use in virtually all oil provinces of affiliated[2] companies;
- the dominance, measured by market shares and geographic spread, of American multinational corporations in the industry's technological core;
- the distinction that exists between those affiliates that provide offshore oil supply services and those that are really only marketing outlets for tools and equipment which are mainly produced by firms in America;
- the American companies' maintenance over the long term of their dominant positions; and
- the limited appearance of non-American multinational firms in the core of the offshore supplies industry.

An objective of the next chapter will be to explain why these facts are so.

Important features of the internationalized offshore oil supply industry

The oil industry first grew to a significant size in the USA (Adelman, 1972) and from an early date the suppliers of the many intermediate inputs were entities separate from their oil company customers. These suppliers, too, were almost exclusively American companies. The earliest census date which relates to vertical integration in the oil industry in the USA is 1939 and a high degree of vertical disintegration is readily apparent (Department of Commerce, 1942).[3] This aspect of industrial structure has changed little if at all since then, for, as was demonstrated in Chapter 3, the oil companies display a high degree of vertical decomposition from inhouse production both of tools and equipment and of services.

According to the 1982 Census of Production (Department of Commerce, 1985), there were 1,005 oil field equipment manufacturing companies in the USA, employing almost 100,000 workers. The companies were mainly located in California and in the three Southern 'oil-patch' states of Texas, Oklahoma and Louisiana.

These American oil field tools and equipment and service companies dominate the worldwide offshore oil supply industry, as can be seen on a country basis in Table 4.1 for 1982, where the US share of oil field machinery imports is shown for sixteen countries. The US share is high in nearly all cases, reaching 91 per cent in Canada and 85 per cent in Pakistan.

Tables 4.2 and 4.3 show world market shares of specific oil tool and equipment markets on a company basis for the years 1976 and 1985. All six companies in these two tables, except Schlumberger, are fully American owned and Schlumberger is 50 per cent American owned.

High rates of market concentration are apparent, with the four-firm concentration ratio over 98 per cent in open-hole logging, 93 per cent in drill bits, 92 per cent in packers and no lower than 55 per cent (in

Table 4.1   *United States shares of country import markets: oil field machinery, 1982*

Country	US share of import market (%)
Algeria	75
Argentina	50
Australia	75
Brazil	49
Canada	91
Ecuador	67
Guatemala	63
India	33
Kuwait	56
Mexico	70
Norway	23
Pakistan	85
Venezuela	75

Source: Department of Commerce, 1985, p. 46.

Table 4.2   Selected major oil contractors and oil equipment suppliers: sales and market shares, 1976

Market Share (%)

Company	Equipment						Logging		Technical services			Total sales of companies (US$m)
	Drilling equipment			Well equipment					Production-related services			
	Bit	Drill pipes	Jointures	Other drilling appliances	Packers	Security equipment	Open hole	Cased hole	Cementing	Acidification	Factoring	
Baker International	12	6	31		56	15		16				553
Dresser Industries	17				12	31	12	6				2,232
Halliburton					24	18	2		58	47	53	4,866
Hughes Tools	38	3	58						10	6	4	383
Schlumberger				10			84	44	13	18	18	1,815
Smith International	25	58		60								308
Others	8	33	11	30	8	36	2	34	19	29	25	
Total (industry)	100	100	100	100	100	100	100	100	100	100	100	10,152

Source: UNCTAD, 1982.

a   Figures refer to the total sales of the companies, including sales not accounted for in the market share columns. All the companies except Schlumberger, which is Franco-American, are based in the United States of America.

Table 4.3 *Market shares of six leading offshore oil supply firms, 1985*

Company	Drill bits	Market share (%) Drilling fluids	Pressure pumps	Wireline	Foreign sales (%)
Baker International	12	11			45
Dresser Industries	12	25	5	13	29
Halliburton		12	52	4	29
Hughes Tools	39	7	5		34
Schlumberger			30	66	66
Smith International	30				27
Value of sales in 1985	$900m	$1.7b	$3.8b	$3.5b	

Source: Standard and Poor's, 1986; Value Line (various).

pressure pumps). In newly developing oil field computer applications the names of the leading firms are also American owned. Thus, in measurement-while-drilling, the leading firms are Schlumberger, Gearhart Industries, NL Industries and two smaller American companies; in seismic services, Gearhart Industries and several smaller American companies. In enhanced recovery, Baker–Hughes, Halliburton, NL Industries, Smith International and Western Company of America dominate (all of them American). The dominant force in the sub-sea well-head and production equipment market is Baker–Hughes. Indeed, American companies have always led the way in state-of-the-art technology in the oil field machinery industry (Department of Commerce, 1985, p. v).

The US oil field machinery industry exports to a large number of countries with no evidence of strong geographic concentration, as can be seen in Table 4.4. Singapore is the largest single export market, a position due to its position as an entrepôt for South-East Asia. The United Kingdom, Canada and Saudi Arabia, with 6–7 per cent US export market shares, are next in order of importance. The Organization of Petroleum Exporting Countries (OPEC) take about one-quarter of US exports and North Sea basin countries about one-tenth.

The dominant American position in the world oil field machinery market is also apparent in Figure 4.1, which shows US export and import ratios, and Figure 4.2, which shows the USA's substantial annual trade surpluses in oil field equipment. Exports as a proportion of industry shipments by US oil field machinery companies varied between 43 per cent and 66 per cent over the period 1972–83, with no apparent trend in the data. Indeed, this export ratio was higher in 1983 than it had been in 1972. This statistic indicates that US companies were successful in maintaining their position as leading suppliers even as many new countries began oil gathering on a large scale and many of their

Table 4.4   *Shares of US export markets^a: oil field machinery, 1983*

Country	Share of US export market (%)
OPEC (25.3%)	
Saudi Arabia	6.6
UAE	6.1
Venezuela	4.4
Indonesia	3.0
Nigeria	2.0
Libya	1.2
Kuwait	1.0
Algeria	1.0
North Sea (10.5%)	
UK	7.4
Netherlands	1.6
Norway	1.5
North America (9.1%)	
Canada	7.3
Mexico	1.8
Latin America (9.9%)	
Brazil	4.4
Peru	2.6
Colombia	1.7
Argentina	1.2
Others (30.5%)	
Singapore	9.4
Japan	2.9
France	2.8
Egypt	2.5
China (P.R.)	2.4
S. Korea	1.7
Australia	1.5
W. Germany	1.5
India	1.2
Trinidad	1.2
Tunisia	1.2
Italy	1.1
Angola	1.1

Source: US Department of Commerce, 1985, p. 20.
^{a} countries with 1 per cent or more.
Note: The countries in this Table account for 85.2 per cent of US exports of oil field machinery for a value of $2.623 billion.

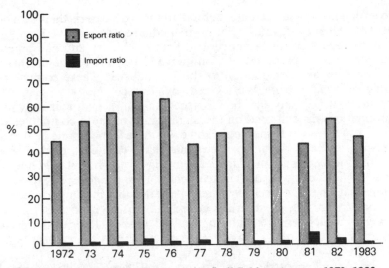

Figure 4.1   *Export and import ratios:*[a] *oil field equipment, 1972–1983*
Source: Department of Commerce, 1985.
[a] Export ratios are exports as a percentage of shipments. Import ratios are imports as a percentage of apparent consumption. Apparent consumption is the sum of product shipments plus imports less exports.

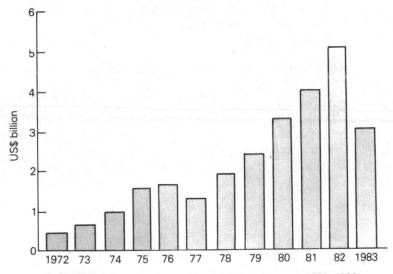

Figure 4.2   *US trade balance: oil field equipment, 1972–1983*
Source: Department of Commerce, 1985.

governments sought to create, behind protective barriers, their own oil field machinery industries. (For more on this see Chapter 11.)

In its report on the American oil field machinery and equipment industry, the Department of Commerce (1985) identified the main foreign company competition to the US industry. These companies came principally from West Germany, France, Norway, Canada, Japan, Holland, Italy and the UK (see Table 4.5). Unfortunately, no information was collected on the significance of these companies to their respective world markets. However, there is then some evidence showing that non-American companies have created a competitive international presence in oil field drilling rigs, drill bits, oil field pumps and oil field controls and instruments. This progress is, at best, somewhat limited, especially in view of the fact that the Department of Commerce sees the most serious competition to US exports of oil and gas equipment coming from foreign subsidiaries of US firms that have taken their technology abroad (Department of Commerce, 1985, p. 39).

The American offshore oil supply firms largely supply foreign markets through affiliates, which they establish in countries playing host to the oil companies. Table 4.6 shows the number of countries in which leading offshore oil field equipment and service companies have established affiliates. One company has them in forty countries and another in thirty-six countries. All leading American firms have affiliates in at least ten countries. Table 4.7 complements this information, showing that the leading offshore oil supply firms are to be found together, often in competition, in many countries.

Table 4.5 *Number of major non-American suppliers of oil field machinery and equipment*

Nationality of ownership	Oil field drilling rigs	Drill bits	Oil field pumps	Oil field controls and instruments
UK	1	3	2	8
Canada	5	0	2	0
France	3	2	4	9
Japan	0	3	2	1
Norway	0	4	1	8
West Germany	2	0	3	4
Mexico	2	0	2	0
Venezuela	0	1	0	0
Other (non-CPE[a])	4	5	5	4

Source: Department of Commerce, 1985.
[a] centrally planned economy.

Table 4.6   *Number of countries in which leading suppliers have affiliates, 1983*

Company	No. of countries
Baker International	36
Dresser Industries	40
Gearhart Industries	19
Gray Tool	17
Halliburton	26
Hughes Tools	22
McDermott	10
NL Industries	11
Schlumberger	16
Smith International	10
Tidewater Inc.	17
Weatherford	23

Sources: Uniworld Publishing Inc., 1984; National Register Publishing Co., 1987.

In offshore drilling – a service activity – this pattern of competition through foreign affiliates repeats itself. Thus, of the thirteen American offshore drilling companies on which it was possible to obtain information, all had at least one overseas affiliate. Seven of them competed through affiliates in the North Sea oil province, eight in the Persian Gulf and ten had affiliates in Singapore to service the South-East Asian market.[4]

The offshore oil supply industry affiliates are unlike the foreign affiliates of American manufacturing companies. Of course, offshore oil supply companies that are entirely service based, with no manufacturing capacity of their own, will establish service-only affiliates. However, several American offshore oil supply firms do have substantial manufacturing capacity in the USA. Nine leading American offshore oil supply parents with manufacturing capacity in their ownership groups together had 201 foreign affiliates, but only 20 of these counted as manufacturing concerns (abstracted from National Register, 1987).[5] In other words, the remaining 181 affiliates were restricted either to the provision of offshore services or to marketing, after-sales service and inventory management functions. In its 1985 review of the competitiveness of the American oil field machinery industry, the US Department of Commerce remained sanguine about the creation of foreign manufacturing affiliates by US companies, but it did warn about the danger of technology transfer to foreign competitors, especially through joint venture companies established with foreign nationalized companies (Department of Commerce, 1985).

Table 4.7 *Seven major oil contractors and equipment suppliers: selected locations of affiliates*

Location of affiliates	Baker Int.	Dresser Inds.	Halliburton	Hughes Tools	Schlumberger	Smith Int.	Weatherford
Argentina	×	·	×	×	·	·	×
Australia	×	×	×	×	×	×	×
Brazil	×	×	×	×	·	×	·
Canada	×	×	×	×	×	×	·
Egypt	·	×	×	·	×	·	·
England	×	×	×	×	×	×	×
France	×	×	×	×	×	×	×
W. Germany	×	×	·	×	×	×	×
Indonesia	×	×	×	×	×	·	×
Libya	×	×	×	·	×	·	×
Kuwait	×	×	×	·	×	·	×
Mexico	×	×	×	×	·	·	·
Nigeria	×	×	·	×	·	·	×
Norway	·	×	×	×	·	×	×
Saudi Arabia	×	×	×	×	·	·	×
Scotland	×	×	×	·	×	×	×
Venezuela	×	×	×	×	×	×	·
UAE	×	×	×	·	×	×	×

Source: as Table 4.5.
× = affiliate in this country.
· = no affiliate in this country.

Services and after-sales service must be distinguished: after-sales service can be considered to be a part of the marketing function (as is inventory management) but services (for example, wireline, logging and geological) are separate intermediate inputs in their own right. To the extent that affiliates perform only the marketing function, they are little more than outlets for the oil field equipment and tools manufactured in the USA (and to a much lesser extent in West Germany, France and the UK). As an example, a leading firm that fits this pattern is Smith International, which has several manufacturing plants in the USA and markets oil field tools through its overseas affiliates (*Annual Report*, 1983). Schlumberger and many other companies are similarly placed.

The economic reasons for the existence of these ownership characteristics, especially the international dominance of the USA and the use of foreign affiliates, will be discussed in the next chapter. Three main questions are immediately provoked:

(1) Why do the American offshore oil supply firms choose to service foreign markets by creating affiliates?

(2) How are the American oil supply firms able to maintain their competitive advantages in foreign countries after having internationalized themselves?

(3) Why is tools and equipment manufacturing capacity retained in the USA?

We continue with a discussion of the theories of the multinational corporation that can give answers to these questions.

Notes

1 The term 'internationalization' is used in the literature on the multinational corporation. It is generally meant to convey that single-firm ownership of multi-plant and other facilities extends beyond international frontiers.

2 An affiliate is defined to be a majority-owned branch or subsidiary of a parent company.

3 For the purpose of this study of economic organization in the offshore oil supply industry, there is really no need to go back further than 1939. However, it is known that the world's first commercial oil well was drilled at Titusville (Pa) in 1859 (US Department of Commerce), that Pittsburgh was the major 'oil-well supply station' in the late nineteenth century (Doheny, 1921) and that oil companies were using independent geological consultants in the 1920s (Special Committee, 1976).

4 This information abstracted from Uniworld (1984).

5 The nine were Baker–Hughes, Gray Tool, Dresser Industries, Gearhart Industries, Halliburton, McDermott, Newpark Resources Inc., Tidewater Inc. and Weatherford International Inc.

5

The multinational offshore oil supply industry: the theoretical aspect

This chapter tries to answer the questions posed at the end of Chapter 4. As these questions are bound up with the internationalization of the offshore oil supply industry, we will seek the answers to them in the literature that has developed on the economics of the multinational corporation. In doing so the emphasis of this book on transaction cost economics will be reinforced because the modern theory of the multinational corporation is a special case of the transaction cost theory of institutional choice, i.e. choice of organizational form.

The chapter begins with a description of the currently most influential transaction cost theory of the multinational corporation: that the internationalization of production virtually always stems from a desire to foreclose international markets. An argument is developed in this chapter that, while foreclosure still occurs when a company goes multinational, there are circumstances in which the emphasis should be placed on internationalization to enhance market efficacy – between the internationalizing firm and its customers. This, it is argued, is both an effect and an objective when the offshore oil service companies set up affiliates to service the oil companies in new offshore oil provinces.

As the efficacy of the markets in offshore oil services and products is to become the focus of this chapter, the discussion later turns to the parameters that are related to this matter: the nature of barriers to entry into the offshore oil supply industry (which explain the continued dominance of the established American offshore oil service companies); and the limitation of asset specificity in reducing the degree of competition in the offshore oil supply markets (where it is argued that a critical mass of transactors is needed for markets to blossom).

Transaction cost theories of the multinational corporation

Transaction cost theories of the multinational corporation have been 'discovered', apparently independently, on three separate occasions: by McManus (1972), Buckley and Casson (1976) and Williamson (1981). In all three cases, appeal is made to the authority of Coase's (1937) seminal paper on the nature of the firm. The transaction cost theory of the multinational corporation is, therefore, a special case of a broader theory. McManus drew explicitly upon measurement costs (which he called 'enforcement costs') and both Buckley and Casson and Williamson drew upon rent appropriation. Later, Casson (1982a) developed his own measurement (or 'monitoring') cost argument for the multinational corporation.

Another landmark in the development of the theory of the multinational corporation is Dunning's eclectic paradigm (Dunning, 1977, 1981, 1988). In this theory, three advantages are necessary for the creation of a multinational corporation: a firm-specific ownership advantage, a transactional advantage of 'the firm' over 'the market', and a locational advantage of a distant site over other sites in the 'home' country. Teece (1986), however, argued that, of the firm-specific and transactional advantages of the firm, only the latter is really important since *all* firms must have some firm-specific advantages in order to exist in a competitive environment. It is also apparent that locational advantages are important only in distinguishing the multi-plant firm that happens to become a multinational corporation from the multi-plant firm that remains as an intra-national corporation. It is only a matter of whether the locational advantage resides in a foreign country or elsewhere in the home country. This leaves just the transactional advantages of the firm over the market as the main argument explaining the existence of multinational corporations.

Rugman (1981, 1985, 1986) seized upon this to claim that 'internalization' was a general theory of the multinational corporation. The multinational corporation exists because it is the most efficient organizational form for 'appropriating rents' (to use Magee's, 1976, terminology), which otherwise would be dissipated through some other organizational arrangement such as international arm's-length commodity or licence markets. Rugman, however, omits to stress that 'internalization' is a general theory of *the firm* (which takes us back to Coase) and that the newly named theory of the multinational corporation is itself a special case of a more general theory.

Meanwhile, Dunning (1988) defended the eclectic paradigm, pointing out that, despite earlier criticisms, the locational and firm-specific factors must remain as arguments in a theory of the multinational corporation. This is the theoretical point of view adopted here. The location of economic activity is obviously an important factor in a firm's investment decision and it plays an especially important part in the 'follow-the-customer' theory of the multinational corporation – which will be discussed shortly. Most certainly, the location of offshore oil provinces is a determinant in whether oil companies and offshore oil service firms become horizontally diversified as intra-national or as international companies.

Moreover, firm-specific advantages must remain important in a theory of the multinational corporation, as differences in the relative quantities of these possessed by a group of firms have been shown to determine which of them will internationalize themselves (Caves, 1974, 1982; Horst, 1972a, b). And, as Casson (1982a) recognized, firm-specific endowments can take the form of either ownership or measurement cost advantages and these too relate to the types of firms that have propensities to internationalize themselves. In particular, it is not necessary for firms to have technologically based 'knowledge monopolies' (the term is due to Johnson, 1970) to have an advantage upon which to turn themselves into multinational corporations. 'Low-tech', patent-denuded firms such as hotels (and many other service-sector firms) may also become multinational corporations because of measurement cost advantages: specifically, because they have a recognised 'name', legally trade marked or not.

'Dominant application' of the transaction cost paradigm to the multinational corporation

However, currently, the dominant application of the transaction cost paradigm to the theory of the multinational corporation draws upon the rent appropriation aspect rather than measurement costs. In this view, the decision to internationalize production is prompted by imperfections in markets for intermediate inputs, especially intermediate inputs that have been created by research and development and are protected by patents or product differentiation or reside in human capital, particularly management. Such knowledge-monopolies take the form of public goods, and markets in public goods are unusually susceptible to market failure. The latter is said to be a characteristic of markets in licences (Buckley and Casson, 1976; Caves, 1982; Johnson, 1970; Magee, 1976, for example), so this avenue for the international transfer of technology (or other firm-specific advantages) is in many circumstances ruled out. In the transaction cost paradigm, the licensing of a foreign agent is susceptible to several potentially costly market failures: impacted knowledge, small numbers bargaining, opportunism, policing costs and free-rider externalities. These transaction costs may be avoided by internalization of the licence market.

Foreign markets can be serviced by exports, but international commodity (and service) markets may also be subject to 'market imperfections'. The import tariff and non-tariff barriers are obvious examples that raise the cost of using the market. Export markets might also be abandoned when foreign locational advantages exist (for example, idiosyncratic local tastes might be identified only if a subsidiary has been established 'close to the market' – this point is stressed by, for example, Ohmae, 1985, and Levitt, 1985). And exporting may be abandoned when scale economies and/or low-cost foreign factors of production can be exploited. The growth of foreign markets, the consequent achievement of scale economies and the eventual transfer of production from the 'home' to the 'foreign' country feature in Vernon's well-known 'product cycle' theory of the multinational corporation (Vernon, 1966, 1971, 1979). The existence of cheap foreign labour may also become important in the decision to transfer production to less-developed country export-platforms. Vernon's product cycle, however, is not usually classified as a transaction cost theory, mainly because it does not give a complete explanation of why international arm's-length markets may need to be internalized.

What is most thoroughly contemplated in what we have called the 'dominant application' of the transaction cost paradigm to the multinational corporation are the reasons for the foreclosure (or internalization) of international markets in intermediate products. Foreclosure has the objective of appropriating rents that would otherwise be dissipated through high transaction cost arm's-length intermediate product markets. Internationalization is *not* seen as a means of creating monopoly positions in either intermediate or final goods markets in order to appropriate rents through monopoly pricing.

Internationalization of production to improve market efficiency

What the 'dominant application' tends not to emphasize is the opposite matter of the internationalization of production, distribution, inventory management or marketing so as to facilitate the creation or maintenance of low transaction cost arm's-length markets in intermediate products or services. Yet, many multinational corporations exist precisely in order to enhance the transactional efficacy of arm's-length markets. This is particularly true in the service sector, including the multinational offshore oil service companies, and it is also true of the companies that supply intermediate goods to the oil companies.

Grubel (1977) was one of the first to discuss a theory of the international service firm – in his case with application to international banking. Firms in this industry, he argued, internationalized themselves so as to create low transaction cost arm's-length markets with their customers. In fact, Grubel did not put the matter exactly in this way, as he seemed to be unaware of the extant transaction cost literature. For Grubel, the decision to go multinational was a means of protecting an established market relationship with a customer that had itself 'gone multinational'. But, as the continued existence of this relationship was seen as being based upon bank-specific knowledge-of-customer advantages, for which arm's-length markets did not exist, the matter is readily reduced to one of the transaction cost efficacy of intermediate product markets (the intermediate product here being that of banking services).[1] This can be taken as originating the *follow-the-customer* theory of the multinational corporation.

More recently, Boddewyn, Halbrich and Perry (1986), Casson (1982a), Dunning (1987) and Dunning and Norman (1987) have argued, from a general theoretical perspective, on the relevance of the transaction cost paradigm to the service sector. The basic point is that, when buyer uncertainty over product quality is high, an arm's-length market is subjected to higher transaction costs than otherwise would be the case. A multinational corporation may then step into the market as a specialist in market-making services, so reducing buyer uncertainty and, therefore, buyer transaction costs. Thus, far from replacing the market, the introduction of a multinational corporation into it raises its transactional efficacy. A case in point is Casson's explanation of the existence of international hotel chains. International travellers have preferences over the qualities and range of services provided by hotels and are willing to incur transaction costs to find a suitable match in a distant city. The existence of a brand name – quality consistent – hotel chain allows an international traveller to economize on these transaction costs and this is a source of competitive advantage for the international hotel.

Additional case studies have appeared on multinational service sector companies and these lend further support to the theory that measurement cost economizing explains the existence of these companies as market-makers in competitive service markets. For example, advertising agencies have been investigated by Anderson (1984), Terpstra and Chwo-Ming Yu (1988) and Weinstein (1977); international banking by Ball and Tschoegl (1982), Brimmer and Dahl (1975), Goldberg and Saunders (1980), Nigh, Cho and Krishnan (1986) and Sabi (1988); and the location of offices of multinational corporations in more than two dozen different service sectors by Dunning and Norman (1987) and Dunning (1987).[2]

Follow the customer in offshore oil gathering

The follow-the-customer theory is highly relevant to understanding the organizational arrangements in the oil-gathering business. As was shown in both Chapters 3 and 4, offshore oil supply firms have a high propensity to follow their customers, the oil companies, to many distinct locations.

What is observed here is the internationalization of two distinct sets of firms: the oil companies and the offshore oil supply firms. The former create new and geographically distinct markets for the outputs of the members of the offshore oil supply industry as they open up new oil provinces around the world. And what is also apparent is that the decision to relocate by the offshore oil supply firms is taken in order to promote marketing advantages – both over one another and over potential host country rivals.

The matter of emphasis is important here. As we have seen, the 'dominant application' stresses internalization as the *raison d'être* of the multinational corporation. The follow-the-customer model also involves an element of internalization but it is the improvement of the efficacy of arm's-length markets with customers that is given most emphasis.

To investigate this further, Figure 5.1 shows organizational relationships between internationalized providers of services and buyers in a foreign country.[3] The 'home' company has internalized the international market (an export and/or licence market) by setting up an affiliate in the foreign country and it supplies buyers through an arm's-length market. Two intermediate service markets (ISMs) are involved: ISM I, which is internalized, and ISM II, the efficacy of which is increased by the foreclosure of ISM I. Indeed, the first market is foreclosed so as to improve the transactional efficacy of the second.

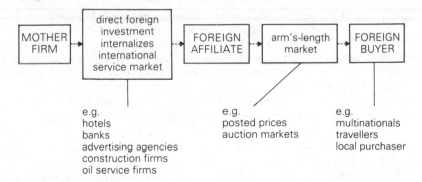

Figure 5.1 *Organization of exchange: offshore oil supply multinationals*

Three main reasons may be identified as propelling the internationalization of offshore oil service firms. First, established offshore oil service firms have a measurement cost advantage over host country rivals (potential or actual). The appeal here is to the Barzel–Casson argument that buyer familiarity with the services of a given set of suppliers, gained at another location, reduces monitoring costs, i.e. there is an 'economy of familiarity'. Secondly, imperfections exist in (potential) licence markets between the home firm and (potential) licensees in the host country. Such licensees of oil service technology, with little experience of the oil industry, are most likely to be ignorant of its true rent potential and the licence market will fail owing to the impacted knowledge problem. Moreover (potential) licensors, noting the unfamiliarity of (potential) licensees with oil-gathering technology, routines and working relationships with oil companies, will anticipate an external diseconomy problem. The cost of reputation failure in one oil province is likely to make itself felt in other provinces because the oil companies – the buyers – operate on a global scale. Thirdly, export markets in many of the oil-gathering services provided by offshore oil service suppliers cannot exist because of the jointness of production and consumption (i.e. the service has to be produced at the same location and time as it is consumed). This is true of all directly productive services such as drilling control, workover, well-site geology and wireline services. An adjacent location is also an advantage in analytical services such as geophysical and geological analysis: it reduces transport costs, it facilitates communication with complementary activities and, in any event, the oil companies usually insist that such analytical work is performed at a close-by location.

These three reasons for the internationalization of American offshore oil service firms can be related to Figure 5.1. The latter two reasons – failure of licence and export markets – account for the internalization of the international service market – ISM I. However, the first reason listed, the measurement cost advantage afforded 'familiar' companies, relates to ISM II. Internationalization in fact increases the efficacy of ISM II and does so in two ways: it reduces buyers' monitoring costs, as already pointed out, and it also has the effect of increasing competition between suppliers in the different offshore oil provinces.

It is because of this complexity that it is wrong to conclude, as does the 'dominant paradigm', that internationalization of production occurs only for reasons of internalization. It is also desirable when it promotes the efficacy of an arm's-length market by reducing the transaction costs of using it.

Because of the importance of ISM II, the arm's-length market between the oil companies and the offshore oil service companies, it deserves closer examination. Why, for instance, do host country firms find it so difficult to enter and what determines whether it will be densely populated by a large number of competitors?

Barriers to entry

When the oil companies first begin exploration in a new oil province, as they did in the northern North Sea in the 1960s, they create a geographically distinct demand for the products and services supplied by the offshore oil supply firms. These demands are supplied from two quite different groups of firms: those firms that constitute the technological 'core' and those that provide what have been called 'locationally determined' inputs.[4] The technological core of the offshore oil supply industry is composed essentially of the thirteen subsectors listed in Table 3.2: that is, logging, well-testing, wireline services, drilling, completion, stimulation, production services, data analysis and the production of tools, equipment and chemicals. The locationally determined inputs are all less specific to the offshore oil supply industry and include outputs from what is known in the business as the 'metal-bashing' industries (heavy items such as storage vessels, pipes, ramps, structures), outputs from the general construction industry, banking and finance services, insurance, transportation and catering. It is in the technological core that the multinational offshore oil supply firms are found, while the indigenous companies are mainly concentrated as providers in the locationally determined sector.

This is because barriers to entry exist into the technological core. These barriers to entry are responsible for the continuance of competitive advantages by the multinational offshore oil supply firms and for restricting indigenous firms to the (largely) internationally non-mobile sectors of that industry. Since barriers to entry as well as transaction costs are important to the internationalization of the offshore oil supply industry, it is appropriate that their nature should be investigated. In fact, the first two barriers to entry that we will list take the form of transactional cost economies: they are examples of existing market relationships acting as barriers to entry to potential rivals.

Indeed, this point has been taken up by Demsetz (1982), who pointed to the primacy of information cost as the fundamental barrier to entry rather than to the need for new entrants to invest in advertising, or overcome economies of scale, or raise large amounts of capital (Bain, 1968; Ferguson, 1974; Stigler, 1968); Demsetz argued:

Information costs are the more fundamental barrier to entry. These costs, not necessarily in identical amounts, constitute hurdles to all who would (and have) enter(ed) the industry. Complete knowledge about products and firms would make brand loyalty useless from both consumer and seller viewpoints. Where advertising and promotion are used extensively, and, therefore, where goodwill and brand loyalty are assets, there must also exist real costs of resolving uncertainties. In the presence of such costs, consumers will find it useful to rely on a firm's experience and reputation, or more correctly, on its *history* or on the fact that it has made sizeable investments specific to this industry. New firms and recent entrants by virtue of their shorter histories or absence of specific investments (in particular, product lines) may not be able to impart to consumers, without some compensating effort, the same confidence as has already been secured by older firms through past investments in good performance. (Demsetz, 1982, p. 50)

Thus, Demsetz uses the term 'information cost', but it would seem that instead 'sorting cost' could be substituted (although Demsetz, 1988, has argued that a theory of the organization of production based upon 'information' cost will eventually be a more complete theory than is admitted by the transaction cost theories which lie behind these concepts).

In the offshore oil-gathering business, even before coming to a new oil province, the multinational offshore oil supply firms have already created goodwill with the oil companies by successfully completing contracts with them either in the USA itself or in oil provinces elsewhere in the world. This goodwill forms a barrier to entry to indigenous firms. The nature of this barrier can be modelled in a manner analogous to that of the Barzel–Casson–Coase–Demsetz–McManus argument on quality sorting. When awarding contracts, oil companies have to appraise rival tender-bids, that is, they sort among tender-bid packages which might well display different quality as well as price offers. An established reputation, or goodwill, reduces this sorting cost;[5] as a supplier's quality can be relied upon, it has a narrower expected probability distribution of out turn without further, potentially costly, investigation. For example, an oil company need not investigate the qualifications or experience of a supplier's personnel or engage in a pre-qualification exercise which involves some cost and may also cause delay.[6] Thus, we may say that established reputations reduce oil companies' measurement costs. As oil companies are expected to try to minimize transaction costs it can be concluded that, *ceteris paribus*, they will prefer to trade with firms that are already known to them rather than with unknown newcomers.[7]

Related to this particular transaction cost based barrier to entry is a second: suppliers that are already familiar with a given oil company's work-practices can be expected to have relatively steep learning curves when taking up a new contract (i.e. they quickly reach maximum efficiency). The oil companies will then have to devote relatively little of their management's or technical personnel's time to advising a new contractor on these particular work practices, and delays or avoidable breakdowns can be expected to be negligible. Newcomers cannot be expected to have such steep learning curves, so trading with them will normally be expected to involve higher transaction costs.

The firms in the technological core of the offshore oil supply industry also have a propensity to be intensive (relative to the providers of locationally determined inputs) in the ownership of patents (see Table 6.5 in the next chapter). Trade marking of items is also widespread in this industry. However, these legal barriers to entry are not of particularly great importance in the oil industry as a whole (i.e. offshore and onshore) because its technology is reproducible. Exceptions to this include the protection of data analysis software and electrical logging (where Schlumberger has a near monopoly of the world market) and in certain specialized areas such as measurement-while-drilling. These observations, however, are less true of the offshore oil supply industry which, as it progresses into deeper waters, sets new technological challenges. Indeed, as was described in Chapter 3, the oil companies and offshore oil supply firms have forged satisfactory relationships for the creation of technological advance. Thus, for example, Baker International, Vetco and Hughes Tools (now all part of Baker–Hughes) have several patents on certain types of sub-sea equipment.

Possibly more important as an entry barrier than patented technology, however, is the very complexity of offshore oil supply business. The intermediate service inputs that are supplied are highly technical and/or highly specific to oil gathering. Thus, while the technology of oil gathering could, potentially, be widely disseminated, the know-how remains concentrated with the multinational offshore oil supply companies themselves. Indigenous non-oil industry companies find that the learning and packaging for sale of this know-how are difficult to accomplish. Thus, when 241 offshore oil supply companies were asked in 1984 what was the main impediment to expansion, even some of the multinational offshore oil supply firms identified shortages of skilled manpower, particularly of the technical and managerial types. To cope with this, the multinational service companies run their own, sometimes considerable, inhouse training schemes.

The question may be raised: why is tools and equipment manufacturing capacity retained in the USA? The answer is bound up with another barrier to entry. Suppliers of tools, equipment and chemicals, in aggregating world market demand, will achieve plant-level scale economies at their factories in America. Unlike the American manufacturers of many consumer goods which have internalized international product markets by establishing manufacturing capacity abroad, the oil field products manufacturers have found it necessary (in large part) to internalize only the foreign marketing function (including after-sales service and inventory management). It is true that they have established some manufacturing plant abroad, but only on a relatively small scale.

The reason for this difference in the behaviour of the American oil field products and consumer goods producers, is bound up with the question of why manufacturing capacity is retained in the USA. It comes about because of differences in relative market sizes. Foreign national markets for American consumer goods (including consumer durables) are often large enough for plant-level scale economies to be achieved, while in oil field products they are not. Individual oil provinces are simply not large enough to absorb the output of efficient-scale plants. Accordingly, direct foreign investment in oil field products manufacturing plant is (largely) avoided and the oil companies' desire for suppliers to be located in close proximity is met by investment in marketing outlets. The scale economies are also barriers to entry to outside firms.

Asset specificity

In Chapter 3 it was pointed out that the oil companies require their suppliers to locate in close proximity to themselves. This was because much of the oil-gathering industry is operated 'around-the-clock' and operating delays can be expensive. Hence, suppliers are often required to contract for immediate twenty-four hour service and this cannot be achieved unless the buyers and suppliers are located close together. These circumstances can be interpreted as the 'high transport costs' which are used to underpin the technological determinism explanation of vertical integration (for example, Bain, 1968). But Williamson (1985) has rejected this explanation. Rather, the governance structure of transactions in intermediate products will be determined on a trans-action cost minimization basis.

Even if transport costs are high, *independent* suppliers may locate in close proximity to the firms which they supply. According to Williamson (1985), the deciding factor in the choice of governance structure is asset specificity (assuming that the degree of uncertainty caused by oppor-tunism is sufficiently low and the frequency of transactions is sufficiently high to amortize the cost of specific assets). Thus, if suppliers have to make investments which are transaction-specific to a particular buyer, the governance structure is likely to be that of vertical integration.

But if the assets are non-specific then a market relationship will suffice, as recontracting with another buyer is feasible.

Two main factors are related to the degree of asset specificity in a given geographic location: the 'density' of the local market and the geographic mobility of the assets. We will discuss each in turn.

Asset specificity and market density
The market density concept refers both to the size of a market and to the number of transactors. Markets in which switching costs are low and large volumes are exchanged between many buyers and sellers may be said to be 'dense', while the opposite is true when the market is 'thin'.[8] In economic theory a dense market is normally a competitive market, while thin markets may display monopsony and/or monopoly powers and price uncertainty features and these may be reasons for replacing the market with an alternative governance structure.

While no absolute standards exist to distinguish between dense and thin markets, their two dimensions (market size and number of buyers) as exhibited in the Aberdeen service base would seem to favour the argument that many markets are relatively dense. In 1984, on the buyers' side, twenty-three oil companies had offices located in Aberdeen, while the market was large enough to support over 1,000 companies on the suppliers' side. Such well-populated markets are in contrast to a thin market such as presented in Venezuela in the 1930s. Thus:

> Because there were no oil-well supply stores in the country, the [oil] companies imported and maintained on hand something like 30,000 different materials and equipment items – everything conceivable from toothpicks to drilling boilers and most such material had to be ordered from abroad at least six months prior to the time when it might be needed on a job. (Special Committee, 1976, p. 227)

In this case, an oil company is backward integrated into inventory management at its Venezuelan location.

On a global scale, Tables 4.6 and 4.7 indicated that the leading offshore oil supply firms have a high propensity to relocate together, and therefore compete with one another, in many countries. Similarly, on a global scale, many buyers exist: between 1953 and 1972 the number of private oil companies increased by about 300 and approximately 50 of these participated in several nations at once. As an indication of the number of oil companies that were buying oil field products and services, in 1972 more than 330 oil companies had exploration rights located in 122 different countries, covering a concession area of 9.3 million square miles. The ownership of oil reserves was similarly widely spread, with over 100 private oil companies each having proven oil reserves of over 100 million barrels. Increasing competition on the buyers' side is also indicated by the fall in the eight-firm concentration ratio in the ownership of rights to concesssion areas, which dropped from 80 per cent in 1953 to 30 per cent in 1972 (i.e. from moderately high to low concentration). Similarly, concentration in the ownership of the non-communist world's crude oil reserves fell from 96 per cent to 74 per cent (Jacoby, 1974; Mancke, 1976).

While here we are looking at market density from the point of view of the suppliers, it is also true that the existence of a large and competitive offshore oil supply industry has reduced entry barriers for the oil companies. The need for vertical integration has for long been seen as a barrier to entry, and its obverse (vertical disintegration) reduces entry barriers by lowering capital and skilled manpower requirements. Thus:

> The capital and human resource requirements of entry were . . . reduced by the increased availability, on a fee or contract basis, of tankers, specialized geological and geophysical services, and foreign contract drilling services. (Jacoby, 1974, p. 124)

What we are observing then is a self-generating process: as the market grows, it provides incentives to both buyers and sellers to use it still more extensively. Thus, if it is true that the 'division of labour is limited by the extent of the market', in this context, *'the extent of the market is limited by the extent of the market'*. This conjecture deserves closer inspection.

Increasing numbers of buyers allow aggregation of demand, and aggregation of demand encourages multiplication in the number of suppliers. Moreover, an increasing number of suppliers encourages multiplication of the number of buyers using the market. To illustrate, as buyers multiply, inhouse activities that do not achieve scale economies, or do not achieve them for long enough to amortize fixed costs, can be decomposed to the market and the market will aggregate these fractional demands. At the same time, multiplication in the number of suppliers enhances competition and encourages buyers to use the market. Furthermore, the effect of large numbers of suppliers is to increase cross-elasticities of demand as the number and closeness of substitutes increase. As a result, in long-run equilibrium, the 'degree of monopoly power' declines and economic rents are reduced. Collusion too is less effective with large numbers. Fraas and Greer (1977) established this as an empirical fact, and O'Driscoll (1986) has observed that cartels are undermined by 'the interloper problem'. That is, the existence of quasi-rent attracts entry and increases competition.

According to Williamson it is asset specificity that creates small numbers bargaining problems and restricts use of the market. But the line of causality can be reversed. Williamson seems not to relate asset specificity to anything other than technological design factors and unique human capital.[9] But asset specificity is, in fact, related to the absolute numbers of potential (or *ex ante*) traders. It is easy enough to conceive of circumstances where the degree of asset specificity is negatively related to the number of buyers or sellers. We will establish this here.

First, how to conceptualize the degree of asset specificity? The relevant concept would seem to be an asset's quasi-rent or appropriable rent. An asset with zero appropriable rent is non-specific (as income equals transfer earnings). Assets can be arranged with increasing degrees of specificity: ascending as the ratio of income to transfer earnings increases.

Secondly, we will assume that, in order to trade, a pair of transactors must install a specialized asset (it could be machinery, equipment or human capital). This is not an unreasonable assumption in the context of the offshore oil supply industry, which is both highly technical and machine dependent. Let it be further assumed that the specialized asset is not homogeneous but can be designed to have one of various forms but, once it is installed, it cannot be redesigned. (In the terminology to be introduced in Chapter 8, a transactor chooses a specific asset with a defined attribute set.) For the sake of illustration, let the asset have a maximum of five attributes: A, B, C, D and E. But for cost reasons let no transactor install the asset with more than two attributes (for example, AB, AC, BD, etc.), and for technical reasons (to give flexibility perhaps) no fewer than two attributes. Also, it will be assumed that, for a pair of specific assets to be able to intermesh on a contract, and so enable the transaction to take place, at least one attribute must be in common (for example, a buyer installs AB and a supplier BE).

Now, if a pair of transactors are engaged in an exchange, asset specificity and potential small numbers bargaining problems will be a lesser problem for either the buyer or the seller if there are many transactors on both sides of the market. With only one transactor on either side of the market, the small numbers bargaining problem is obvious: one side may be able to appropriate the rent of the other's specific asset. But, in the circumstances supposed, consider the effect of increasing the number of transactors in the market. Ten combinations of attributes can be drawn two at a time from a universal set of five attributes, and seven of these combinations will have at least *one* attribute in common (only one in common is necessary to trade). Thus, the number of potential trading partners must grow as new transactors join the market even if, when first entering the market (in a new location say), transactors are paired off through contracts and have installed specific assets for the purpose.

This argument establishes that asset specificity and small numbers bargaining problems are reduced as the number of transactors on both sides of the market grows. In a very real sense then, 'the extent of the market is limited by the extent of the market': increasing numbers of transactors in a market can reduce the perceived (by those who have yet to join it) transaction cost of using the market so encouraging them to join it. Or, put another way, the transferability of specific-attribute assets increases with the number of transactors and the potentiality of rent appropriation will decline. Or, again, the existence of increasing numbers of potential transactors has the effect of increasing transfer earnings and reducing the rent portion of income, so reducing asset specificity and small numbers bargaining problems.

Asset specificity and geographic mobility

Asset specificity is also reduced if the assets are 'mounted on wheels' (Williamson, 1985, p. 89); that is, can be moved with little cost to another place. For then

> contractual problems between independent buyer and supplier are limited since contracts can be terminated and productive resources relocated at negligible cost. Given the unspecialized nature of the investments and the mobility that has been ascribed to them, neither buyer nor supplier operates at the sufferance of the other. (Williamson, 1985, p. 89)

It is one of the main conjectures of this chapter that the firms in the technological core of the offshore oil supply industry are indeed 'mounted on wheels'. This is one of the effects of the internationalization of the industry. The multinational offshore oil service firms have a 'global vision',[10] are geographically diversified and do not devote specific assets of any substantial value to a given oil province. This global vision is evidenced by the wide geographic spread of the oil suppliers' operations. Tables 4.6 and 4.7 have already established this fact. Moreover, the offshore oil supply firms' assets located in the Aberdeen area often amount to little more than manpower (sales, technical and managerial) and inventory, as only two or three of them have established a manufacturing presence. Of course, both manpower and inventory can be 'mounted on wheels' – or wings.

In the next chapter attention turns to an examination of structural and other relevant features of the offshore oil supply industry in the Aberdeen location. We will be looking in particular for support for the underlying theories outlined in this chapter relating to the international-ization of the offshore oil supply industry.

Notes

1 Grubel argued the case in the following way: 'The continuous business carried on between, for example, a US bank and US manufacturing firm in the United States, is made highly efficient by the use of informal operations procedures built on trust, which in turn is based on continuous personal contacts and the resultant flow of information vital for decision-making. *The continuous commercial contacts between the bank and manufacturing firm permit the bank to have access to information about the firm's financial conditions at such low cost and high speed that it is in a better position than any other competitor to evaluate and respond to the firm's demand for loans*' (Grubel, 1977, p. 352; emphasis added). It is the italicized portion of this quotation that is interpreted as a monitoring (measurement) cost advantage of an established supplier over its potential rivals.

2 Dunning (1987) listed the following service sectors which have the feature of internationalized production: restaurants, car rental, telecommunications, tourism, transportation (shipping and airlines), hotels, legal services, licensing, managerial consultants and public relations, medical services, motion picture production, live entertainment, educational services, engineering, architecture and surveying services, data transmission, insurance, investment banking, accounting and auditing, data processing and construction management.

3 Thanks are due to Mark Casson for stressing to me the importance of the organizational relationships shown in Figure 5.1.

4 The term 'locationally determined' is due to Cameron (1986).

5 Sorting cost is an aspect of an oil company's tender-bid assessment cost, which is discussed at length in Chapter 9.

6 By passing 'pre-qualification', a supply company is certified as being fit to perform the work. It does not, of course, guarantee that a given contract will be won by that company.

7 Barzel (1982) reached the opposite conclusion: *suppliers* sort for quality for transaction cost reasons. His conclusion is valid for both posted-price and flexible-price commodity exchanges. But with the invited tender-bid auction operated by the oil companies, it is the buyers that sort for quality between the rival bids. In Chapters 9 and 10, among other matters, reasons are given for the oil companies' avoidance of purchases on posted-price markets and tender-bid cost optimization is modelled.

8 High switching costs alone are enough to create a thin *ex post* market.

9 For example, Williamson (1985) writes: 'parties to a transaction commonly have a choice between special purpose and general purpose investments' (p. 54). He also uses the terms 'unique' (p. 53) and 'almost unique' (p. 53) when referring to the nature of an asset.

10 The term 'global vision' is used by Vernon (1979) and is meant to convey that a multinational company will scan the globe for profitable investment opportunities. Vernon applied this concept to manufacturing industry, and the manufacturing company as 'global scanner' is of fairly recent vintage in his view. It is apparent, however, that the manufacturing and service companies in the oil supplies industry have been 'global scanners' for several decades. Their 'market analysis' is, perhaps, simplified as the geographic relocational moves of the oil companies are fairly easy to read.

6

The offshore oil supply industry in its main British service base

The preceding chapter's discussion of the transaction cost theory of the multinational corporation, together with Chapter 4's description of the internationalized technological core of offshore oil supply industry, leads one to expect that certain features will be present in a given offshore oil supply service base. We will call these expectations 'propositions' and we want to see if they are supported by the evidence. Attention here will focus on the Aberdeen area of north-east Scotland where, in the early 1970s, a major service base was established to serve the British sector of the northern North Sea oil province. We may list the propositions as follows:

(1) Since it has been established as a matter of theory that the companies in the technological core prefer to service overseas markets by establishing affiliates, then affiliates (rather than head-quartered firms) will predominate in a supply base.
(2) Since oil companies, as buyers, require, for transaction cost reasons, that suppliers are located in close proximity to their own facilities and since market failure is thought not to be a problem, independently owned affiliates will serve in an oil province.
(3) Since American companies predominate in the global industry, American ownership groups[1] will be found in the technological core of the offshore oil supply industry while indigenous firms will be found mainly as providers of locationally determined inputs.
(4) Since the American offshore oil supply firms follow on the heels of the oil companies, American affiliates in the technological core will be among the first to arrive in a new supply-base.
(5) Since American leadership in the offshore oil supply industry is at least partly based upon firm-specific advantages, patent owner-ship will be more prevalent with them than with the non-American firms.

(6)   Since there is no evidence of a decline in the American leadership role in the offshore oil supply industry, American ownership groups will be at least as research and development intensive as the less specialized ownership groups.

(7)   Since affiliates are established to serve oil companies' needs in different oil provinces, it is unlikely that a given affiliate will be an important decision-making centre for an ownership group in the wider global industry.

(8)   Since the leading offshore supply companies have affiliates in many countries, any given affiliate in the technological core is unlikely to be important (as measured by share of sales) within its ownership group.

If these features are indeed prevalent in the Aberdeen service base, we can take this as support for the underlying theories presented in earlier chapters, which relate to:

- the importance of firm-specific advantages to direct foreign investment;
- the transactional cost efficiency of the offshore oil supply markets; and
- the role of barriers to entry in excluding indigenous companies from the technological core.

How then does the offshore oil supply industry in the Aberdeen supply base measure up to these expectations? To answer this question, a sample survey of 241 offshore oil supply firms was undertaken in the Aberdeen area. A questionnaire was designed and interviewers sent out to each firm in the summer months of 1984. At this time, oil production in the British sector of the North Sea was nearing its peak and the sample survey pre-dated the collapse of oil prices in December 1985. What we were observing then was an offshore oil supply base operating in the prime of its life-cycle.[2] Attention now turns to a presentation of the findings of this sample survey as they relate to the hypotheses laid out above. We begin with some definitions of the terms used.

Some definitions

The companies which constitute the offshore oil supply industry in Aberdeen were defined as:

- 100% oil-related affiliates;
- 100% oil-related non-affiliates (i.e. headquartered firms with or without facilities located outside the city);

- less than 100% oil-related affiliates; and
- less than 100% oil-related non-affiliates.

The 100% oil-related companies are gathered together into *group A* and the less than 100% into *group B*.

The data file

A total of 241 offshore oil supply companies replied to the questionnaire. These were selected by a stratified random sample with replacement. The total population of 807 group A and 251 group B companies was divided between the main standard industrial classifications.[3] The number of establishments selected from each classification was in proportion to the relative size of each classification. Within each classification, establishments were divided into four groups according to their size (small, medium, large and very large) as measured by the number of employees, and selection within the classification was in proportion to the relative weight of these size groupings.[4] Among group A companies, 23 per cent of their total population completed the questionnaire, and 22 per cent of group B companies did so.

The predominance of affiliates: propositions 1 and 2

As the offshore oil supply industry is global in its organization, it is to be expected that affiliates will make up a large proportion of the firms located in the Aberdeen service base. This was indeed the case: affiliates made up 70 per cent of the entire sample – 71 per cent of group A and 65 per cent of group B companies. Moreover, of the 133 group A affiliates in the sample, over 90 per cent reported that they were set up especially for North Sea oil activity. This is a higher proportion than for non-affiliates: of 54 such group A companies, 72 per cent were set up especially to exploit opportunities arising from the development of the North Sea oil province. The remainder of the group A sample were firms that had already arrived in the local area before diversifying completely into the offshore oil supply industry.

The location of parents of group A affiliates is shown in Table 6.1. Most of these affiliates were of parents located in the UK (excluding Scotland) or in America – both with about one-third of the total sample. In fact, Scottish parents accounted for only about 14.3 per cent of group A affiliates, little more than the proportion for Europe (areas 4 and 5 together). It is among the less specialized, group B, companies that

Table 6.1   *Location of parents of group A affiliates*[a]

Location of parent companies	(%)
(1) Local area	8.3
(2) Scotland (excl. 1)	6.0
(3) UK (excl. 1 and 2)	34.6
(4) Norway	5.3
(5) Europe (excl. 1–4)	8.3
(6) America	33.1
(7) Other	4.5

Source: Questionnaire.
[a] Based on 130 replies by 100% oil-related companies.

the Scottish parents were mainly to be found – accounting for 28 per cent of group B affiliates. This tends to confirm the unspecialized nature of the Scottish parent companies, which is not at all surprising given the discussion in Chapter 5 covering the matter of barriers to entry into the core of the offshore oil supply industry. By contrast, 88 per cent of North American affiliates were 100 per cent specialized in the offshore oil supply industry. It is also revealing that the industry base of British (areas 1, 2, and 3 together) parent companies was overwhelmingly from non-oil related industries.

Subsectors of the offshore oil supply industry: proposition 3

The offshore oil supply industry was divided into twenty-one main subsectors, which are listed in Table 6.2. For example, row number 15 – distribution and supplies – is made up by combining SIC numbers 610, 612, 614, 615, 616 and 619. The subsectors that are most heavily specialized in oil exploration, development and production are rows 1, 2, 3, 4, 5 and 6, while a lesser degree of specialization arises in rows 8, 9, 10, 11, 12 and 15. Relatively low oil industry specialization is the case with the remaining rows.

The expectation is that affiliates of American parents will be found in the specialized subsectors. The main finding was that this was indeed so. The American parents' ownership of group A and B affiliates taken together was about 33 per cent. Of the 168 affiliates in the sample it was above average in eight subsectors (see Table A6.1 in the Appendix to this chapter). Three of these are included in the 'highly' specialized grouping, three more were of lesser specialization, and American ownership was virtually absent in the 'low' specialized sectors.

The reverse expectation is that Scottish and other UK companies would be over-represented in those subsectors that were less specific

Table 6.2 *Twenty-one subsectors of the offshore oil supply industry and related activities: SIC groupings*

Row number	Description	SIC grouping
1	General exploration	130
2	Oil production	131
3	Drilling	132
4	Diving	133
5	Surveying	134
6	Well stimulation	135
7	Miscellaneous metal goods	310
8	Mechanical engineering	320
9	Miscellaneous machinery production	324 + 328
10	Electrical and electronic engineering machinery	340 + 343 + 344
11	Marine engineering	361
12	Instrument engineering	375
13	Miscellaneous manufacturing	475 + 493
14	Construction	500–504 inclusive
15	Distribution and supplies	610 + 612 + 614 + 615 + 616 + 619
16	Retail distribution	640 + 651 + 653
17	Catering	644
18	Transport	740 + 763 + 770 + 750
19	Banking, finance, insurance, business services	814 + 820 + 835 + 836 + 837 + 838 + 839
20	Renting and hiring of movables	840 + 849
21	Other services	932 + 940

Source: Hallwood, 1986.

to the offshore oil supply industry. Thirteen of the twenty-six affiliates which fell into subsectors where the Scottish ownership share was greater than the Scottish average ownership share did indeed fall into the 'low' specialization category (see Table A6.2). Only four of these Scottish affiliates fell into the 'highly' specialized group. These features, of course, reflect the fact that those Scottish parent companies diversifying into providing intermediate inputs to oil companies did so from production bases that were unconnected with the oil industry. Moreover, what these data also show is that a dozen or so years after the offshore oil supply industry came to Scotland, Scottish companies had made little headway in penetrating the technological core.

If anything, this picture of a lack of specialization in the most highly specialized subsectors of the offshore oil supply industry is a stronger characteristic of British companies taken in their entirety (areas 1, 2 and

3 together; see table A6.3). The ownership share of these companies was above average in nine subsectors, all of which were of 'low' or 'lesser' specialization. Of the sixty-three British companies that fell into this category, twenty-eight were in banking and finance, ten in construction, nine in transport and three in retail distribution. Again, the view is confirmed that British companies have been generally unable to establish an interest in the technological core.

Who got in when? proposition 4

The first oil discovery in the northern North Sea was in 1967 and Shell Oil Company was the first oil company to establish offices in Aberdeen. Other oil companies followed; for example, Mobil in 1972, Amoco and Union Oil in 1973, and Chevron in 1976. With the recognition that oil in commercial quantities was recoverable from this oil province, the American offshore oil service companies also established affiliates in the Aberdeen service base. Table 6.3 shows the time-profile of entry by a sample of these companies. The years 1970–5 were the most prolific, with twenty companies in the sample being established, and these were to account for the bulk of employment by American affiliates when activity in the Aberdeen service base was at its height in the mid-1980s.

The average age of 130 group A affiliates in 1984 was 7.9 years, and affiliates of American parents had on average been the longest established in the Aberdeen area (longest by two years). Although the average age of American affiliates in the aggregate data is higher than in any of the three categories of British companies, the differences cannot be shown to be so at an acceptable level of statistical significance.

Table 6.3 *American subsidiaries in Aberdeen: year of entry*

	1965–9	1970–1	1972–3	1974–5	1976–7	1978–9	1980–1	1982–4
No. of American affiliates established	2	5	12	3	8	7	5	3
Employees in 1984 of firms in row above	325	337	1997	1398	525	82	145	123
Percentage of 1984 US affiliates' employment	6.6	6.8	40.5	28.3	10.6	1.7	2.9	2.5

Source: Questionnaire.

However, significant differences do show up when the aggregate data are divided into smaller items. Thus, in the eight subsectors where the American ownership share of affiliates is greater than the average American ownership share (which turns out to be the technological core), the American affiliates' average age was 9.3 years compared with only 6.6 years for the British affiliates. This difference is significant at the 1 per cent level. Further evidence of early entry by American affiliates was found in SIC 612 (wholesale distribution of industrial materials). Here the average age of the twelve American affiliates was 10.4 years compared with a British (excluding Scotland) average of 6.4 years (this difference is significant at the 10 per cent level.

Thus, what we have established is that the subsectors in which the American affiliates have concentrated themselves (the technological core) are also the longest established in the Aberdeen service base.

The arrival of American affiliates also seems to be *more bunched in time* than is the arrival of the affiliates of British parents. The standard deviation of age since entry (in 1984) of American affiliates was only 4 years, while that of geographic areas 2 and 3 was 4.4 and 8.7 years respectively. Using an 'F' test for differences in population variances (Yamane, 1970, pp. 651–3), American entry is significantly (1 per cent level) more bunched than is entry by the affiliates of UK (non-Scottish) parents. This suggests that when the offshore oil supply industry in the Aberdeen area was in its infancy the American parent companies both were the most sensitive to the development of new marketing opportunities, and/or were the most competent to meet the companies' needs.

This finding is informative because, in the literature on the multinational corporation, entry-bunching has been associated with oligopolistic interaction between the firms that take the decision to establish foreign affiliates (Knickerbocker, 1973). Here the direct foreign investments by the rival American parent companies are essentially defensive in nature. The necessity to establish an affiliate in a new service base is especially marked given the oil companies' preferences for dealing with suppliers that have facilities located in close association with their own. Moreover, the relative absence of entry-bunching by firms outside of the technological core is also entirely expected. These affiliates have been established by parents from diverse industries and marked oligopolistic interaction between them would not be expected. Moreover, these latter companies are most unlikely to have a 'global vision' of events in the international oil industry, whereas the members of the technological core have been hypothesized to have such a view of marketing developments in this industry.

This evidence on age and entry-bunching is telling in its support for the view that when the offshore oil supply industry in the Aberdeen supply base was in its infancy it was the American parents that were most sensitive to the development of new opportunities to market the specialized intermediate inputs. This is not surprising, as it is the American companies that have created firm-specific advantages in the offshore oil supply industry and are the longest established as specialist suppliers of both material inputs and services.

Patent ownership: proposition 5

Details of patent ownership in the offshore oil supply industry are shown in Tables 6.4 and 6.5. Among group A affiliates in Table 6.4, 57 per cent reported possession of at least one patent within their ownership group. This was markedly higher than the 37 per cent reported by group A non-affiliates. Group B affiliates were less well endowed with patents, with just 33 per cent owning them. This was more than group B non-afiliates, of which only 9 per cent possessed patents.

Table 6.5 shows group A ownership of patents by location of parent company. The third column is most revealing, showing that affiliates of American parents are dominant in the ownership of patents, with 42 per cent of all patents owned by group A affiliates.

There is strong evidence that the American ownership groups are intensive in the possession of patents. This can be seen by comparing the final two columns of Table 6.5. The American share of patents is greater than their share of group A affiliates. British (excluding Scottish) companies show the opposite tendency. A significance test was performed on the difference in the proportion of American affiliates belonging to ownership groups possessing patents and the British companies with the same. Among American affiliates, 70.5 per cent possessed patents, while the proportion for British affiliates was only 49.2 per cent. The difference is significant at the 1 per cent level.

Table 6.4   *Ownership of patents (Group A companies)*

	All companies		Affiliates[a]		Non-affiliates[b]	
	No.	%	No.	%	No.	%
Own patents	93	51.1	74	56.9	19	36.5
No patents	89	48.8	56	43.1	33	63.5
Missing cases	5		3		2	
	187		133		54	

Source: Questionnaire.
[a] Affiliates using patents possessed by their ownership group.
[b] Independent firms.

Table 6.5   *Group A affiliates' ownership of patents by location of parent*

Location of parent	No. with patent	% with patent	% of all companies with patents	% of affiliates (130 total)
(1) Local	8	72.7	10.8	8.5
(2) Scotland	6	75.0	8.1	6.2
(3) UK	18	40.9	24.3	33.8
(4) Norway	3	42.9	4.1	5.4
(5) Europe	4	40.0	5.4	7.7
(6) America	31	70.5	41.9	33.8
(7) Other	4	56.7	5.4	4.6
Total	74	56.9	100.0	100.0
Without patent	56	43.1		
Total sample	130	100.0		

Source: Questionnaire.

Research and development: proposition 6

The relative failure of the British companies to penetrate the technological core of the offshore oil supply industry is at least partly due to their failure to invest in R&D as well as to their later start in the industry. Most group A affiliates belonged to ownership groups that undertook some form of R&D. American ownership groups, despite their lead in the technological core (or perhaps because of it), also performed more R&D than did the British companies – see Table 6.6.

Aberdeen as a decision-making centre: proposition 7

Ninety-eight per cent of affiliates reported that they had decision-making powers covering the local area. But only 18 per cent of group

Table 6.6   *Possession of R&D capabilities by parents of group A affiliates*

Location of parent companies	% of all parents with R&D
(1) Local area	8.9
(2) Scotland	5.6
(3) UK	26.7
(4) Norway	5.6
(5) Europe	8.9
(6) America	38.9
(7) Other	5.6
	100.0

A affiliates had decision-making powers reaching out to overseas affiliates in the same ownership group, and most of these were just across the North Sea in Norway, that is, dependent upon essentially the same oil province.[5] Of the forty-four American affiliates in the sample, twenty-eight reported that decisions over capital investments were made in the USA, with a further eleven reporting that these decisions were made at regional headquarter offices located elsewhere in the UK, most usually in England. Thus, only five American affiliates in the sample at the Aberdeen service base had independent powers over capital investments (i.e. little more than 10 per cent).

The Aberdeen affiliate within its ownership group: proposition 8

The questionnaire revealed that the contribution of affiliates in the Aberdeen service base to group sales was not very large. Thus, 55 per cent of affiliates located there accounted for 10 per cent or less of their respective ownership group's total sales, and almost one-third of affiliates accounted for 1 per cent or less of their group's sales. The picture is similar with group employment: two-thirds of affiliates accounted for 10 per cent or less of group employment, and 30 per cent of them accounted for 1 per cent or less of group employment.

Conclusions

The determinants of the internationalization of production were discussed in Chapter 5 and it was the main objective of this chapter to assess whether the features of the offshore oil supply industry as found in its main British base were consistent with the transaction cost theory of the multinational corporation. In order to perform this task, eight propositions were deduced from the theory, and the facts (as revealed in a stratified random sample of offshore oil service companies) were compared with these propositions.

The facts correspond with expectations in the case of each proposition, and this is taken as offering support for the transaction cost theory of the multinational corporation, albeit support limited to a case study. In particular, it was found that affiliates of multinational companies heavily predominated amongst the firms active in the Aberdeen service base; furthermore, in the technological core of the offshore oil service industry it is American multinational companies that dominate. These companies were shown to be the earliest entrants and to have bunched their entry, while host country firms tended to straggle their entry over a longer time period. These two findings are consistent with the view that the American headquartered offshore oil service companies are 'global scanners', seeking out profitable investment opportunities wherever they may arise. The slower response of British companies to the investment opportunities offered by the growth of the Aberdeen service base is consistent with their origins outside of the oil industry, as this is likely to have delayed both their recognition of the existence of profitable investments and/or their speed of reaction to them.

The peripheral nature of the Aberdeen service base to the world oil industry was evidenced by the predominance of affiliates rather than headquartered firms; in addition the American, technological core, companies retained their research and development expenditures in the USA as well as their decision-making over investment expenditures. Indeed, the decision-making powers of the vast majority of the oil-related companies located in Aberdeen either were limited to the local area or extended to other areas (such as Norway) that are anyway dependent on the longevity of the North Sea oil province.

As a general conclusion the features found in the Aberdeen offshore oil service base which relate to the eight propositions discussed in this chapter are entirely consistent with the picture of the global offshore oil supply industry described in Chapter 4. If a caricature of the global offshore oil supply industry were to be offered, it would be one akin to the old silk route caravans that travelled Eurasia. At the head of the caravan are the oil companies, which decide in which direction the caravan is to move, and behind them come the multinational offshore oil service companies. Each member of this caravan is but a part of a wider ownership group and other members of these groups are off on other trails. The caravan sets itself down from time to time at a watering-hole (a service base) and there it is tended by providers of the locally produced goods and services needed by the caravan members. The caravan will eventually move on, leaving the service base behind, but this is no small matter for the inhabitants of the service base or its government. Both would like to enjoy the profits of the caravan when it settles in a new service base. However, the difficulties of joining the caravan are immense because of barriers to entry. We will discuss the position of local firms and host/multinational corporation relationships in greater detail in Chapter 11.

Notes

1 The term 'ownership group' simply means the group of firms held in common ownership.
2 The life-cycle of an offshore oil supply base is discussed in Chapter 8.
3 The populations were composed of the lists of firms published by the Manpower Services Commission, the North East Scotland Development Authority and Grampian Regional Council.

4 Small firms employed 1–25 employees, medium 26–100, large 101–500 and very large over 501.
5 The decision-making domains of the 130 group A affiliates were as follows: local area only – 60.8 per cent of all group A affiliates; UK only (including local area) – 20.8 per cent; UK and overseas – 13.8 per cent; and overseas and local (excluding UK) – 4.6 per cent (questionnaire responses).

Appendix

Table A6.1 *Ownership of 100% involved affiliates by American parent companies grouped by SIC (1980)*

Average North American ownership share across all SIC (1980) = 33.1%

Row number	SIC description	American owned (No.)	Sample size (No.)	Percentage N. American
Rows where N. American ownership % is greater than N. American average %:				
1	General exploration	2	4	50
3	Drilling	2	5	40
6	Well stimulation	4	4	100
8	Mechanical engineering	7	11	63
10	Electrical & electronic engineering	2	5	40
15	Distribution & supplies	17	40	42
17	Catering	1	1	100
20	Renting and hiring of movables	3	7	41
Rows where N. American % is below N. American average but significantly greater than nil:				
4	Diving	1	7	14
5	Surveying	1	5	20
18	Transport	2	14	14
Rows where N. American % is nil or very low:				
2	Oil production	0	1	0
7	Misc. metal goods	0	1	0
9	Misc. machinery production	0	7	0
11	Marine engineering	0	3	0
12	Instrument engineering	0	1	0
13	Misc. manufacturing	0	2	0
14	Construction	1	13	8
16	Retail distribution	0	3	0
19	Banking, finance, etc.	1	34	5

Table A6.2 *Ownership of affiliates by Scottish parent companies grouped by SIC (1980) (100% and less than 100% weighted sample)*

Average Scottish ownership share across all SIC (1980) = 20.36

Row number	SIC description	Scottish owned (No.)	Sample size (No.)	Percentage Scottish
	*Rows where Scottish ownership % is greater than Scottish average %:*			
1	General exploration	1	4	25
3	Drilling	1	5	20
4	Diving	2	7	28.6
7	Misc. metal goods	1	1	100
8	Mechanical engineering	3	11	27.3
9	Misc. machinery production	2	7	28.6
10	Electrical & electronic engineering	1	5	20
11	Marine engineering	3	3	100
16	Retail distribution	2	3	66.6
18	Transport	3	14	21.4
19	Banking, finance, etc.	7	34	20.6
	*Rows where Scottish % is below Scottish average but significantly greater than nil:*			
14	Construction	1	13	7.7
15	Distribution & supplies	6	40	15
	*Rows where Scottish % is nil:*			
2	Oil production	0	1	0
5	Surveying	0	5	0
6	Well stimulation	0	4	0
12	Instrument engineering	0	1	0
13	Misc. manufacturing	0	2	0
17	Catering	0	1	0
20	Renting & hiring of movables	0	7	0

Table A6.3 Ownership of affiliates by British parent companies grouped by SIC (1980) (100% and less than 100% weighted sample)

Average British ownership share across all SIC = 55%

Row number	SIC description	British owned (No.)	Sample size (No.)	British %
Rows where British ownership % is greater than British average %:				
7	Misc. metal goods	1	1	100
9	Misc. machinery production	4	7	57
10	Electrical & electronic engineering	3	5	60
11	Marine engineering	3	3	100
13	Misc. manufacturing	2	2	100
14	Construction	10	13	77
16	Retail distribution	3	3	100
18	Transport	9	14	64
19	Banking, finance, etc.	28	34	82
Rows where British % is below British average but significantly greater than nil:				
1	General exploration	1	4	25
3	Drilling	2	5	40
4	Diving	2	7	29
5	Surveying	2	5	40
8	Mechanical engineering	4	11	36
15	Distribution & supplies	15	40	38
20	Renting & hiring of movables	3	7	43
Rows where British % is nil:				
2	Oil production	0	1	0
6	Well stimulation	0	4	0
12	Instrument engineering	0	1	0
17	Catering	0	1	0

7

Legal and customary practices in the offshore oil supply industry markets

Oil companies in the Aberdeen offshore oil service base display high degrees of vertical *dis*integration. The average external procurement index was calculated in chapter 3 to be over 91 per cent, which implied that less than 10 per cent of the intermediate inputs used in offshore oil gathering (exploration, development and production) were produced 'inhouse' by the oil companies. Three main reasons were put forward for the oil companies' choice of the market over inhouse production. First, many of the intermediate input markets used by the oil companies were perceived by them to be competitive in the sense that the markets were populated by a good number of competitors (for example, see Table 3.8). Secondly, the oil companies' choice of vertical integration was constrained: as the requirement for an input was often either for a limited quantity or for a relatively short period of time, the amortization of fixed costs would have been unduly burdensome. The solution was to turn to the market to procure these inputs. An alternative solution of selling surplus output produced inhouse to other oil companies seems to have been precluded because it is not possible to isolate the transaction from a potentially costly exchange of information.

The third reason for the choice of market over inhouse production is bound up with the particular market arrangement that the oil companies have chosen through which to procure inputs from arm's-length suppliers, i.e. a variant of the first-price sealed-bid auction. Many of the markets in the technological core of the offshore oil service industry display such high levels of market concentration (see Tables 4.2 and 4.3) that a strong propensity for non-competitive pricing might exist. However, it was argued in Chapter 2 that a choice of a market organizational arrangement might be made that could be expected to diffuse a supplier's scope for monopoly pricing. This, in particular, is true of competitive auction arrangements that induce bidders to compete with one another and bid the true worth of a contract to them.

The oil companies have, in fact, chosen as a market organizational arrangement the 'invited tender-bid auction system' through which to procure intermediate inputs and our attention now turns to an examination of this market form.

Before an economic assessment can be presented, a description of the institutional laws, norms and practical mechanics of the invited tender-bid auction is necessary. This is the purpose of this short chapter. Its contents owe a debt to the work of Professor Arvid Frihagen of the Institute of Public Law, Bergen, Norway, who conducted an assessment of offshore tender-bidding practices from a lawyer's point of view (Frihagen, 1983). During the course of interviewing many oil companies and offshore oil service firms for the sample surveys which have been referred to in Chapters 3 and 6, we were able to confirm some of the legal–institutional features that Frihagen has described.

The oil companies enter into agreements contracting for products and services that are worth millions of pounds sterling. The invited tender-bid process which they operate is their chosen means of obtaining competitive prices. Frihagen comments that the oil companies' 'worldwide standard pattern [is] using only closed tenders' (p. 42) and he quotes as follows from an oil company's internal manual:

> competitive tendering must always be sought for contracts of any value, except where very strong justification can be made for single tender action, such as a technical monopoly. (p. 24)

These outline facts are easily verifiable. In practice, potential suppliers seal bid-prices in envelopes which are subsequently opened at a predetermined time. The winning bidder is the one with the lowest price. Table 3.4 showed that a large oil company may use the invited tender-bid auction arrangement up to 2,000 times during the course of a year. Smaller companies may use it anything between 70 and 1,000 times per annum.

An oil company seeking a tender agreement will invite bids from only those contractors in which it has confidence. The number of invited contractors is usually kept small. The advantage here, according to Frihagen, is that it promotes a competitive environment while, at the same time, minimizing the need for long, and possibly complex, comparative analysis of bids. (In Chapter 9 a formal economic model of the optimum number of invited tender-bidders is presented.) Likewise, Frihagen ventures that the individual contractors will take a tender-invitation more seriously when there are fewer firms with which it must compete. Preparing a tender-bid is often a time-consuming and costly venture in itself and it is likely to be begun only if there is a good probability of winning the contract. These reasons also explain why the oil companies prefer to issue invitations rather than operate an 'open' bidding system. With open bidding, the number of bidders for a contract may be so large as to involve an oil company in excessive (i.e. non-optimum) tender-bid assessment costs. (Tender-bid assessment cost is one of the transaction costs relevant to the determination of the optimum number of invited tender-bidders – see Chapter 9.)[1]

The matter of restricting the bidding to a limited number of invited bidders may be assessed in another way. Following Demsetz (1968a) and Schelling (1956, 1960), a competitive environment may be created in a situation of sealed bidding. In ignorance of what the others are bidding, each bidder will be induced to bid up to its own private valuation of the contract. However, the more bidders there are, the greater are aggregate bidding costs, which will ultimately be at least partly incident on the oil companies (see Chapter 9) and the greater will be the complexity – and cost – of assessing the rival bids. Williamson (1976) and Goldberg (1977) have considered the question of bid assessment complexity and the choice between an auction and fixed-price negotiation. When many variables have to be assessed – in the determination of a kind of weighted average price – there is a cost advantage in restricting the number of bidders. In the limit, when complexity is very great, it may be advantageous to abandon the auction method altogether and negotiate with a single supplier.

As national laws generally do not require that oil companies use any particular form of bidding system for procurement purposes, the adoption of the invited tender-bid system has come about as a matter of free choice. Potentially there are several market arrangements in which exchange prices could be determined. If it is assumed that oil companies are profit maximizers, then their unanimous adoption of the invited tender-bid auction ought to be taken as indicating something about their belief in its efficacy as a market arrangement. That is, revealed preference is indicative of the existence of a belief on the part of the oil companies in its comparative advantage over other market arrangements.

It is interesting to note that the invited tender-bid auction has advantages other than those connected with its transactional cost efficiency. First, as several suppliers are usually invited to submit tender-bids for a given job, the scope for finding the most technically capable contractor is broadened (Frihagen, 1983, p. 15). Secondly, Frihagen points out that the invited tender-bid arrangement reduces the chances of fraud by a buyer's own employees.[2] Thirdly, competitive bidding assures co-licensees that fair prices are being paid (Frihagen, 1983, p. 15). This could be important when an operator makes purchases from firms in the same ownership group as itself. And, finally, open competitive bidding may allow entry for indigenous national contractors to participate (Frihagen, 1983, p. 16). This would be less likely if the oil companies were much more highly backward vertically integrated than they in fact are, or if they habitually made purchases from only a small, unchanging, group of suppliers. In fact, national governments will sometimes insist that large contracts be broken down into component parts so as to give relatively new indigenous entrants to the offshore oil supply industry an opportunity to compete with the dominant multinationals.

The invited tender-bid system as operated by the oil companies can, for descriptive purposes, be divided into four broad phases: the pre-selection phase, the invitation phase, the bidders' reply phase and the award phase. Each of these plays a role in the formation of the prices affixed to the goods and services that are exchanged between the oil companies as buyers and their suppliers in the offshore oil supply industry. Each phase is given consideration in the formal arguments presented in the next two chapters. A brief description of these four phases is now given.

The pre-selection phase

The oil companies keep extensive lists of potential vendors on file, which they frequently update. The information is gathered through direct representations by new entrants to the offshore oil supply industry, as a result of experience gained by working with chosen suppliers and through other channels including the news media, trade magazines and trade fairs or conferences. It should be clear that all potential suppliers must have their names placed on the oil companies' *vendor lists*. As only those suppliers that are deemed to be competent can have their names on these lists, such a listing can be seen as being a form of low-grade pre-qualification.

Pre-qualification
Formal pre-qualification, however, is somewhat more demanding. All *invited bidders* will have pre-qualified: that is, the purchaser will have satisfied itself prior to sending out the invitations to bid that a supplier is capable of carrying out the work for which it is to be invited to tender.[3]

The pre-qualification procedure usually involves a potential supplier in the provision of detailed information about its technical qualifications, financial standing and manpower commitments to other jobs, and even about the specific personnel to be used on a given contract.[4] Additionally, a résumé of similar work experience will often be requested. The main point of pre-qualification is then that 'the operator wants some assurance that the contractor will not over-extend himself'

(Frihagen, 1983, p. 118) in the technically and financially demanding offshore oil supply industry.

From the vendor lists, a *bidders' list* of pre-qualified companies will be drawn up. As a matter of practice, anything between one and ten companies will be invited to place tender-bids.[5] The drawing up of a bidders' list is not necessarily the sole responsibility of a single buyer. When an offshore leaseblock concession has been granted to a consortium, the lead company, known as the operator, will often consult with its partners. Also, as national interests might be at risk, a specially created governmental entity (such as Britain's Offshore Oil Supplies Office) will have to be informed. This obligation is incurred under articles written into the leaseblock concession agreements by the statutory powers. If no national suppliers have been included on the bidders' list, then the Offshore Supplies Office may require that one or more such suitable companies be added to the list.

In the economic model of the invited tender-bid system presented in Chapter 9, the pre-selection phase is modelled in the following way: a buyer is deemed to know exactly the number of pre-qualified firms in any given offshore oil supply industry subsector (e.g. $n = 7$, where n is the number of potential suppliers). Each of these is also deemed to be pre-qualified. Selection of m firms ($m \leq n$) from the bidders' list is modelled in two different ways: first, as a matter of random selection, where each of the n firms has equal probabilities of being invited to bid; and, secondly, after a limited process of market surveillance has been conducted.[6] As the main objective in Chapter 8 is to assess the allocative efficiency of the invited tender-bid system, governmental involvement in the drawing up of a bidders' list is not discussed further: such involvement is motivated by the objective not necessarily of improving allocative efficiency, rather of promoting national interests.

The invitation phase

Each firm appearing on the bidders' list will be sent a preliminary enquiry letter and, following an expression of interest on a supplier's part, a formal letter of invitation. The work description and accompanying terms and conditions will be stated in detailed annexes to the invitation letter. These annexes provide information on matters relating to the scope of the work, specifications, articles of agreement, exhibits and drawings. The tender forms on which a tenderer's tender-bid is to be written will also be sent out at this stage. This documentation forms the basis of the tender. It is up to the bidder to examine these documents so as to know exactly what is to be bid for. Mistakes or misunderstandings due to a bidder's negligence are unlikely to be compensated by the buyer.[7] The buyer, however, is ready to answer enquiries prior to the bid closing date and the answers will be communicated to all bidders so that each is equally well informed.

Replies by bidders

On the tender form the bidder will enter the details of its tender-bid. These details include, where relevant, statements of lump sums payable, unit time-rates, fixed fees and any reimbursable costs, as well as estimates of required manhours and rates for extra work. Usually bids will be made in the currency of the host country and, when exchange rate conversions are involved, the basis of these will be stated. The completed tender form will be accompanied by a parent company's guarantee of the bidder's financial viability (unless these matters have been settled in the pre-qualification phase). When alternative technical proposals are presented, the practice required by the oil companies is that a supplier submits two separate tenders: one to the oil company's own specifications and the second to the alternative specifications.

In the following chapters it is assumed that bidders understand fully the nature of the work for which they are bidding, and that the tender-bid is represented by the statement of a single lump-sum contract price. In reality, such a single price may not exist. Alternative technical specifications may have been provided and a bidder may have entered alternative contractual clauses. In such cases, Frihagen points out that the oil companies use detailed points-scoring systems so as to facilitate comparisons. For our purposes, these can be thought of as being a means of calculating a weighted average price, where both the weights and the translation method of turning non-pecuniary into pecuniary values are chosen by the buyer. Thus, despite the added complications, contracts can still be thought of as being awarded on the basis of a comparison of single valued price-bids.

Contract award

On the due date the buyer will open the envelopes containing the tender-bids. The bidders will not be present; indeed, this little 'ceremony' will be shrouded in secrecy. While the unsuccessful bidders will be shortly so informed, usually no reasons will be given for their failure. Nor is it likely that they (or the winning bidder) will be told of the names that appeared on the bidders' list. Although, in law, acceptance of the winning bid may itself constitute a contract, a formal signing of contracts with the winning bidder usually follows.

Throughout the tender-bidding process, the oil companies seek to reduce information flow between the rival bidders to the very minimum. In the next chapter, the economic model that is developed reflects this feature with alternative specifications. First, the bidders are not allowed to know either each other's identities or the cost levels of any single firm in their subsector; secondly, and less restrictively, the rivals are allowed to know each other's cost levels but do not know the identity of any of their rivals in any given tender-bid contest.

Conclusions

This chapter has outlined some of the important institutional arrangements and practices chosen by the oil companies by which the prices for the intermediate inputs that they purchase are determined. In the invited tender-bid system, the oil companies seek to minimize information flow, both pre- and post-auction, between the rival auction bidders. Thus, they seek to create (and have been successful in achieving) a world of uncertainty for their suppliers. Not only is outright collusion between suppliers illegal, but typically an invited bidder will not be told the identity of its rivals in any given bidding contest, nor are the losing bidders told the value of the winning bid.

A resource allocation system that does not publish prices and is so restrictive of information flow might be expected to be inefficient. This contention is examined in the next three chapters, where it will be shown that, in fact, the invited tender-bid system is an efficient means of allocating resources within and between the oil companies and their suppliers in the offshore oil supply industry.

Notes

1   On the matters mentioned in this paragraph Frihagen has commented that 'the prime reason for limiting the number of bidders has probably been to simplify the administrative task of choosing the final contract' (1983, p. 41). And 'as the cost of preparing bids could be considerable, limiting the number of participants could, in addition, tend to hold the price level down as the tendering costs somehow will have to be a general cost factor covered by the tender prices' (p. 42).
2   'The contracts will involve such great sums of money and other interest, that it would be in the operator companies' interests to have a system where the choice of contractor is made on the basis of competing and comparable offers *so as not to leave too much up to a few employees*' (Frihagen, 1983, p. 15; emphasis added). Milgrom (1989) supports the view that auctions are more fraud-resistant than is negotiation. Thus, 'as compared to bargaining, auctions have the additional advantage of being institutions whose conduct can be delegated to an *unsupervised* agent. Public auctions offer fewer opportunities for kickbacks and behind-the-scenes agreements between the seller's

agent [buyer's agent in a procurement auction] and a single buyer [seller] than do negotiated agreements' (Milgrom, 1989, p. 19; emphasis added).

3   Frihagen points out: 'in the North Sea offshore development business . . . pre-qualification arrangements as a general rule will be more-or-less automatic' (p. 44).

4   Sometimes an oil company may not have enough time prior to a tendering to perform an entire pre-qualification exercise. Bidders will then have to provide information pertaining to their competence along with other bid documentation.

5   This information was confirmed in my own detailed interviews with ten oil companies having interests in the British sector of the North Sea.

6   A distinction between the concepts of 'market surveillance' and the better-known concept of 'market search' is drawn in Chapter 10.

7   Of course, if a misunderstanding has arisen owing to some sort of failure on the part of the buyer, the successful bidder will, if necessary, be compensated financially.

8

Bid prices, rent distribution and adjustment in the long run

This and the following three chapters present an economic analysis of the invited tender-bid auction system as operated by the oil companies in their purchasing relationships with their suppliers in the offshore oil supply industry. These chapters pay attention to bid-price optimization and economic organizational problems in the offshore oil-gathering business (this chapter), optimization of (measurement cost) expenditures on running an invited tender-bid auction (Chapter 9), the role of buyers as market-makers (Chapter 10), and the transactional problems to which product idiosyncrasy and related matters give rise when an organizational form is being chosen (Chapter 10, but more particularly Chapter 12).

One of the main arguments that will be developed is that the oil companies, having already taken the decision to avoid the organizational transaction costs that would be incurred with vertical integration into the many facets of oil exploration, development and production, in fact face a trade-off between the transaction costs thereby avoided and the transaction costs of using the market. That is, vertical disintegration, while reducing the costs of internalized economic organization, does not necessarily come free of additional costs of other kinds. Thus we are taking a comparative-institutions approach here.

These additional costs can take several forms. First, there are the costs of running the invited tender-bid system that are *directly* incurred by the oil companies. These are defined as 'tender-bid assessment costs'. The sellers of goods and services to the oil companies also incur bidding costs, which we call 'tender-bid assembly costs', and at least a part of these are likely to be *incident* upon the oil companies as buyers. Secondly, it will also become apparent that, as the dissemination of price information is suppressed, the invited tender-bid auction as operated by the oil companies has an element of informational inefficiency. This informational inefficiency tends to hinder resource allocation in the offshore oil supply industry and, in an expansionary phase, allows the suppliers' quasi-rents on fixed assets to persist longer than otherwise. These quasi-rents are a cost to the buyers. Thirdly, it will be shown that, in the model of the invited tender-bid auction, buyers will not necessarily find the lowest *potential* price-bidder for a given contract. Indeed, it will be demonstrated that the *expectation* is that this bidder will not be found. This too might seem to be another cost of utilizing the invited tender-bid market arrangement. It will be shown, however, that the invited tender-bid arrangement is in fact a Pareto optimal market organizational form. When costs are incurred in affixing prices to idiosyncratic quantities, it does not necessarily pay to extend invitations to bid to all potential contractors.

In this world where information flow is restricted, the firms invited to place tender-bids for a contract are assumed to try to maximize the monetary value of expected profit. This is an obvious choice of objective function for shareowner-owned firms operating in a competitive environment. We begin by demonstrating the bidding problem that the offshore oil service firms have to cope with. The chapter then moves on to consider buyer behaviour and to assess the effects of changing market conditions (market demand relative to installed supply capacity) on both the level and variability of bid-prices and supply firms' profits. This is followed by a discussion of the long-run adjustment of the offshore oil supply industry (i.e. as installed capacity in a given geographic location is induced to vary over time).

Thus, in this chapter five main issues are to be discussed:

- supply companies' price-setting behaviour under conditions of uncertainty;
- the relationship between bid-prices and market conditions;
- the level and variability of bid-prices and supply-firm profits;
- the distribution of natural resource rents derived from oil production between the oil companies and the firms in the offshore oil service sector; and
- the existence of quasi-rent and the adjustment of the size of the offshore oil service industry in the long run.

Attention first turns to modelling the suppliers' and the buyers' side of the offshore oil-gathering business, beginning with an explicit list of the underlying assumptions.

The assumptions

As there are buyers and suppliers standing in a market relationship, we assume:

(1) A market has to be made between

buyers: B_u, the set $u = 1 \ldots v$ is internally homogeneous; and

sellers: E_j, the set $j = 1 \ldots n$ is internally homogeneous.

As inputs into offshore oil gathering are complex, it is assumed that:

(2) The intermediate input exchanged is variable multi-attribute (i.e. idiosyncratic) but, to simplify matters, homogeneous between suppliers for any given subset of attributes. (Quality screening matters will be considered later.)

The next ten assumptions are designed to standardize the invited tender-bid auction as operated by the oil companies.

(3) Contracts awarded at each tender-bid auction are of equal size and for a limited period of time.
(4) A buyer 'makes' a market by inviting tender-bids from a selected set of m suppliers, $m \leqslant n$.
(5) Tender-bid 'contests' are arranged by buyers sequentially. (This assumption allows us to avoid determining multiple bids at a given point of time.)
(6) Only one buyer at a time invites tender-bids. (Again avoiding the need to consider the placing of multiple bids.)
(7) The buyer will always select the tender-bid with the lowest price and suppliers know this. (This is a reasonable assumption given the attribute-homogeneity assumption.)
(8) Buyers have no information as to where each supplier is operating on its variable cost curve.[1]
(9) Information flow between rival tender-bidders as to each other's tender-bid price does not occur. (This is most likely to be true in the absence of collusion, as both suppliers and buyers favour price secrecy.) Collusion is also illegal under British monopolies' legislation.
(10) Contracts are large in relation to a supply firm's 'normal' capacity output. That is, a contract gained will move a supplier significantly up its variable cost curve. (This is a reflection of limited short-run installed capacity and shortages of appropriate skilled labour.)

(11) 'Normal' capacity is defined as being the output level that can be sustained by a firm's fixed inputs without marginal costs rising sharply.
(12) An invitation to bid will not be refused. In fact, invitations to bid are nearly always accepted both because a refusal might generate 'bad-will' and because of the profit expectation.

The objective lying behind these assumptions is to homogenize (i.e. minimize differences) as much as possible so as to concentrate only on the pure processes of the invited tender-bid price formation system without other differences being responsible for certain features of the outcome. Relaxing some of the assumptions does give rise to qualitative differences in the model, but it is shown later (particularly at the end of Chapter 10) that altering assumptions does not detract from the model's major conclusions on the allocative and distributional efficiency of the invited tender-bid auction system. Thus, the objective of the assumptions is to simplify a complicated real-world market organizational form. Accordingly, assumption (2) rules out quality differences between the rival suppliers; assumptions (3), (10) and (11) together imply that the winning of a contract will have the same effect on each supplier's level of variable costs; assumptions (5) and (6) simplify a seller's bidding problem, as multiple bidding at a given point in time is ruled out; and assumptions (8) and (9) indicate that information flow in the oil industry is highly circumscribed – an assumption that is meant to reflect the intention of the legal contracts drawn up by the oil companies.

Supply firms

Supply firms are assumed to be risk-neutral profit maximizers. Accordingly, in a world of uncertain outcomes, a risk-neutral firm trying to maximize profit will equivalently try to maximize expected profit. Put another way, the risk-neutral firm ignores risk and is concerned only with maximizing the expected value of profit. This is the function that our supply firms attempt to maximize.

A supply firm, firm j, has a clearly defined total cost function:

$$C_T{}^j = C_V{}^j + C_F{}^j, \tag{8.1}$$

where the subscripts V and F refer to variable and fixed costs respectively. Additionally,

$$C_T{}^j = C_V^j (W_V{}^j, Q^j, F^j) + C_F{}^j (W_F^j, F^j), \tag{8.2}$$

where the W's are the prices of factor inputs, Q^j is output and F^j the quantity of fixed inputs.

Profit (π) is earned by winning a contract with a bid of $\bar{P}^j$ to supply an oil company with intermediate inputs. More exactly, it is defined as 'contribution to profit and fixed-cost expenses', i.e.

$$\pi^j = \bar{P}^j - C_V{}^j, \tag{8.3}$$

and, to avoid the clumsiness of the phrase 'contribution to profit and fixed-cost expenses', $\bar{P}^j - C_V{}^j$ will be called 'unit profit'. Since winning a contract in competition with rivals is by no means certain, a supplier will attempt to maximize *expected* unit profit, i.e.

$$E(\pi^j) = Pr_W (\bar{P}^j - C_V{}^j), \tag{8.4}$$

where Pr_W is the probability of winning a contract in a given bidding contest.

A supplier will be aware that the selection of a bid-price, P^j, will affect both unit profit and the probability of winning a contract. If a very low bid is made, the probability of winning will be high but unit profit will be low, while if a very high bid is submitted, unit profit will be high but the probability of winning will be low. The problem that a supply firm faces is to select the bid-price that will maximize expected profit. So some consideration is needed of the problem of choosing an optimum bid.

Finding the optimum bid
It has been pointed out that the bid-price chosen affects both unit profit and the probability of winning. Thus, for a given level of variable costs, unit profit increases as $\bar{P}^j$ increases but Pr_W decreases. For likely probability distributions of rivals' bids (such as the normal distribution), as firm j raises its bid-price from a low to a high level, the proportionate rate of *decrease* in the probability of winning will increase. So, with the bid-price being increased, the proportionate rate of increase in unit profit might at first increase faster than the probability of winning decreases, and expected profit will at first increase along with the bid-price. Eventually, however, the proportionate rate of decrease in Pr_W will come to swamp the proportionate increase in unit profit, so expected profit would then decline.

For any bidder the calculation of unit profit is an easy matter since it is assumed that variable costs are known with certainty. Much more difficult is to calculate the probability of winning with any given bid, for this depends upon the rivals' bids. In fact, it will be shown that the oil companies (the buyers) restrict the amount of information flow between themselves and the sellers and between the sellers to such a great extent that it seems to be impossible for a bidder to adopt a well-informed bidding strategy. Each bidder, though, will still have to choose a bid-price using such information as is available. This information consists of:

- an observation of the state of market demand relative to the supply industry's existing supply capacity; and
- knowledge of where each rival supplier is on its own cost curve.

But there will be no knowledge of any of the rivals' previous bid-prices or of exactly which rivals a particular bidder will be bidding against in any bid contest.

In order to illustrate the extent of a bidder's bid-price selection problem it is informative to compare it with the situation envisaged in Friedman's (1956) seminal paper, where more information than in our case was available. In particular, Friedman assumed that the records were available of each rival's bid-prices on previous contracts for which a given contractor had bid. Friedman's technique for finding the optimum bid required that firm j constructed a frequency distribution of the ratios of each rival's actual bid, X^{j-1}, to firm j's own cost estimate, C_V^j, of these jobs. Thus, if firm j bids X^j, scaled relative to its own cost estimate for the job, its probability of winning is the sum of the probabilities of beating each firm separately, i.e.

$$Pr_w = Pr(A) + Pr(B) + Pr(C),$$

where the right-hand-side probabilities are those for beating each rival separately.[2]

By restricting the information on bid-prices, the oil companies keep their suppliers in the dark. But the suppliers will, naturally, still be concerned to find bids that will maximize an expected profit function.

What Friedman's and related approaches to the bidding problem achieved was to turn a situation of *uncertainty* into one of *risk*, in the sense first defined by Knight (1957). What enabled him to consider the bidding problem as an aspect of decision-making with risk was the availability of information on previous bids. Without this information, the 'certainty' of decision-making under conditions of risk (i.e. with known probability density functions) is transformed into a problem of decision-making with uncertainty because the relevant probability distributions remain hidden. This greatly complicates the decision-making problem, for as Hey (1979) has observed:

under *uncertainty* the decision procedure is not so simple [as under risk]. Indeed, there is no universally agreed 'best' procedure (nor is one ever likely to be found; perhaps this, more than any other reason, is why economists have steered clear of the analysis). (p. 42)

Nevertheless, an attempt must be made if the understanding of the economics of the offshore oil supply industry is to be advanced. The approach will be to construct a conditional subjective probability distribution of rivals' lowest bids. The conditions will be set by the 'state of the market'.

Given the complexity of finding the optimal bid for a given bid-contest in this world of uncertainty, a solution based on an explicit probability distribution of rivals' bids cannot be sought. Fortunately, it will be possible to indicate in a simple model how bid-prices are likely to behave as market conditions change in the short run and supply industry capacity changes in the long run. Thus, what will be shown is the likely direction of change of optimum bid-prices under varying circumstances. The more demanding problem of defining optimal bid-prices for explicit probability density functions is not attempted. However, this less ambitious task is at once tractable and will provide valuable insights into the matters raised above: the distribution of rent between the oil companies and their suppliers; the existence of quasi-rent on fixed resources; the long-run adjustment of the supply industry; and the trade-off faced by the buyers between the transaction costs avoided by not vertically integrating production and the costs of using the market.

However, before these issues are broached it is necessary to model the behaviour of the oil companies – the buyers of intermediate goods and services supplied by companies in the offshore oil supply industry.

The buyers

According to the assumptions listed earlier, on the demand side of the market there are firms $B_u, u = 1 . . . v$, that sequentially arrange tender-bid 'contests' and award contracts to the low bidders. Each buyer invites m firms to bid from the n firms in the supply industry, with $m \leqslant n$ (just why m is most likely to be less than n is explained in the next chapter, where the subject of the optimal number of invited bidders is discussed). Buyers have no information as to what point each of the n suppliers is currently operating at on their respective variable cost functions. The effect of this assumption is that the selection of the m firms to submit tender-bids is random. However, within the set of m bidders, a buyer will award the contract to the lowest bidder. As the m firms are drawn at random, the lowest bid-price need not be the lowest tender-bid price had all $j = 1 \ldots n$ supply firms been invited to bid: the buyer had set $m = n$.

With these assumptions, the sequential random selection of m firms to submit tender-bids can be expected to result in firms $j = 1 \ldots n$ gaining from an incremental batch of contracts in an unevenly distributed manner. Accordingly, some firms will move further up their variable cost curves than others. The probability of this happening is quite high. Suppose that $n = 5, m = 3$ and that five incremental contracts (d) have to be distributed. It can be asked: what is the probability of any one firm being awarded two contracts before any one other firm has been awarded a single extra contract (i.e. what is $Pr(2–0)$)? The problem may be solved using conditional probability.

In this case $Pr(2–0)$ is 46 per cent; while, as will now be shown, with $n = 7, m = 3$ and $d = 7$, $Pr(2–0)$ is 74 per cent.

Bayes' theorem is used to calculate the probability of events conditional upon one or more preceding events. As an example of a calculation of $Pr(2–0)$ we will work with the second case mentioned above: there are seven firms in an offshore oil supply industry subsector, i.e. $n = 7$; three of these firms are to be invited to bid on any contract ($m = 3$); and seven new (or incremental) contracts are to be awarded in sequential order.

In these circumstances we can draw up the tree diagram shown in Figure 8.1, where $Pr(2–0)$ is defined as the complement to Pr (not $2 – 0$), i.e. the terms A^c, B^c, C^c and D^c are the probabilities of the fourth, fifth, sixth and seventh contracts, respectively, of $Pr(2–0)$ occurring.

Calculation of the probabilities in the tree's branches is as follows. Given that a contract will always be awarded to the firm with the fewest

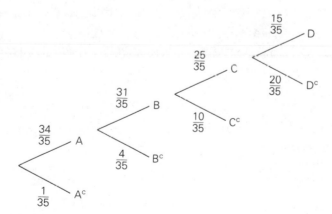

Figure 8.1   *Tree diagram: calculation of* $Pr(2–0)$, m = 3 *and* n = 7

number of contracts among the $m = 3$ firms selected to bid (remember that winning a contract moves a supply firm appreciably up its variable cost curve), after three contracts have been awarded three supply firms must have one contract each: the universal set is:

$$[1,1,1,0,0,0,0.]$$

There is $\binom{3}{3} = 1$ way in which the three firms with one contract in this set can be selected when the fourth contract is awarded, but there are $\binom{n}{m} = \frac{7!}{3!4!} = 35$ ways of selecting *any* three firms from the seven in the industry subsector. Hence, $Pr(A) = 34/35$ and $Pr(A^c) = 1/35$. That is, the probability of one firm obtaining two additional contracts before some other single firm has obtained one additional contract is 1/35.

   If the fourth contract is awarded to a fourth firm, we have the universal set:[3]

$$[1,1,1,1,0,0,0,]$$

and there are $\binom{4}{3} = 4$ ways in which these four firms with contracts can be selected to bid on the next contract. Hence, $Pr(B) = 31/35$ and $Pr(B^c) = 4/35$. If the fifth contract is awarded to a fifth firm, the universal set becomes:

$$[1,1,1,1,1,0,0,]$$

and there are $\binom{5}{3} = 10$ ways in which these five firms with contracts can again be selected to bid. Hence, $Pr(C) = 25/35$ and $Pr(C^c) = 10/35$. If the sixth contract is awarded to a sixth firm, the universal set now becomes:

$$[1,1,1,1,1,1,0,]$$

and there are $\binom{6}{3} = 20$ ways in which these six firms with contracts can be selected. Hence, $Pr(D) = 15/35$ and $Pr(D^c) = 20/35$.

   Now from Bayes' theorem we simply add the four conditional probabilities to find $Pr(2-0)$ across all $d = 7$ additional contracts.

Calculation of $Pr(2-0)$: n = 7; m = 3; d = 7

$Pr(A^c)$	= 1/35		= 0.029
$Pr(B^c)$	= $Pr(B^c\|A).PrA = (4/35).(34/35)$		= 0.111
$Pr(C^c)$	= $Pr(C^c\|B \cap A) = (10/35).(31/35).(34/35)$		= 0.264
$Pr(D^c)$	= $Pr(D^c\|C \cap B \cap A) = (20/35).(25/35).(31/35).$		
		(34/35)	= 0.351

$$Pr(2-0) = Pr(A^c) + Pr(B^c) + Pr(C^c) + Pr(D^c) \qquad = 0.755$$
$$Pr(2-0) = \qquad\qquad\qquad = 75.5\%$$

It is instructive to notice the role played by d, the incremental number of contracts to be awarded. In the above example, $d = n$ and $Pr(2-0) =$ 75.5%, but, as d is reduced below n, $Pr(2-0)$ declines, viz:

$$d = 6, Pr(2-0) = 40.4\%$$
$$d = 5, Pr(2-0) = 14.0\%$$
$$d = 4, Pr(2-0) = 2.9\%.$$

The implication is that it needs a surge in demand – defined as d being relatively large in relation to n – to raise the probability of an uneven number of contracts being distributed to high levels. Or, put another way, it is when market conditions are fluctuating (again defined as d large in relation to n) that the probability of contracts being distributed unevenly among the rival suppliers becomes high.

As we have seen, in the technological core of the offshore oil supply industry, concentration of suppliers is sometimes high. As the oil companies taken together typically run thousands of tender-bid procurement contests in a given offshore oil service base, it is not unreasonable to assume that the number of contracts to be distributed in a subsector may sometimes be greater than the number of supply firms (i.e. $d > n$).

The probability of contracts being awarded unevenly among the suppliers would be further increased if contracts were not awarded for equal periods of time (assumption 3). Then firms would move to different points on their variable cost curves as contracts were run off at different times. This factor would further complicate the calculation of $Pr(2-0)$, but would seem to raise it. We will continue with the assumption that contracts are awarded for equal periods of time.

Bid-prices

What is now sought is the behaviour of bid-prices under various conditions. Firm j is assumed to treat other bids in any state of the market as a random variable and its subjective probability distribution over these bids is conditioned by the cost levels that it thinks each potential competitor to have. It could be assumed that firm j knows those cost levels exactly. But this might appear to introduce an unjustified dichotomy into the analysis: buyers have no knowledge of any potential supplier's costs, while the suppliers have complete knowledge of each rival's cost level. But what could be asserted is that *even if* suppliers had such complete knowledge they would still have probabilistic expected profit functions because they would not know the identity of any of the $m - 1$ rivals when bidding for a contract. Any supplier would still be uncertain as to the cost levels of the rivals in question. While, in fact, a supply company in a clearly defined subsector of the offshore oil supply industry will, through experience and alertness, have some idea of how many contracts each of its potential rivals is currently working upon, we will work with the assumption that this is not so. In other words, it is being assumed that supply companies are as ignorant as the oil companies regarding the cost levels of their potential rival bidders.

Now let P_L be a random variable, the *lowest* bid of the other bidders stated in a given bid-contest. The jth bidder has a subjective probability distribution over P_L. This subjective probability distribution is conditional upon the 'state of the market', $D_M - \bar{S}_M$. Thus, as D_M rises relative to $\bar{S}_M$ (because d is positive), the market is becoming 'tighter', contracts will get distributed unevenly among the supply companies (as was argued earlier). Thus, a cumulative probability distribution can be defined:

$$F = (P^j, D_M - \bar{S}_M) = Pr(P_L < \bar{P}^j \mid D_M - \bar{S}_M), \qquad (8.5)$$

which shows the probability of losing a contract (bidding $\bar{P}^j$) in a given state of the market. It is further assumed that $F_{DM-\bar{S}M} < 0$, meaning that an increase in D_M relative to $\bar{S}_M$ (a tighter market) will decrease the subjective probability of losing with any given bid P^j. This is shown in Figure 8.2, where market conditions become tighter so that the cumulative probability function shifts from F^1 to F^2. Notice that for a given bid, P^j, the probability of losing a contract (the height of the F function above P^j) declines as market conditions become tighter.

The jth bidder wins the contract if $\bar{P}^j < P_L$ and unit profit will be $\pi^j = \bar{P}^j - C_V{}^j$. *Expected* unit profit going in to the 'contest' is:

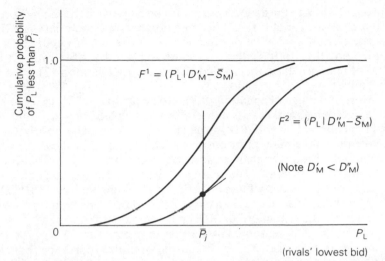

Figure 8.2   *Subjective probability distribution of being the low bidder*

$$E(\pi) = \{1 - F(P_L < P^j \mid D_M - \bar{S}_M)\} (\bar{P}^j - C_V{}^j),   (8.6)$$

where the term in the braces is the probability of winning with a bid of $\bar{P}^j$. In principle, the bidder should choose the bid P^j that yields the maximum expected profit, $E(\pi^*)$.

As was stated earlier, unless a bidder can uncover information that enables it to calculate the probability density functions of rivals' bids, it is very hard indeed to see how the bidder can objectively choose the expected profit-maximizing bid.

The expected profit-maximizing bid-price, P^{*j}, can in principle, however, be found by differentiating equation (8.6) and setting the result equal to zero, viz:

$$\frac{\theta E(\pi)}{\theta P^j} = \{1 - F(P_L < \bar{P}^j \mid D_M - \bar{S}_M)\} + (\bar{P}^j - C_V{}^j)$$
$$\{ - \theta F/\theta P^j \, . \, (P_L < \bar{P}^j \mid D_M - \bar{S}_M)\} = 0.   (8.7)$$

Implicitly differentiating equation (8.7) one can solve for the effect of changing market demand, D_M, on the optimum bid-price. Thus,

$$\frac{\theta P^*}{\theta D_M} = \frac{[\frac{\theta F}{\theta D_M} + (\bar{P}^j - C_V^j)] \, . \, (-\frac{\theta^2 F}{\theta P^j \, \theta D_M})}{2 \, (-\frac{\theta F}{\theta P^j}) - [\bar{P}^j - C_V^j \, . \, \frac{\theta^2 F}{\theta P^{j2}}]} \, .   (8.8)$$

In equation (8.8) the denominator must be negative if the second-order conditions are to hold in (8.7). Remember that the denominator in (8.8) is the second derivative of equation (8.7), i.e. of $\theta E(\pi)/\theta P^j$. But if equation (8.7) truly is the maximum expected profit (rather than the minimum), then the second derivative of equation (7) must be negative.

Now, if the sign of equation (8.8) is to be positive – bid-prices to rise in a tightening market – its numerator must also be negative, but this will only be so if $\theta^2 F/\theta P^j \theta D_M$ is negative (or not greatly positive as to make the whole numerator positive). This latter term shows how the slope of the F function changes when D_M changes at any given bid-price, as shown in Figure 8.2. The change in the slopes of the tangent to the cumulative probability functions, F^1 and F^2, is shown by $\theta^2 F/\theta P^j \theta D_M$. However, as we do not have an explicit cumulative probability function of $P^L < \tilde{P}^j$, the sign of $\theta^2 F/\theta P^j \theta D_M$ must remain unknown.

However, it is reasonable to argue that equation (8.8) is in fact positive. If it were otherwise, then firm j would be seen to be reducing its bid-prices as the market tightened, i.e. as rival firms gained extra contracts and moved up their variable cost curves, so becoming higher-cost competitors to firm j. This would seem to be counter-intuitive, although it is possible that firm j could choose to exploit its improving competitive position by increasing quantity sold rather than raising unit profit. But, if we were to assume that suppliers' short-run output capacity is sharply circumscribed, it is most likely that, as the market tightens, suppliers will raise bid-prices. Moreover, as market conditions were tightening, it is to be expected that the suppliers' state of optimism would be rising and they would be much more likely to put in higher than lower bids; after all, when the market is tight, if the current contract bid is not won, another invitation to bid will likely soon be received. Hence, we will work with the assumption that the cumulative subjective probability functions such as in Figure 8.2 will always take on a shape that justifies the belief that the sign of equation (8.8) is positive.

One other possibility is that the relevant subjective probability density functions are rectangular. Then all terms in the numerator of equation (8.8) are negative or zero, rendering the equation positive. Such circumstances could arise if firm j thought that the rivals would put in different bids but could not distinguish differences in the probabilities of these bids.

Hence it is expected that firm j's bid-price will increase (for given variable costs) as the market becomes tighter. *The important implication is that expected profit increases as the market becomes tighter.* This is shown by partially differentiating equation (8.6) with respect to D_M, viz:

$$\frac{\theta E(\pi)}{\theta D_M} = -(\bar{P}^j - C_V^j).\frac{\theta F}{\theta D_M} > 0. \tag{8.9}$$

As a unit profit is positive and $\theta F/\theta D_M$ negative (i.e. the probability of losing falls), the sign of equation (8.9) must be positive: expected profit rises if the market becomes tighter.

But what is true of firm j is also true of the other $n - 1$ firms. Thus, all bid-prices will tend to rise relative to variable costs: all suppliers expect that their profits will increase as market demand rises relative to fixed normal supply capacity.

It is now time to bring in an observation about the behaviour of demand for the inputs supplied by the offshore oil supply industry. During the last fifteen years or so many tens of leaseblock concessions were passing unevenly through various stages of exploration, development or production, so that market demand for the various inputs fluctuated from year to year. In the model developed here fluctuations in demand, θD_M, can also be represented by changes in the discrete variable d, which, it will be recalled, is the incremental number of contracts to be distributed by the buyers. At any given time the suppliers will be currently working on the outstanding stock (D) of contracts (i.e. those that have been let earlier but have not yet been completed). Thus, as market demand in each of the subsectors fluctuates, d, can take on positive or negative values ($-d$ is the rate of run-off of contracts as they are completed). When d is positive, and greater than $-d$, D increases, but when d is negative D falls.

Hence, from equation (8.9) it follows that, as demand fluctuates (relative to installed supply capacity), suppliers' unit profit will fluctuate and so will prices paid by the buyers. These prices will fluctuate above $C_V^j, j = 1 \ldots n$ because a supplier would choose not to supply if $P^j < C_V^j$.

Quasi-rent

It follows from the above observations that if all potential suppliers raise prices when the market becomes tighter then a buyer's purchase prices must also increase. The oil company buyers have for long earned significant economic rents from their position as leaseblock concessionaires of productive oil fields (Kemp and Rose, 1982). It can now be seen that at least some of this rent must be shared with the supply companies when market demand for inputs from the offshore oil supply industry rises relative to installed capacity. The share of rent obtained by the suppliers takes the form of a quasi-rent on the locationally devoted assets that they own. However, this is only a temporary (the meaning of 'quasi') rent because its existence will attract entry into the supply sectors.

Adjustment of the supply industry in the long run

As we have seen in earlier chapters, the core of the offshore oil supply industry is composed of multinational corporations, mainly, but not only, American, which are organized on a global scale. That is, they seek out profitable opportunities in oil provinces wherever they may be located in the world. In pursuit of profit, a multinational corporation will locate a new affiliate, or expand the capacity of an existing affiliate, when it identifies a profitable opportunity to do so. Such an opportunity arises if the existing supply capacity in a given location is earning a quasi-rent. The assertion that quasi-rent attracts entry is nothing more than the 'traditional' neoclassical assumption on this matter.

It is further assumed that there is a time-lag between the appearance of positive quasi-rent and the adjustment of installed capacity in a given location, so allowing a tight market $(D_M > \bar{S}_M)$ in the short run. This assumption is reasonable because, it will be recalled, contract prices are never published. Thus, as the existence of quasi-rent cannot be signalled through market price signals, it will be passed on through informationally less efficient channels, such as rumour of a buoyant market or as recorded profits in company annual reports, which anyway appear with a time-lag.

The effect of entry, that is increasing S_M in the long run, on prices bid can be found by implicitly differentiating equation (8.7) and has already been done in equation (8.8) for the effect on bid-prices of changing market demand. In equation (8.7), $\bar{S}_M$ enters with the opposite sign to D_M so $\theta P^{*j}/\theta S_M$ is opposite in sign to $\theta P^{*j}/\theta D_M$. Thus, while in the short run an increase in market demand relative to fixed installed capacity will increase bid prices, a rise in installed capacity relative to market demand (i.e. reduced excess demand) will, in the long run, decrease bid-prices. This is intuitively plausible: increased competition among suppliers causes bid-prices to fall.

The effect of changes in installed capacity on supply firms profits is negative:

$$\frac{\theta E(\pi)}{\theta S_M} = - (P^j - C_V{}^j) \cdot (\theta F/\theta ED) \cdot (-1) < 0, \qquad (8.10)$$

where ED is excess demand (or $D_M - \bar{S}_M$). The term $\theta F/\theta ED$ is negative because the probability of losing declines as excess demand increases. However, excess demand is negatively related to changes in installed capacity, so increased installed capacity must reduce supply firms' profits and they gain a lower share of an oil province's economic rent.

In the beginning . . . and in the end

Ultimately the reserves of an oil province will be exhausted and the offshore oil supply industry that was created in that location will have to be dismantled. (Any fragments of it that remain to supply inputs to the oil companies at some other location are not being discussed here.)

The level of oil production and suppliers' installed capacity in a given location is shown schematically in Figure 8.3. Over time, oil production may be assumed to build up gradually from nothing to reach a peak and then to fall away, at some time in the future again reaching zero output.

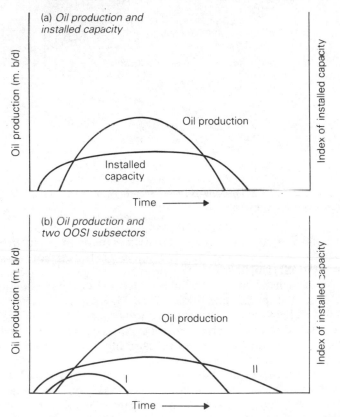

Figure 8.3   *Schematic time-profiles of oil production and indexes of installed capacity*

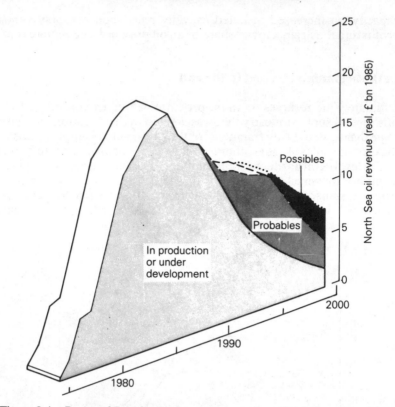

Figure 8.4   *Projected British government revenue from North Sea oil production*
Source: Aberdeen University (David Rose)

Indeed, this is what is projected for British revenue from North Sea oil production – see Figure 8.4. Installed capacity in the offshore oil supply industry (OOSI) will have a more extended time-profile since capacity will have to be installed ahead of oil production to meet the demand for inputs into the initial exploration and development work. Final shutdown will post-date the cessation of oil production, either because supply firms do not have perfect information as to the exact day that oil production will come to an end or because there will be some residual demand for inputs into oil exploration.

The time-profiles of the installed capacity of the separate offshore oil supply industry subsectors will differ from that shown in Figure 8.3a, which can be thought of as representing the time-profile for the industry as a whole. In Figure 8.3b two important subsectors have been separated out. Profile I could represent that for offshore structures construction, while Profile II that for geological and geophysical services. The latter subsectors are needed for a longer period of time than are those of the former sector.

What can be deduced from this schematic representation is that, in any subsector, a period of secular expansion will be followed by a period of secular contraction. As was argued earlier, entry is induced by positive quasi-rents, while exit will occur when quasi-rent is negative. From equation (8.9) it is known that there is a positive relationship between expected profit and the level of market demand (for given supply capacity). Now it can be seen that expected profit must be high enough to attract entry during a subsector's expansionary phase. Then, when demand for inputs starts to decline, expected profit will decline and, presumably, the decline will be sufficient to provoke exit. Which affiliates will exit first is not entirely clear, since a multinational corporation could practise cross-subsidization if it so wished. However, if this is ruled out, and as the contracts which have been awarded by the oil companies are completed at different dates, there will be a growing pool of supply firms in a subsector that are unable to obtain another contract to replace the one that has been completed (this must be so, as with d negative D will be falling). It is entirely plausible that it will be one of these firms that will make the decision to exit, so closing down installed capacity in the location in question.

It can also be seen, from equation (8.10), that exit by some suppliers will increase the expected profits of those that remain. Only when excess demand is zero is the offshore oil supply industry in long-run equilibrium, and such an equilibrium may or may not be long lived. This depends, ultimately, upon the shape of the oil production time-profile shown schematically in Figure 8.3. As drawn, entry will be followed almost immediately by exit. But if peak production was to be maintained for some years (a flattening of the time-profile), some subsectors might be maintained at a constant level of installed capacity for some years.

Having described how the offshore oil service firms in principle arrive at optimum bid-prices and how the offshore oil supply industry adjusts itself in the long run to oil company changing demands, our attention is turned in the next chapter to an important optimization problem faced by the oil companies: the optimization of the number of invited tender-bidders. Here the transaction costs of operating a specific market arrangement will be laid out.

Notes

1   As stated, assumption 8 is almost certainly true but, in reality, an oil company might have some idea of which potential suppliers are high- or low-cost firms. In Chapter 10 the concept of 'market surveillance' is developed, which is related to an oil company's search for information on this type of matter.

2   Friedman later refined this approach for the situation where the number of rival firms competing for a contract was unknown. The bidding distribution of the 'average bidder' was found by combining all previous $X^{j-1}/C_v{}^j$ observations. When plotted, a probability density function is constructed and the probability of winning a contract for which a given bid has been submitted is the area contained in the right tail of the distribution. Broemser (1968) applied the Friedman technique for a contractor in the Californian construction industry. Simulated results derived from his bid-optimizing model, when compared with those actually achieved by the contractor, showed that a significant advantage lay in using the model. More contracts could have been won and profits would have been larger. In order to economize on the amount of information needed, it is possible to find the optimum bid by using the value of the winning bid, P_L (scaled relative to C^j), rather than that of all bids submitted.

3   We ignore the possibility of 2,1,1,0,0,0,0, because the probability of its occurrence is very low.

9

Measurement costs and optimization of the number of invited tender-bidders

Posted or fixed pricing by suppliers of intermediate inputs into the oil-gathering (exploration, development and production) business is, generally, not practised. The oil companies, therefore, can do relatively little comparative 'shopping' or searching for bargains offered at fixed prices by rival suppliers. Nor do flexible-price commodity exchanges exist for any intermediate inputs into offshore oil gathering. Nor, again, is face-to-face negotiation over prices of any importance. Rather, as we have already seen, the oil companies put out to competitive tender virtually all purchases above just a few thousand dollars. In fact, these purchases will total millions of dollars during the economic life of a single offshore oil field. The unique competitive auction arrangements – the invited tender-bid auction – that the oil companies employ for procurement purposes is the dominant market form in offshore oil gathering.

As was described in Chapter 3, the oil companies are characteristic-ally vertically disintegrated from the production of most of the intermediate inputs required for oil gathering. We have argued (again in Chapter 3) that this feature is consistent with the rent appropriation version of the transaction cost paradigm. In this view the internalization of production is due to fear of the consequences of unfriendly behaviour by an opportunistic contractual partner. We have also argued that the suppression of price information under the invited tender-bid auction arrangement may help to ameliorate threats of opportunistic or monopolistic price behaviour.[1]

Since the oil companies have chosen to rely upon a market to procure most of their needs of intermediate inputs, what needs to be explained is how they go about minimizing the costs of using the market. It is argued in this chapter that the oil companies' choice of the invited tender-bid auction can be explained within the context of the measurement cost branch of transaction cost economics (i.e. within the framework of those ideas emanating from seminal papers by, *inter alia* Barzel, 1982, Casson, 1982a, Cheung, 1983, Coase, 1937, and McManus, 1975).

It is hypothesized that the oil companies are concerned simultaneously with the cost of executing transactions (finding with whom to trade and the cost of making and assessing tender-bids) and maximizing the advantages to be derived from exchange (i.e. finding the lowest price available). Thus, the oil company is seen as a market-maker – arranging auctions, and incurring measurement costs in seeking to maximize the *net* advantage of exchange. As a profit-seeking organization, it will attempt to minimize prices paid, while, at the same time, seeking to economize on measurement costs. However, it is apparent that there is a trade-off between these variables, such that the oil company will rarely 'sample' the potential price offers of *all* suppliers on any given trade.

Attention in this chapter is focused on the determination of the optimal number of invited tender-bidders, optimal expenditure on tender-bid costs and the expected gross and net benefits to be derived from measurement. It will be shown that expected *net* benefit from exchange is maximized when the number of invited bidders is optimized. It will be made clear that, on average, an oil company does not expect to find the lowest potential bid-price on any contract.

The treatment here of the optimal number of bidders is somewhat similar to that by French and McCormick (1984) who considered this optimization problem in the context of an open first-price, sealed-bid auction (i.e. the bidders are not invited and they separately and independently decide whether to bid or not). However, their model has some differences compared with the one presented here: the French and McCormick model does not provide a convincing mechanism through which the potential bidders sort themselves out between bidders and non-bidders – it is just assumed that they can do so – while in the invited tender-bid auction it is the oil company running the auction that provides this mechanism. (On the matter of the problem of the transference of theoretical models into practical price determination mechanisms, see Loasby, 1986b; Richardson, 1959, 1960.) Also, when considering invited tender-bidding, the French and McCormick model is not entirely different from fixed-price search models as first developed by Stigler (1961).

Before continuing further it is useful to recognize explicitly that the tender-bids usually transfer more information than just that on price. Each bid will specify details relating to product quality, delivery dates, possibly extra legal clauses or alternative technical solutions and, sometimes, even the names of the personnel who will work on the contract.

Goldberg (1977) has discussed the matter of competitive bidding and the transfer of information *before* contracts are signed. Only in the case of the simplest of homogeneous goods are buyers interested only in price information. When goods (or services) are not homogeneous the ranking of suppliers needs to be performed in more dimensions than just price: for example, durability, quality and style. Hence, extra information needs to be transferred from the potential suppliers to the buyer.

Sometimes the non-price information is at least as important as is the price information. This could be the case, for example, in the oil industry where breakdown of a faulty intermediate input would lead to the interruption of production (or exploration/development) activity with consequent high financial costs (the cost of 'downtime' and/or the cost of lost oil output). However, non-price information, just like price information, is itself costly to transfer and the cost is likely to vary according to the channel through which the transmission takes place. These channels include the competitive auction, negotiation, posted pricing (with non-price information being made available to enquirers) and, of course, vertical integration. The latter is more likely to be chosen the more difficult and expensive it is to transfer non-price information between arm's-length transactors.

It is to be expected, therefore, that arm's-length transactors will attempt to design a contract that will allow for the transfer of 'appropriate' information at relatively low cost. The oil companies have solved this problem by specifying as often as possible desired quality (and other non-price attributes) before potential suppliers make their bids. This has the advantage of reducing the amount of non-price information that might be transferred, since bidders might otherwise put in price–quality bids that differed in both of these dimensions. The buyer's bid-assessment difficulties would, therefore, be increased. Besides, if the buyer knows from the beginning what quality it will accept, unnecessary (costly) information transfer can be avoided by stating the desired quality in advance. This is why, presumably, the oil companies run the invited tender-bid auction in the way that they do: we saw in Chapter 7 that when seeking bids they define what quality of provision is wanted.

Two other questions which relate to the arm's-length transfer of non-price information have had to be dealt with by the oil companies. First, information on the ability of a supplier to render what they contract to supply is of great importance. Interruption of a single supplier's service may cause costly delay. The oil companies' solution is to verify the ability of potential suppliers through the process of pre-qualification whereby potential suppliers have to confirm their technical and financial capabilities (see Chapter 7). Secondly, there is the problem of quality development once a contract has been awarded. Sometimes a supplier will see a new solution to a particular problem once it has become engaged on a contract. In such circumstances, an oil company is often prepared to work with the contractor in ironing out any difficulties with the new solution and to make appropriate post-contractual price adjustments in the contractor's favour.

The chapter proceeds on the assumption that the arm's-length transactors have found a contractual solution to the cost-efficient transfer of non-price information and concentrates on the optimization of expenditure on running the tender-bidding system.

The buyers

When an oil company in its role as a buyer of inputs from the offshore oil supply industry invites suppliers to bid for supply contracts it does so with the intention of minimizing as far as possible the purchase price that it must pay. *A priori* the more supply firms that it invites to bid, the greater is the probability of it finding the lowest of all possible bid-prices. However, a cost is associated with running the invited tender-bid system and this is positively related to the number of suppliers that are invited to bid. This cost is composed of two components:

(1)   an oil company's cost of assessing tender-bids; and
(2)   the supplier's cost of assembling tender-bids, which will be passed on to the buyer.

The optimal number of invited tender-bidders is determined by the price-benefit and transaction cost functions which arise in the contracting process. Each of these is presented in turn.

The expected benefit function
The expected benefit function is derived from the expected loss function, where 'loss' is the probability weighted expected cost to the buyer of *not* finding the lowest potential bidder had all firms been invited to bid. Expected loss, $E(L)$, is:

$$E(L) = (1 - m/n) . A(m,n); A_M < 0, A_N > 0 \qquad (9.1)$$

The term $(1 - m/n)$ is the probability of *not* including the lowest price-bidder in the selection of m firms invited to bid from a subsector of the offshore oil supply industry of size n firms $(m \leq n)$.[3] The term A is the probability weighted average cost of accepting a low bid, which is greater than the lowest potential bid-price had all n firms been invited to bid, i.e.

$$A = \sum_{i=2}^{n} Pr_i\,(P_i - P_1), \qquad\qquad (9.2)$$

where Pr_i is the probability of a given excessive bid $(P_i - P_1)$ winning. P_1 is the lowest bid-price possible from the n firms and P_i is the lowest bid actually received. By way of an example, if $n = 7$ and $m = 3$; there is only one low bidder if the probability distribution of prices bid is rectangular. Firm 1 is the potential low bidder with a bid of P_1 and there are six potential high bidders with bid-prices of $P_2 \ldots P_7$.

The term A is the probability weighted average cost incurred if $m <$ n, and it can be calculated by answering the question: what is the probability that any one of the six high bidders will be the low bidder among the $m = 3$ firms randomly invited to bid by an oil company? There are twenty possible combinations of three high bidders being selected from the six possible. The probabilities for each of the $P_2 \ldots$ P_7 being the low bid-price are shown on the left of Table 9.1 and the opportunity cost to the buyer in the right-hand column.

In equation (9.1), A is a function of both m and n. If m increases, with n fixed, A declines because the probability of not finding the low bidder falls. For example, if $m = 4$ and $n = 7$, the probability of firm 2 (the firm with the next lowest bid) winning rises, while that of firms 3 . . . 5 falls (that of firms 6 and 7 is already zero). Thus, what is happening is that, as an oil company increases the number of firms that it invites to bid, it is increasing its chances of finding the lowest bid-price from the set of all firms, n, in the supply industry.

The effect of increasing n (with m fixed) is the opposite: the probability of finding the lowest possible high bid (i.e. P_2) declines while the probability of finding one of the higher bid-prices as the lowest bid in a given contest increases.

Table 9.1   *The weighted average expected cost of not finding the lowest bid*

Probability P_i lowest	Cost if P_i is lowest
$P_2 \ldots = (10/20)$	$(P_2 - P_1)$
$P_3 \ldots = (6/20)$	$(P_3 - P_1)$
$P_4 \ldots = (3/20)$	$(P_4 - P_1)$
$P_5 \ldots = (1/20)$	$(P_5 - P_1)$
$P_6 \ldots = (0/20)$	$(P_6 - P_1)$
$P_7 \ldots = (0/20)$	$(P_7 - P_1)$

$$A = \sum_{i=2}^{n} Pr_i\,(P_i - P_1)$$

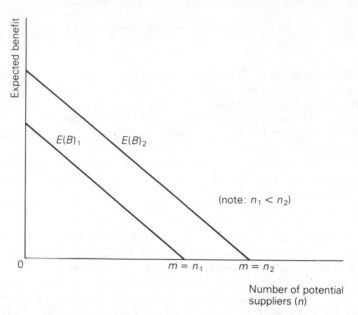

Figure 9.1   *The expected benefit function, E(B)*

Differentiating equation (9.1), the loss function, with respect to m and n yields:

$$\theta E(L)/\theta m = (1 - m/n) . A_m + A(m,n) . (-1/n) < 0 \qquad (9.3)$$

$$\theta E(L)/\theta n = (1 - m/n) . A_n + A(m,n) . (m/n^2) > 0. \qquad (9.4)$$

Thus, loss is a decreasing function of the number of firms invited to bid (for fixed n) and an increasing function of the number of firms in the supply industry (for fixed m).

Let us now define a reduction in the expected loss brought about by increasing the number of suppliers invited to bid from m to $m + 1$ as the expected marginal benefit, $E(B)$, of increasing the number of invited bidders (i.e. $\theta E(B) = -\theta E(L)/\theta m$. The negative relationship between marginal benefit and m is shown in Figure 9.1. Notice that:

- $E(B) = 0$ when $m = n$, which follows from equation (9.1) as the term $(1 - m/n)$ will be zero; and
- an increase in n shifts the benefit function outward from the horizontal axis (i.e. equation (9.4)).

Tender-bid transaction cost functions

There are two tender-bid transaction cost functions: the buyer's tender-bid *assessement cost* function, and the tender-bidder's tender-bid *assembly cost*.

The costs of assessing the tender-bids can be significant in the case of the variable multi-attribute intermediate goods that oil companies purchase. Indeed, it is not unusual for an oil company to pay in excess of $100,000 for engineering consultants to assess tender-bids. Total assessment cost will be an increasing function of the number of invited bids. The marginal assessment cost function could also be an increasing function of the number of bids to be assessed because of the complexity of the growing number of comparisons that have to be made in order to compare the bids. Increasing marginal tender-bid assessment costs are shown in Figure 9.2.

If $m = 4$ then, on average, a tender-bidder will be awarded a contract once in every four tender-bid submissions. Each tender-bid submission incurs a cost, which is called here a tender-bid assembly cost. This is a 'cost of telling' or a communication cost. Tender-bidders can be expected to recoup the variable cost component of this cost on contracts that they are successful in obtaining. That is, the desired attribute, low price, will not be found with zero marginal cost to the buyer. Total

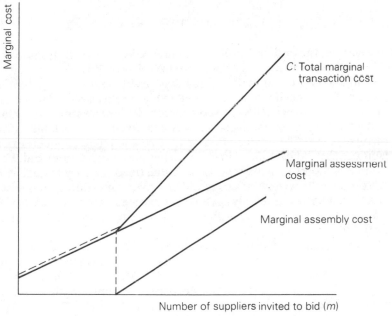

Figure 9.2   *The total marginal cost function,* C

assembly costs are an increasing function of the average per contract number of invited tender-bidders. The marginal assembly cost can for simplicity be assumed to be increasing (see Figure 9.2).

A tender-bidder's tender-bid assembly cost may have both a fixed and a variable component. It is a fixed component which could explain an x axis positive intercept of the marginal assembly cost function. As in any tender-bid contest, a given supplier is either invited to bid or not invited to bid we can use the binomial distribution to model the expectation of invitations to bid in a given time period (say a year). Thus the probability density function is:

$$\binom{d}{r} K^r . (1 - K)^{d-r}; r = 0, 1, 2 \ldots d, \tag{9.5}$$

where d is the total number of trials (i.e. contracts to be distributed during the year); K is the constant probability of obtaining an invitation to bid (i.e. m/n); and the variable r is the total number of successes in d trials – the annual number of invitations received. It is assumed that the trials are independent of each other, which is a correct assumption given that the oil companies randomly invite suppliers to bid.

The easiest way to derive the marginal assembly cost function is by way of an example: if $m = 3, n = 7, d = 7$, we have

$$Pr(r) = \binom{7}{r} (3/7)^r . (1 - 3/7)^{7-r}; r = 0, 1 \ldots 7.$$

For example, the probability of receiving exactly $r = 3$ invitations to bid is 29.4 per cent and $r = 4$ is 22 per cent (see Figure 9.3).

A supply firm could install 'fixed capacity' to bid on all potential contracts for which it might be invited to bid, in this case 7. However, it need not incur such a large fixed expense. Rather a supply firm may divide tender-bid assembly costs between fixed and variable components. A variable tender-bid assembly cost is incurred when extra resources have to be utilized in order to put together a tender-bid. For example, a supply firm may choose to install fixed capacity to deal with a maximum of three invitations to bid in a given time-slot. In this case, variable tender-bid assembly costs will be avoided with a probability of 0.65, i.e. the area under the probability density function and to the left of $r = 4$ in Figure 9.3.

However, if more than three invitations to bid are received, marginal assembly costs will be incurred. Extra resources will have to be obtained so as to be able to put together a tender-bid. Managerial work-power might be diverted from some of its other tasks, replacing it with less specialized, lower-productivity, non-managerial labour. Or, management might have to be rewarded with extra payments for overtime

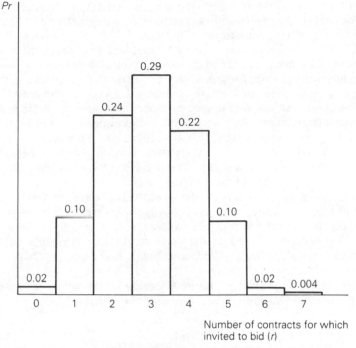

Figure 9.3   *Probability density function:* m = *3;* n = *7;* d = *7*

working. Or, again, the opportunity cost of assembling a tender-bid may be measured in terms of the discounted value of work postponed by management as it is diverted to the tender-bid assembly task.

If a supplier chose to install fixed tender-bid assembly capacity to cope with three invitations to bid in a given time-slot, the marginal cost function will become positive at $m = 3$ in Figure 9.2. How much capacity of this type a supplier will install is a choice variable and will be related to its risk aversion for carrying fixed costs. If it is assumed that suppliers are identical in this respect, then if one firm chooses to install fixed capacity to cover three invitations to bid per period of time, then all other suppliers will do so.

The optimum number of invited tender-bidders

The optimum number of invited tender-bidders is $\bar{m}$ in Figure 9.4. This is determined where marginal benefit and total marginal costs are equal. The optimal number of bidders is less than n with any total marginal cost function so long as, if the total marginal cost function is of negative slope, it is not geometrically steeper than the marginal benefit function, for then $m = n$ would always be optimal.

Changes in the cost and benefit functions will affect the optimal number of bidders. A rise in costs will reduce the optimum number. Product (and service) idiosyncrasy requires that a unique price be formed each time an item is exchanged. And idiosyncrasy raises transaction costs because tender-bid specifications have to be redrawn on each transaction. Assessment of, and comparisons between, rival bids will be made more complex and, therefore, expensive than when the price-bids are identical across attributes. Higher transaction cost raises the total marginal cost function in Figure 9.4, and so will reduce the optimum number of firms invited to bid.

The optimum number of bidders would also be reduced if the spread of bid-prices declined, perhaps because supply firms became more alike in their cost conditions or ability to solve technological problems. Such developments would reduce the value of A (the probability weighted average cost of not finding the lowest bid from the universe of potential bidders).

The world of Walrasian market clearing is one with zero marginal assessment and assembly costs. The auctioneer is assumed to gather and

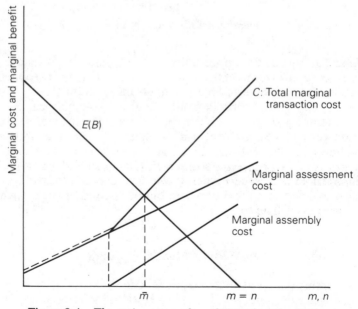

Figure 9.4   *The optimum number of invited tender-bidders*

process information without cost. Thus, here, the optimum number of bidders is where the marginal benefit function falls to zero, i.e. $\bar{m} = n$ and all potential suppliers have their prices sampled – they get to bid. This is the ideal, unfortunately unobtainable, 'state of nature'. However, the oil companies face very real positive transaction costs and because of these they optimally economize on the number of bid-prices that they sample.

It is apparent that, at the optimal $\bar{m}$ in Figure 9.4, expected benefit, $E(B)$, remains positive. This is because the term A in equations (9.1) or (9.3) is itself still positive. Since A has been defined as 'the probability weighted average cost of not finding the potential lowest price-bidder', it is implied that on average the oil companies do not expect to find the potential lowest price-bidder on any contract. Quite simply, the transaction costs of finding this particular bidder are too great.

An important feature of the Walrasian tatonnement price-determination process is that, as an exchange mechanism, it does achieve Pareto optimal resource allocation: no single extra transaction can improve the transactors' welfare. The exchange of information without any cost of doing so ensures that, on every transaction, price equals the marginal cost of the lowest-cost supplier as well as the marginal valuation of every buyer.

However, when transaction costs are positive, as with invited tender-bidding, the bid-prices of all potential suppliers do not get inspected. This is because the expected net benefit of observing the bid prices of firms $n - m$ is negative. While m is the optimal number of invited tender-bidders as far as the oil company is concerned, m is also Pareto optimal so long as some other agent (the winning bidder perhaps) is unable profitably to identify a still lower cost supplier.

Comparison of the optimal properties of the invited tender-bid auction with an open tender-bid arrangement is less straightforward. However, it was argued in Chapter 7 that failure to restrict the number of bidders to a shortlist of those that are invited may increase the number of bidders on a given contract. Moreover, the financial, technical and productive capacity capabilities of these bidders are likely to be less well known than those of the invited bidders – because the invited bidders will have been scrutinized by an oil company *before* the invitation to bid is issued. Now, if the attributes of the potential suppliers differ widely – or are thought to by the oil companies, the complexity of tender-bid assessment will be increased. An increase in the complexity and, therefore, the cost of tender-bid assessment will raise the marginal assessment and total marginal transaction cost function in Figure 9.4, *reducing* the expected benefit and net expected benefit derived from the tender-bidding process.

The oil companies say that they use the invited sealed-bid procurement auction because it gives them greater control over their suppliers, which, in turn, induces the supply companies to greater endeavour in fulfilling the terms of a contract: poor performance risks non-invitation to subsequent auctions.

Certainly the supply companies themselves are well aware of the importance of being invited to join a bidders' list and many of them do in fact feel that the oil companies have a great deal of leverage over them. However, it is difficult to see why buyer leverage really is greater, because poor performance can be punished by non-award of a subsequent contract with non-invited bidding.

But there are still other reasons for preferring invited bidding which are related to the equilibrating properties of the non-invited sealed-bid model. In the latter model, as French and McCormick (1984) point out, there is no guarantee that the optimal number of bids for any given contract will always be submitted. But they argue that over successive auctions there will be a tendency for the optimal number of bidders to establish itself. The argument is that excess returns will attract entry to and losses will attract exit from the next auction. However, it is not convincingly explained just how the correct number of firms happen to enter or exit as bidders. Richardson (1960) made this same point in connection with the familiar model of perfect competition, pointing out that a firm's entry or exit plan depends not only upon industry profits but also upon the entry or exit plans of rival firms. For example, even if revenue does not cover variable cost, a given firm may not choose to exit an industry if it believes that a sufficient number of its rivals are about to do so. Contrariwise with excess profits: if a firm suspects that there will be a rush of new entrants, which would drive profits down, it may refrain from making the necessary investments. But the French and McCormick model of non-invited tender-bidding, like that of perfect competition, is silent on this crucial matter of interactions in decision-making by rivals. As a result, there is no guarantee that excess returns or losses will induce an appropriate equilibrating adjustment. It could be that excess profits earned on the last contract will induce a monumental rush of bidders at the next auction, driving returns down and so discouraging bidders on the following auction so that very few submit bids.

What is being described here is a type of cobweb in expected returns, realized returns and number of bidders, and such a cycle may be convergent to $\bar{m}$, divergent or regularly repeating. Thus, if the number of bidders depends on last period's return (R_{t-1}) we can write $m_t = f(R_{t-1})$, $f' > 0$ and $R_t = g(m_t)$, $g' < 0$ showing returns to be a negative function of the number of bidders. (Holt, 1979, established the negative relationship between returns and number of bidders.) The first of these functions is the 'supply of bidders' and the second is a kind of demand schedule (or an outcome function). Graphing the two functions, and noting that the number of bidders always adjusts to last period's returns, results in a cobweb cycle in number of bidders. Only if $m_t = \bar{m}$ from the beginning, or after a possibly long time lapse with a convergent cycle, will the actual number of bidders equal the optimal number.

Nor would it seem to be at all possible to correct this fault in the long-run adjustment properties of the non-invited tender-bidding model by, for example, making available to all potential rival bidders the appropriate information on each others' bidding intentions as this information would seem to be impossible to collect. Thus, with the equilibrating properties of non-invited tender-bidding being held in question, it follows that the desirable equation between the actual and the optimal number of bidders might rarely happen. Consequences follow for both the buyers and the sellers.

A risk-averse buyer will not be indifferent to the fluctuations in suppliers' returns because these depend upon the prices paid by the buyer. The placing of invitations is an obvious means of overcoming this particular problem. Nor is risk aversion a necessary assumption, as average returns over a run of auctions could be, or may be thought by a buyer to be, higher in non-invited that in invited-bidding – this depends upon the 'shapes' (actual or supposed) of the functions in the cobweb.

The supply companies, too, are unlikely to be indifferent to the ebb and flow of the number of bidders in non-invited tender-bidding: perhaps they too are risk averse or expect average returns to be low. It is argued, therefore, that the invited-bidding arrangement can have the effect of looking after the interests of both the bidders (by reducing the variance of expected returns and, perhaps, raising the average level of returns) as well as the buyers (by optimizing the number of bidders on each auction and also, perhaps, reducing the average level of prices paid).

But this is not all. The peculiarities of the globalization of the offshore oil-gathering industry must also be recognized. If non-invited tender-bidding was in fact used and suppliers generally preferred not to involve themselves at a given offshore supply base because of the adverse features of that arrangement that have just been described, the oil companies would have little choice but to integrate backwards and carry the extra transaction costs of doing so. Or, if a few independent supply companies were to establish affiliates in that particular supply base, the oil companies might find that there were insufficient firms to invite to an auction, so that m was always less than $\bar{m}$ – an obviously undesirable outcome, which again might provoke costly vertical integration on the part of the oil companies. All the better then for the oil companies to adopt the invited tender-bid arrangement, so encouraging the supply companies to join them at a supply base, and attempt themselves to set $m_t = \bar{m}$ on each contract.

Whether they were successful in doing so could, in practice, only be assessed qualitatively as full information about the bidders' marginal assembly cost functions and an oil company's own expected benefit function would not be available. However, the oil companies can observe their own expenditure on tender-bid assessment costs as well as the general profitability of their offshore oil-gathering activities. They can also observe the number of suppliers that they may draw upon in each subsector. If they are satisfied with what they see, then they have probably gauged m_t at about the level of $\bar{m}$. Experiments raising the number of invited bidders will, on average, reduce prices paid but also raise assessment costs. Repeated often enough, information could be gathered so as to judge approximately the number of invited bidders that maximizes the net benefit of exchange. Of course, the oil companies are not known to behave in this way; instead they have adopted a 'rule of thumb' and invite between two and ten bidders, with the mode being five bidders.

Conclusions

This chapter has used measurement costs to explain the choice of market organizational form in the offshore oil-gathering industry. From a range of potential market organizational forms, the oil companies have chosen to use a unique auction-bidding arrangement – the invited tender-bid system. The principal hypothesis that has been discussed is the prediction that markets will be organized so as to economize on transaction costs. Product (or service) idiosyncrasy was identified as a main factor increasing transaction costs, since unique prices had to be calculated, communicated and assessed each time a buyer wished to make a purchase. From the preceding discussion it can be concluded that the organization of markets in the offshore oil-gathering business is consistent with the hypothesis of transaction cost minimization.

Our attention next turns to a discussion of some other features of oil company market behaviour – their surveillance of potential suppliers and the practice of price secrecy. These too will be shown to be consistent with the measurement cost paradigm.

Notes

1　Although instances of each have arisen. J. Ray McDermott and Brown and Root Inc. pleaded no contest to federal grand jury charges that they conspired to allocate contracts between themselves and to rig bids. Each company was fined $1 million (*Wall Street Journal*, 15 December 1978).

2 This finding is consistent with that of Stigler (1961), who also pointed out the cost of costly information.

3 The term $(1 - m/n)$ is the probability of *not* finding the lowest of all potential price-bids because m/n is the probability of finding *the* lowest potential bid-price. That this latter statement is true is easily demonstrated.

Let $n(S)$ be the population space with:

$$n(S) = n(E) + n(E^c),$$

where $n(E)$ is the number of random selections of size m that contain the single lowest price-bid and $n(E^c)$ is the complementary event that it is not so contained. Hence,

$$n(E) \quad = n(S) - m(E^c)$$

and

$$n(S) \quad = \binom{n}{m}$$

$$n(E^c) \quad = \binom{n-1}{m}.$$

Thus, dividing through by $n(S)$,

$$Pr(E) \quad = 1 - n(E^c)/n(S).$$

For example, with $m = 3$ and $n = 7$, $n(E^c) = 20$ and $n(S) = 35$. Thus,

$$Pr(E) \quad = 1 - 20/35 = 3/7 = m/n.$$

And $(1 - m/n) = 4/7$ is the probability of *not* finding the lowest potential price-bid firm, given that $m = 3$, $n = 7$ and there is a single lowest potential price-bidder.

10

The buyers as market-makers

This chapter investigates further the subject of the buyer as market-maker. As was discussed in Chapter 9, buyers seek to minimize prices paid but, with positive transaction costs, they may not want to 'investigate' the prices that would be asked by all potential suppliers. This observation led to the concept of the optimum number of invited tender-bidders, which was investigated in the previous chapter. It will be argued in this chapter that the oil companies have become the market-makers for many of the goods and services that they purchase from the offshore oil supply industry because this is the most transaction cost efficient means of pricing the idiosyncratic items which are exchanged. With idiosyncratic (or variable multi-attribute) intermediate inputs, both posted pricing and pricing on organized commodity exchanges are ruled out on grounds of high transaction costs.

Other issues to be discussed here include: the function of *market surveillance* by the oil companies as a means of increasing the transaction cost efficiency of the invited tender-bid auction system. However, investment in surveillance is also shown to be limited by the usual marginal cost and benefit rules. The topic of subcontracting is also briefly investigated. Subcontracting is known as being a means of improving the efficacy of the auction (Engelbrecht-Wiggans, 1980). However, it is argued that in the offshore oil-gathering business the potential benefits of subcontracting are unlikely to be garnered because there is no reason to suppose that a winning bidder has better knowledge of the whereabouts of lower-cost suppliers than do the oil companies themselves.

Market-makers

Goldberg (1977) observed that competitive bidding is a device for transmitting information between firms and as such it can either be a substitute for or complement to alternative devices such as negotiation, advertising and vertical integration. In the simplest case, bidding is a price-searching device, but the complexity of the search (hence the cost) increases if product quality or specifications are variable.

However, if the non-price dimensions can be conveyed accurately and cheaply between the buyer and the bidders, complexity ceases to be a problem. One way of transmitting such information to the potential sellers is for the buyer to determine the non-price factors and to tell the potential sellers what is wanted by way of blueprints or with reference to recognized industry standards. Goldberg calls this a 'sampling rule' (1977, p. 253) and this one is particularly effective in reducing the 'choice of supplier problem' to one of ranking bids according to price (lowest being the most desirable). Thus, here an oil company invests in blueprints so as to reduce post-contract bid-assessment costs.

However, this sampling rule is not well suited to coping with non-standard technical solutions to a production problem, because knowledge of these solutions may not be known to an oil company in advance of allocating a procurement contract. This is particularly true when oil-gathering techniques are going through a process of technical progress. In offshore oil gathering many new technical solutions have been developed as a response to the desire to cut costs as well as in the form of breakthroughs in previously unresolved areas such as working in water depths that once could not be operated.

Thus, for the oil companies, promoting technical progress is desirable and the question arises of how to promote the development of new solutions. Sticking rigidly to one sampling rule is not necessarily optimal. At the same time, an oil company is often in the position of not knowing in which technical areas a breakthrough may occur. If it knew that, then it could tailor the sampling rule for these special cases accordingly. Allowing bidders to offer their own solutions (along with price-bids) is tantamount to jettisoning the chosen sampling rule and complicating (at cost) the bid assessment process. The oil companies, therefore, have rejected this alternative and have chosen a two-part sampling rule for the special cases. Bids are invited in the usual way, with the oil companies defining the technical solutions. Post-bid submission discussions are then entered into and suggested novel solutions investigated. Sometimes these discussions will occur after an offshore oil supply firm has begun work on a contract – the supplier itself only finding (perhaps incompletely) the new solution once work has begun (a facet of on-the-job learning). The oil company will assess the suggested technical improvements using its own personnel and, perhaps, contribute further to their development. If the new solution is accepted and it is more costly than allowed for in the original contract, the oil company is almost always prepared to negotiate a higher price (some technical advances in offshore oil gathering that have been developed through processes such as described here are listed in Chapter 3, p. 51).

It has been made clear then that the oil companies incur costs running the invited tender-bid auction system and that on average they do not expect to find the lowest potential bid-price on any contract. Why then have they adopted such an apparently costly system for discovering prices?

Vickrey has pointed out that

a system of perfect competition is a system of markets in which uniform divisible commodities are traded in by large numbers of participants who accept the market price generated by the forces of supply and demand. (1976, p. 13)

A problem arises, however, when the commodity or service to be exchanged is not uniform or when the number of participants is few. On both counts this is the case with many exchanges between the oil companies and firms in the offshore oil supply industry. In particular, the goods or services to be exchanged often have a large number of attributes, only subsets of which need to be packaged together on any given exchange. Thus, unlike formal exchange markets where prices are set for largely homogeneous products (for example, on commodity, currency and stock markets) on an hour-to-hour or even minute-to-minute basis by the weight of thousands of buy and sell orders passing through an exchange's market-makers (the brokers, jobbers, etc.), *the buyers in the invited tender-bid model have to make their own markets*. That is, a buyer has literally to bring itself and potential suppliers together *before* price (and other contract attributes) can be decided upon. This type of price-formation process is also quite different from that of fixed-price markets (for example, the retail market for chocolate bars) where sellers determine a selling price and buyers make quantity offers.

The essential difference between contracting for intermediate inputs by invited tender on the one hand and formal market exchanges and fixed-price markets of the type mentioned on the other is to be found in the *uniqueness* of the items exchanged. These unique items are not only multi-attribute but also variable in the attributes that need to be combined in any one transaction. It is this latter feature that largely rules out posted pricing or agreement of prices through repeated contracting on a commodity exchange.

The extent of the problem of arriving at an agreed exchange price may be appreciated in the following example. Consider a product which has, say, twenty atributes. Attribute 1 may represent the basic item (the mainframe or a no-frills service), attributes 2–10 could be 'extras', which can accompany the basic item but do not necessarily have to. All of these attributes may also incorporate different grades or quality or may be varied in details of design. An obvious example of such a variable multi-attribute good is an oil rig or platform, and many geological and geophysical services are similar in nature. Accordingly, literally hundreds of prices might have to be posted if sellers were not informed in advance about exactly which attributes buyers wished to purchase. The number of combinations of all size that can be drawn from a set of twenty is very large indeed. In such circumstances, posted pricing would be resource intensive and, therefore, expensive. To avoid this expense, the oil companies have devised the invited tender-bid system, where a seller states price only after receiving notification of a buyer's needs.

The assumption of homogeneous input (assumption 2 listed in Chapter 8, p. 106) in fact reduces the richness of the invited tender-bid system of price formation because product idiosyncrasy requires that a unique price be formed each time an item is exchanged. Idiosyncrasy can be assumed to raise transaction costs since tender-bid specifications will have to be redrawn on each transaction. Thus, assessment of and comparisons between rival bids will be more complex and expensive than when the price-bids are identical across attributes. Higher transaction cost raises the total marginal cost function in Figure 9.4 and so will reduce the optimum number of firms invited to bid.

But suppose that the goods and services provided by offshore oil supply firms were homogeneous, would the oil companies still wish to use an auction arrangement or would posted pricing be preferred? There is a strong presumption that they would still prefer to use the auction procurement method.

As several subsectors of the offshore oil supply industry show high levels of market concentration – especially in the technological core of the industry – the possibility exists that the oil companies will at least sometimes have to pay prices near the monopoly level. Demsetz (1968a) was one of the first to suggest that an auction process could be used to negate a monopoly pricing potential. His argument was made with reference to monopoly pricing by a public utility and his answer was to have potential suppliers compete in an auction (low bidder winning) to win the franchise to supply customers.

The oil companies with their use of the invited tender-bid auction do something very like what Demsetz had suggested: contracts to supply an oil company with particular inputs for a period of time (often of three years or more) have to be won in a competitive auction. The winning firm is never in a position to set monopoly prices, even though it becomes the sole supplier.

Both Williamson (1976) and Goldberg (1977) criticized Demsetz's suggestion, arguing that certain transaction costs, ignored by Demsetz, could be substantial. As we have seen, Goldberg in particular stressed the problem of comparing bids when bidders suggested different technological solutions or offered services of different qualities. Moreover, at a later bidding contest an incumbent supplier might have an advantage over rival bidders if it had accumulated specific capital assets and/or consumer-specific knowledge. Certainly, because of factors such as these, Williamson was sceptical of Demsetz's idea, at least as far as public utility franchising was concerned.

However, these potential difficulties are not that great in the offshore oil-gathering business. One reason for this is that the oil companies are particularly careful in defining (through blueprints) exactly what they require, so problems of comparing bids composed of bundles of prices and qualities (and technical solutions) are minimized. Problems of specific customer knowledge are also not great for, as was discussed in Chapter 3, switching costs are often low. When the matter of specialized capital assets could be a problem, the oil companies practise quasi-vertical integration – owning the assets themselves and engaging an outside firm to operate them.

Surveillance

The oil companies keep records compiled from mainly publicly available information pertaining to developments in the various subsectors of the offshore oil supply industry. These records include: information on contracts awarded to the individual supply firms; changes in the individual supplier's managerial or technical personnel; any involvement that a supplier might have had in promoting productivity or technical advancement in oil exploration, development or production; anything else that might relate to the cost levels or efficiency of the potential suppliers in the offshore oil supply industry.

It has so far been assumed that the intermediate inputs exchanged are variable multi-attribute but homogeneous across suppliers in any given subset of attributes. The only distinguishing feature between the suppliers in a bid contest is in the prices that they ask. Market surveillance can be thought of as an investment by the oil companies to identify high-cost suppliers prior to the distribution of invitations to bid, and this would be worthwhile if it meant that contracts would not be awarded to the higher-price suppliers in a bidding distribution.

However, this homogeneity assumption reduces somewhat the true richness of the economic benefits that an oil company may gain from market surveillance. Product (or service) heterogeneity (within a given attribute subset) complicates a buyer's problems in comparing bids, since both pecuniary and non-pecuniary elements are included in the tender-bid quotations. In these circumstances an oil company must either explicitly or implicitly construct a weighted average price index, where the weights will be chosen by the buyer according to its own preferences over quality differences, reliability, operating lives, etc. This weighted average price index can still be referred to as the tender-bid 'price' asked by a particular bidder. And, as before, the objective of market surveillance is to identify potential low price-bidders prior to the distribution of invitations to bid. Or, put another way, the effect of market surveillance is to reduce the degree of randomness in the distribution of bid invitations.

We will assume, however, that market surveillance does not yield perfect information to the oil companies on the distribution of bid-prices. Rather, the market intelligence gathered will help in identifying the potential highest price-bids.

Elimination of potential high price-bidders prior to invitation to bid is tantamount to reducing the number of suppliers in a subsector. This effectively restricts choice of firms to bid from n_1 to n_2. Thus, in Figure 10.1, the expected benefit function will be shifted inward from $E(B)_1$

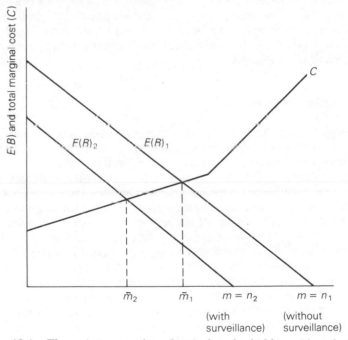

Figure 10.1   *The optimum number of invited tender-bidders with and without surveillance*

to $E(B)_2$. This follows from equation (9.4) where expected *loss* and the number of firms in a subsector are positively related. Importantly, the optimum number of invited tender-bidders is reduced from $\bar{m}_1$ to $\bar{m}_2$, so the tender-bid transaction costs incurred by the oil companies will also be reduced. Thus, investment in market surveillance can be viewed as a substitute for investment in tender-bid transaction costs. Both investments, of course, are made with the objective of identifying the potential low price-bidders. The optimum investment in market surveillance is where marginal surveillance cost is equal to the marginal reduction in tender-bid transaction cost brought about by the investment in surveillance.

If marginal surveillance cost is always very low, then surveillance might replace tender-bidding as a means of finding prices and initiating exchanges. This is most likely to be the case when the particular market under surveillance provides standardized items that carry posted prices. In this case, market surveillance reduces itself to a type of market search. (For a discussion of market search models, refer to Okun, 1981.) These models assume that a price-searcher knows the probability distribution of prices asked, but this is not the same as with market surveillance where, in the limit, surveillance reveals all of the prices that are being asked. However, when prices are not posted by suppliers, the best that surveillance can do will be taken to be the identification of potential high price-bidders and, thus, the truncation of the subjective bid-price distribution.

The problem of publicity

As the publication of prices reveals marginal valuations (as has been pointed out by Smith, 1976, in his experimental work on the institution of contract, for example) and is generally beneficial for efficient resource allocation, it may be wondered why the oil companies insist upon the non-publication of bid-prices. The publication of past bid-prices would have the effect for the supply firms of turning the price-setting environment into one of decision-making with risk rather than with uncertainty, as has already been pointed out. A priori, in the short run, there seems to be no reason to suppose that this transformation would have a definite adverse effect on the average level of prices that the oil companies would have to pay for intermediate inputs. Indeed, if the publication of prices enhanced information flow on the existence of quasi-rents, then the speed of adjustment of installed capacity to changing demand in the long run could be increased, which would be to the advantage of the oil companies.

The answer to this seeming paradox lies with the oil companies' fear of collusion, either implicit or explicit, between their suppliers. In the British sector of the North Sea oil province, the oil companies do appear to face a small numbers problem: some subsectors in the technological core of the offshore oil supply industry are populated by as few as three – seven rival suppliers. It is taken as being almost axiomatic in the literature on industrial organization that small numbers enhance the possibility of collusion.

The effect of collusion on the efficacy of the invited tender-bid system can be assessed by assuming that its effectiveness is negatively correlated not only with the number of firms in an industry, n (the generally accepted view in the literature on industrial organization), but also with the number of firms, m, invited to bid. This is not unreasonable because small numbers are thought to enhance collusion and, in this context, small numbers enhance the chances of all invited bidders finding one another. If m is small, it would be all the easier for the invited bidders to arrange a price ring amongst themselves. In Figure 9.4 the optimal $\bar{m}$ may be small enough for collusive suppliers to extract large profits from an oil company. If so, the buyer would benefit from increasing the number of suppliers invited to bid above $\bar{m}$. But then marginal net benefit would be negative. Thus, buyers would find it more efficient to deal with collusion directly – both through legalistic codes and price secrecy – rather than by the informationally inefficient means of defeating it by raising the number of firms invited to bid.

Multiple bids and subcontracting

Multiple bids
A multiplicity of auctions at a given point in time can complicate the analysis (developed in Chapter 9) of finding the optimum bid-price: a supplier may have to determine two or more bid-prices at once. The following discussion relates to firm j receiving simultaneous invitations to bid on two contracts at the same time.

It should be borne in mind that all supply firms face rising variable costs. So, if a supplier is invited to bid on two contracts at once and gains both of them, it will end up with different variable costs than if only one extra contract had been obtained. Thus, a supplier faces a dilemma when simultaneously bidding for two new contracts. To price both on the assumption that only one will be gained might mean that losses are incurred on one of the contracts if both are won. Yet to price both on the assumption that both will be won risks not winning either because of the higher cost levels that have been built into the bids.

In the following analysis a supplier, firm j, is asked to bid on two identical contracts, with market conditions and firm j's own subjective probability distribution of rivals' bids taken as given. The two bid-prices will then depend only upon the variable costs of executing each contract. The supplier, though, will have a notion of expected variable costs of contracts 1 and 2:

$$E(C_{V1}) = [\text{Pr. win contract 2}] . [C_{V2}] + [\text{Pr. lose contract 2}] . [C_{V1}] \qquad (10.1)$$

and

$$E(C_{V2}) = [\text{Pr. win contract 1}] . [C_{V2}] + [\text{Pr. lose contract 1}] . [C_{V1}], \qquad (10.2)$$

where $E(C_{V1})$ and $E(C_{V2})$ are the expected costs of fulfilling contracts 1 and 2 respectively.

Thus, there are four possible outcomes for firm j when asked to bid simultaneously on two contracts. These are:

(1)   loses both contracts: $\pi_1 = 0; \pi_2 = 0$;
(2)   loses contract 1, wins 2: $\pi_1 = 0; \pi_2 = p_2 - C_{V1}$
(3)   wins contract 1, loses 2: $\pi_1 = P_1 - C_{V1}; \pi_2 = 0$
(4)   wins both contracts: $\pi_1 = P_1 - C_{V2}; \pi_2 = P_2 - C_{V2}$.

Then the expected profit on the first contract is the sum of items 3 and 4 above, viz:

$$E(\pi_1) = [\text{Pr. win contract 1}] . [\text{Pr. lose contract 2}] . [P_1 - C_{V1}] + \\ [\text{Pr. win contract 1}] . [\text{Pr. win contract 2}] . (P_1 - C_{V2}), \qquad (10.3)$$

while the expected profit on the second contract is the sum of items 1 and 2 above, viz:

$$E(\pi_2) = [\text{Pr. lose contract 1}] . [\text{Pr. win contract 2}] . [P_2 - C_{V1}] + \\ [\text{Pr. win contract 1}] . [\text{Pr. win contract 2}] . [P_2 - C_{V2}] \qquad (10.4)$$

Expected total profit on the two contracts bid for is simply the sum of equations (10.3) and (10.4) viz:

$$E(\pi_T) = E(\pi_1) + E(\pi_2). \qquad (10.5)$$

The two bid-prices, P_1 and P_2, should be identical as there is no reason to distinguish between the two contracts at the time of placing the bids. They should be chosen so as to maximize equation (10.5).

However, as has already been pointed out in Chapter 9, firm j will have only subjective information on the probabilities contained in equations (10.1) and (10.2): firm j will simply have to guess at these probabilities. This task could very easily be viewed by a supplier as involving too much uncertainty, in which case it may settle for a 'rule of thumb' bidding strategy. Two possible cases are:

(1) Refuse to accept one of the invitations to bid, or bid at a price that maximizes expected profit earned from one of the contracts and, simultaneously, at a price that will almost certainly lose the other contract.

(2) Set step-wise tender-bid prices: bid for contract 1 on the assumption that contract 2 is not won and for contract 2 on the assumption that contract 1 is gained.

With case (1) only one contract at best can be won; while with case (2) it is probably going to turn out that, again, only one contract at best will be won if the rival bidders happen to be bidding for only one additional contract at that point in time. Indeed, for the case of simultaneous bids, Engelbrecht-Wiggans (1980) has pointed out that submission of one 'high' and one 'low' bid may be optimal, but that the strategy chosen will vary with the exact circumstances of the investigation. This conclusion agrees with the analysis presented here.

Subcontracting
The analysis in Chapter 9 was developed with an implicit assumption that subcontracting by a contract winner is not allowed. But, if it is allowed, some new alternatives open up for the tender-bidder invited to bid on two or more contracts at once. Such a bidder can know its future supply costs with certainty (provided that it is confident of finding a subcontractor). Firm j can now bid for both contracts at once, assuming that the relevant costs are C_{V1} ($C_{V1} < E(C_{V2})$ as before). This will increase the probability of winning at least one of the contracts. And, should two contracts be won, the losses that might be incurred by supplying contract 2 at the higher variable costs, C_{V2}, may be avoided by subcontracting the work to another supplier.

Both Engelbrecht-Wiggans (1980) and Vickrey (1976) have pointed out that the use of subcontracting shows up a weakness in the auction arrangement for setting prices. It is a weakness in our case because the additional transaction necessitates that additional transaction costs will be incurred. That is, if subcontracting by firm j is *both* desirable and feasible (because C_{V2} is greater than the variable costs of some other supplier), the first tender-bid auction will have turned out to be non-Pareto optimal.

It will be apparent from this argument that it is in the buyer's interests to allow subcontracting, for, as we have said, firm j will feel free to place price-bids on both contracts that are related to the lower of its variable costs (i.e. C_{V1} rather than C_{V2} or $E(C_{V2})$).

It will also be noticed that, if the winning bidder can increase profits by subcontracting to a still lower cost supplier, then the buyer too could reduce price paid if it could only find this lower-cost supplier for itself. However, it has already been established, when discussing the optimal number of invited tender-bidders, that the cost to the buyer of finding this lower-cost supplier will exceed the expected benefit of the lower price paid. This must be so if the buyer has already optimized for the number of invited tender-bidders as in Figure 9.4. The corollary is that a supplier invited to bid for two contracts at once will abandon its rule of thumb bidding strategy only if it is confident that the transaction costs of finding a lower-cost subcontractor are not prohibitively high. But there is little reason to believe that a supplier would really incur lower transaction costs than do buyers in searching for a still lower cost alternative supplier. If this is true, the advantage of subcontracting is non-existent.

Thus we reach another strong conclusion on the economics of the invited tender-bid auction system: with positive transaction costs the arrangement produces Pareto optimal outcomes provided that winning bidders do not have better information on the whereabouts of still lower cost suppliers.

Conclusions

This and the previous chapter have attempted to lay out the economic determinants of choice of market form by transactors which have, or choose to have, to make a market each time an item is exchanged between sellers in the offshore oil supply industry and the oil company buyers of these intermediate inputs. The model that has been developed rests on the transaction costs theory of the firm. Optimization within this environment, both of choice between organizational forms, and within the chosen organizational form, is based upon the transaction costs incurred and expected benefits gained from investigating price offers. The model was laid out in a probabilistic framework. The main focus of attention has been the invited tender-bid auction system and the main intention was to analyse its properties in its 'pure' form. The pure form was delineated by the twelve assumptions listed at the beginning of Chapter 8 and carried over into this chapter. Short-run price behaviour in the pure invited tender-bid price determination model was compared with price formation under tatonnement as the base case. Not surprisingly, given the absence of transaction costs in the latter model, price determination with invited tender-bidding was shown to be less efficient in ensuring that contracts would be awarded to firms with the lowest variable costs. As a result the oil companies, it was argued, have to share some of the economic rent derived from an oil province with their suppliers in the offshore oil supply industry. Despite this, it was shown that, provided that the oil companies, as buyers, were optimizing the number of invited tender-bidders, the invited tender-bid auction does yield Pareto optimal resource allocation. It is the existence of transaction costs (positive tender-bid assessment and assembly costs) that accounts for the apparent inefficacy of the invited tender-bid auction. Given the existence of these costs, it was shown that, on average, on any contract an oil company does *not* expect to find the potential lowest variable cost supplier. However, it has also been argued that the invited tender-bid auction has transactional cost advantages for the market-maker over posted pricing by suppliers or an arrangement of more open information flow between the market participants. The latter could open up the possibility of collusive monopoly pricing and the extraction of even larger rents from the oil companies.

Some interesting implications have been shown to follow from the relaxation of certain of the assumptions that define the pure form. In particular, design idiosyncrasy of items exchanged was shown to be a factor encouraging pre-invitation surveillance activity on the part of buyers. Investment in surveillance was shown to be a substitute for transaction costs incurred in running the invited tender-bid auction. Surveillance enables buyers to reduce the number of invited bidders without a consequent loss of expected benefit.

It has also been argued that, if invited bidders were permitted to refuse an invitation to bid, this would also increase the efficacy of the invited tender-bid auction. This follows because invitation-refusal amounts to a mechanism of self-surveillance. As it is high-cost suppliers that would be most likely to disqualify themselves from a given auction, the way will be left open for more lower-cost suppliers to be invited to bid.

The alternative to assumption 1 (Chapter 8) – the existence of market exchange – is either backward vertical integration by the oil companies, or, perhaps, forward integration by some major offshore oil supply firms. The reason why the oil companies have chosen market rather than hierarchical relationships with their suppliers has been dealt with in an earlier chapter. In most offshore oil supply industry subsectors, vertical integration by the oil companies is not a cost-effective choice and nothing needs to be added to this conclusion at this point.

Relaxation of assumption 2 (the homogeneity across suppliers of the attribute subsets) was shown to further enrich the discussion. The existence of design idiosyncrasy and/or quality differences between the suppliers has the effect of further raising transaction costs. This especially affects the oil companies' tender-bid assessment costs, since comparisons across the suppliers' non-standard set of attributes is made more complicated. The effect of this was shown to reduce the optimum number of invited tender-bidders and to encourage the oil companies to invest in market surveillance.

Assumptions 5 and 6 together ruled out the occurrence of two or more auctions at a given point in time. Relaxation of this condition, however, led to a most interesting further conclusion: the Pareto optimality of the invited tender-bid auction is maintained on condition that a winning bidder does not have superior information on the whereabouts of potential lower-cost suppliers. If this is the case, then subcontracting cannot be profitable and there is no argument in favour of incurring the costs of a second auction.

Assumption 8 was that buyers lacked any information on the suppliers' cost levels; the effect of this was to turn the buyers into 'random number machines'. Perfect information on the part of buyers would, of course, entirely negate the need for the invited tender-bid auction and we would be returned to the world of Walrasian market clearing. However, buyers do engage in surveillance activity so as to improve their information set, and the transactional advantages of this have been discussed.

11

Host countries and the international offshore oil supply industry: problems of entry and exit

The oil-gathering industry was shown earlier to be composed of the oil companies and the offshore oil supply firms that provide intermediate goods and services inputs to the oil companies. Virtually all of the oil companies and many of the leading firms in the supply industry operate multinationally, and this has created the somewhat unusual feature in a globally organized industry as both the buyers and the sellers operate as internationalized producers – connected to one another through market relationships simultaneously in several locations. (This is more unusual in the oil-gathering industry's manufactures branch rather than its service branch, as there are several examples of service industries being organized on a similar basis – see Chapter 5.) The objective of this chapter is to point out some of the more important consequences of the globalization of the supply industry for the economic development of localities and the wider national economies that have been chosen as service bases for offshore oil provinces.

In the UK, even after about fifteen or so years of operation, indigenous firms have largely failed to create a strong presence in the technological core of the supply industry. (The 'core' of the supply industry was defined earlier to include drilling, mud logging, well-testing and wireline services, geological exploration services, completion and well stimulation, production services, production of specialized down-hole chemicals (known as muds) and specialized oil field tools and machinery manufactures.) Indeed, the record of failure is even longer than this because the development of the northern North Sea beginning around 1969 was preceded by about six years by large-scale gas production in the southern North Sea, which provided similar opportunities to develop an indigenous presence in the exploitation of offshore hydrocarbons. In fact, according to one estimate, British companies won only about one-quarter of the business offered by the exploitation of this resource (Cook and Surrey, 1983). This failure, as was argued in Chapter 5, was largely due to barriers to entry into the core, which are themselves primarily caused by the possession of protected, or at least not easily reproducible, firm-specific knowledge by the existing, largely American, multinational supply industry firms. This knowledge has often been created through long experience in the oil-gathering industry and through research and development, and is sometimes protected by patents and trade marks. Firm-specific advantages also reside in the possession of specialized capital equipment, employment of superior skilled specialized labour, and superior management techniques that cut costs and enable the established supply firms repeatedly to win contracts under conditions of competitive invited tender-bidding. Without a presence in the technological core, indigenous British companies and those of other host countries will probably not be able to service the supply industry's substantial global markets in the longer term – as an oil province's production begins to decline. Quite simply, it will be difficult to break into export markets. They will remain as peripheral providers of locationally determined inputs, i.e. inputs that are not specific to the oil industry and are relatively easily reproducible by other host countries' indigenous enterprises. These locationally determined inputs include heavy non-oil industry-specific items such as storage vessels, cranes, ramps and other rig-top structures (including housing for personnel, outputs from the general construction industry, banking and financial services, insurance, transport, and catering.

Organization of the offshore oil supply industry

We have already seen in Chapter 4 that the oil industry first grew to a significant size in the USA and from the earliest date the suppliers of the myriad intermediate manufactured and processed inputs were entities separate from their oil company customers. American offshore oil supply firms thereby gained a first mover advantage. There appear to be no official published American data relating to the commercialization of the services provided by the supply industry, but we know that the oil companies rely heavily upon purchases from independent suppliers (see Chapter 3). This market-based relationship has been transferred by American oil companies to many other countries and has been reproduced by the non-American oil companies (see Chapter 4).

We have also seen that several powerful reasons exist for this choice on the part of the oil companies of a market relationship over one of vertical integration – the subject matter of Chapters 1, 2 and 5. One explanation, originating in the transaction cost literature, is that ownership and operation of supply companies would take the oil companies away from their main business, thus involving them in excessive transaction costs (since perhaps several hundred separable inputs are used in oil exploration, development and production). The second explanation, also rooted in transaction costs, derives from the oil companies' fear of opportunism. An oil company would not wish to purchase the surplus output of, say, geological services from another oil company for fear of giving away valuable knowledge to the supplier (see Mead, 1986).

When the oil companies first begin exploration activities in a new oil province, as they did in the northern North Sea in the late 1960s (the first commercial field discovered was the Montrose field in 1969), they create a geographically distinct demand for the intermediate products and services provided by the supply industry. These firms then face a classic choice as to how to service the new market. They may export from their home production facilities in the USA, license a foreign supplier, or go multinational by establishing a foreign affiliate (on these matters see the discussion in Chapter 5 on the theory of the multinational corporation). Disembodied services cannot be exported in a manner similar to manufactured goods when they must be applied on site, as is very often the case with the services used by the oil companies. So service companies will be found in close proximity to the oil companies. Besides, even when it is possible to provide services at a distance (e.g. with laboratory-based services), the oil companies will usually deal only with suppliers that have facilities located close to them, as this tends to facilitate cooperation and communication and speeds turnaround. Licensing of local firms has not been popular either, both because indigenous companies with the requisite skills do not exist and because the licenser fears that a licensee might free-ride on the licenser's reputation, so denuding goodwill with the oil companies and creating a global external diseconomy.

With oil field equipment and machinery, the American suppliers have chosen the export route with greater frequency than is the case with service inputs, but they still nearly always establish a non-manufacturing affiliate in a new location. These overseas affiliates act as sales offices, inventory holders and managers and providers of after-sales services, while the parent companies retain their manufacturing capacity in the USA. (A few American manufacturers of oil field equipment, however, sometimes set up additional manufacturing capacity, as Baker International, Combustion Engineering and Halliburton have done in Aberdeen, Scotland.)

Government policies towards the offshore oil supply industry

We would expect that, since the existence of multinational corporations is based upon firm-specific knowledge, economy of scale cost benefits and measurement cost advantages, if host country firms are to penetrate in to the industry, some form of special help would be needed from governmental sources. The forms that this help could take are, as we shall see, varied but, to have any success at all, must offer some form of protection to nascent indigenous competition to the multinationals. The infant industry argument has often been invoked to justify such protectionism. Indeed, protectionism has had some success in countries such as Brazil, China, France, Norway and Venezuela in raising the share of indigenous firms in oil company procurement expenditures, while, at the same time, in the one country that has most refrained from protectionism, the UK, the penetration of indigenous firms is quite limited.

However, this is not to say that protection of the indigenous offshore supply industry is automatically desirable. The infant industry argument for protection readily admits that, in the short term, production costs are likely to rise as production is shifted from the competitive foreign firms to protected indigenous companies. Clearly, they are protected because they are relatively inefficient, at least in the beginning. Only in the longer term might relative production costs equalize. Dynamic–economic arguments are also usually employed to justify the infant industry argument; for example, for countries with narrow commodity (and service) export bases, entry into oil field services and equipment export markets might reduce a foreign exchange constraint on economic growth. Be that as it may, the adoption of protectionist policies is likely to involve an intertemporal trade-off of economic welfare, which necessitates the choice of an appropriate discount rate by the responsible governmental authorities before any sensible policy approach can be put together.

We will see that the UK has followed an 'open door' policy towards the multinational offshore oil supply firms. At quite the opposite extreme, China has followed politico-economic policies that have lain entirely outside of the international market economy system. Until quite recently, it had chosen not to rely in any way upon multinational enterprise in the oil-gathering industry. It is also true that Venezuela and, to a somewhat lesser extent, Brazil have pursued strongly protectionist measures but within the international capitalist system. Multinational companies have been allowed a presence, particularly in the areas of specialized, firm-specific technology and techniques, while tariffs, the tax system and other measures have been used to promote indigenous enterprise in the more peripheral subsectors.

Norway is following a more cautious protectionist course inter-mediate between the British open door policy and Latin American strongly protectionist approaches.

As we can think of no good reasons (such as more adaptable indigenous enterprise) that would suggest that Venezuela and Brazil have a more favourable intertemporal trade-off than do either Norway or Britain, then their more protectionist policies can be justified on the basis of either a lower rate of time preference (which is hardly likely given their substantially lower per capita incomes) or a belief in relatively strong dynamic benefits from import substitution. This latter is entirely plausible given that the external economies derived from incremental industrialization (e.g. labour training, foreign exchange saving) may be greater in these countries and that, ultimately, a viable indigenous offshore supplies industry may help to diversify their relatively narrow export structures.

However, it is not the objective of this chapter to go into any detailed analysis of the relationship between the development of an indigenous offshore oil supply industry and a country's rate of industrialization and economic development. Rather, the objective is more limited: to establish that the existence of multinational offshore oil supply firms – based upon their transactional and economy of scale advantages – has constituted a competitive barrier to indigenous firms around the world and that governments have had to decide what they should do about it. We will observe the response of some governments to the inability of indigenous companies to overcome the advantages enjoyed by the multinational offshore oil supply firms.

We have also tried to make clear that the application of protectionist government policy is likely to have some adverse welfare cost effects for the host country in the short run. These welfare costs may be regarded as the opportunity cost of overcoming (if the protectionist measures are ultimately successful) the relative transaction cost disadvantages of indigenous industry. The counterpart to this observation is that failure to protect indigenous firms from foreign competition at least avoids the short-term costs of doing so, but then the long-term benefits – if any – will be forgone.

British policy
Until 1984, successive British governments gave priority to the speedy development of the oil and gas resources of the British continental shelf and ran an open door policy towards foreign direct investment. This policy was not without its costs, however; Cameron (1986, p. 27) reflected the widely held impression that 'although the UK industry probably ranks second or third among the world suppliers of offshore goods and services by oil companies, it has so far failed to become a large-scale exporter'.

The British government's policy towards the offshore oil supply industry is embodied in the Memorandum of Understanding and Code of Practice (1975, modified 1981) agreed with the member oil companies of the UK Offshore Operators Association (UKOOA). The policy is described one of 'full and fair opportunity' for British suppliers and amounts to an open door for foreign suppliers. In this respect, British policy is unique among offshore oil-producing nations: all other countries give substantially more protection to their indigenous oil supply firms.

The Memorandum of Understanding agrees the objective of non-discrimination *against* UK suppliers and the Code of Practice enumerates the means through which discrimination is to be avoided. Central to the application of these arrangements is the Offshore Supplies Office (OSO), which has the role of ensuring that the agreements are applied in practice. Thus, the oil companies must inform the OSO of purchases that will be made from overseas and the OSO will vet the bidding procedures and contract award decisions.

The Memorandum of Understanding and Code of Practice, therefore, do little more than ensure that a competitive environment exists. British companies are to have no less than (or more than) an equal chance of being awarded a supply contract. There is no provision for positive discrimination in favour of British companies. Besides, as was discussed in Chapter 7, there are other pressures on the leaseblock operators that encourage them to place contracts with the most competitive suppliers. The reference here is to the interests of an operator's leaseblock partners who stand in a type of principal–agent relationship with the operator and have a strong interest in seeing that production costs are minimized. They would not, for example, want to see an operator award a contract to a subsidiary company (or company related to it some other way such as nationality) at anything more than the most competitive bid. To some extent then, the 'full and fair opportunity' policy is redundant. However, there are provisions in the Memorandum of Understanding that might have some effectiveness. For example, operators are not allowed to write the bid documents in a way that excludes British industrial specification standards, which would have the effect of being discriminatory against British firms.

An aspect of the Code of Practice that has been much criticized is the target that operators must place 70 per cent, or more, of purchases by value with UK companies. The criticism arises because a 'UK company' is defined with reference to its location rather than to the nationality of its ownership. The difference is by no means trivial: if nationality of ownership mattered, then the discriminatory effect in favour of procurement from indigenous British companies would be enormous. As it stands, all a foreign supplier needs to do is to set up an affiliate in the UK and give it a minimal function such as inventory management. The latter is obviously of little use to the development of indigenous British enterprise.

In fact, it is claimed by the OSO that, in 1984, 74 per cent of orders by value for offshore goods and services were placed with 'UK companies' (the remaining 26 per cent being placed directly abroad). A much more interesting statistic is the share of the value of orders placed with indigenous British supply firms.

The government has published no information on this, but a sensible estimate can be made by using information gathered in the sample survey discussed in Chapter 6. The sampled firms employed a total of 13,250 workers, of whom 53 per cent were employed by indigenous British companies. Assuming that sales and employment relate proportionately, then only 39 per cent of sales must have been made by indigenous companies, with 26 per cent being placed overseas and 35 per cent with the affiliates of foreign companies located in the UK (total purchases of goods and services by the oil companies in 1984 amounted to £3.61 billion). Moreover, if we allow foreign-affiliated companies a 10 per cent labour productivity (output per worker) advantage over indigenous firms to allow for their greater experience in the offshore oil supply industry (e.g. because they can share in the overhead facilities provided by their overseas headquarters), then the indigenous share falls to 36 per cent of all purchases placed in the UK.[1]

In exploration contracts (mainly drilling – the core activity of the oil industry), the share going to British companies is particularly poor. Only about one-third of contracts (by value) in the 1980s were going to companies that could be designated as 'British' and most of these were won by foreign affiliates (*Financial Times*, 9 March 1984). Commenting on the performance of indigenous British companies in the international offshore industry, the chairman of perhaps Britain's most successful indigenous company, the John Wood Group, lamented the failure of these companies to win even 1 per cent of the total world market and described this performance as 'miserable' (*The Scotsman*, 23 January 1984).

Successive British governments have, in fact, chosen to ignore the recommendations of a commissioned report for the Department of Trade and Industry undertaken in 1972 (International Management and Engineering Group). In the report it was observed that:

In overcoming the severe technological and operational difficulties of the North Sea environment, non-British enterprise is becoming progressively more entrenched. *The time for British firms to establish is now or not at all* (p. 5, emphasis added).

An interventionist policy was advised, with the main elements being:

- the establishment of a petroleum industries board under the Department of Trade and Industry to assist in the development of internationally competitive British equipment and service contracting companies;
- joint venture partnerships to be established as a means of transferring technology and know-how to British enterprise, which then would be able to compete in international markets;
- a wholly owned British contractor to be set up in offshore drilling;
- insurance – through a government body – of risk capital invested by British companies in the offshore oil supply industry;
- purchase of equipment by the British government for lease to British contractors;
- the creation of an information service for British equipment suppliers;
- subsidized credit;
- government-supported research and development;
- government financial support for the education of petroleum engineers and the creation of university courses in petroleum engineering.

The approach to be embodied in policies such as these may be described as 'the spawning of internationally competitive indigenous private enterprise'. As such, the suggested policy was not protectionist in the sense of reserving the British offshore oil supply market for British companies. Such an exclusion of foreign multinational companies would have served to raise production costs and to have left British companies at a competitive disadvantage in world markets. One could characterize the International Management and Engineering Group's arguments and suggestions as an infant industry argument for protection. The cost disadvantages faced by British firms were not insurmountable, given that patented technology is not so important in the offshore oil-gathering business and anyway might be reproduced by British investment in research and development or might be obtained through joint venture arrangements with the multinational companies. But what was essential for the strategy was that British offshore oil supply firms could gain an early start so as quickly to develop a competitive position.

As it has turned out, no British government has accepted this infant industry argument. By 1983 – as British-sector North Sea oil production neared its peak – Cook and Surrey concluded that it was by then too late to adopt 'radically new nationalistic policies' (1983, p. 89). Indeed, surveying the 1973-7 period, Gaskin and MacKay pointed out that failure of British companies then to penetrate the market would have long-term adverse consequences (1978, p. 94). What had come out of the consultants' study was limited in relation to the wider objectives: the Offshore Supplies Office (OSO) was established as a part of the Department of Energy and some small interest payment subsidies were paid directly to the oil companies when they made purchases from some British suppliers – as an offset to subsidized export credits given by, for example, the USA's Export–Import Bank (this scheme was withdrawn in 1980). The OSO's main function is as an information broker: brokering information on the oil industry's current purchasing and technological needs as well as British industry's offshore services capabilities (for an early discussion of British information services relating to the offshore oil supply industry, see International Marketing Research Association, 1975, and any number of OSO brochures). In recent years it has acquired a £5.5 million research and development budget for investment in targeted technologies – especially in sub-sea systems, exploration, drilling and production and offshore weight reduction – but it is admitted that this budget is small in relation to existing private sector (foreign company) expenditures (Offshore Supplies Office, 1987). And, as Table 11.1 below shows, the British have been far less assertive than the French and Norwegians in promoting an indigenous offshore supplies industry.

By 1984, the British government began to shift its 'full and fair opportunity' policy towards one of more active discrimination, with the objective of promoting the British supply industry as a major competitor in world markets (Financial Times, 12 February 1985). With government approval, UKOOA set up the Quality Appraisal Service Company (QUASCO) in 1985, whose function is to investigate companies for pre-qualification. Pre-qualification costs constitute a barrier to entry for a new firm, especially when it has to pre-qualify with each of several potential oil company customers. The QUASCO may reduce these pre-qualification costs by investigating a potential new entrant on behalf of the UKOOA members.

Somewhat more significantly, in the ninth round of licensing (1984/5) the British government adopted more stringent criteria with respect to oil company purchases from British-based companies. An oil company that failed to reach the 70 per cent target mentioned above would not be looked upon favourably in later licensing rounds. This new policy might have affected the allocation of certain platform design contracts to British companies and away from the leading US suppliers – an act that provoked a protest of trade discrimination from the US Secretary of State (Cameron, 1986; Financial Times, 19 October 1985). But in view of the British government's late start in favouring indigenous British supply companies, combined with the widespread

Table 11.1 *Government policies towards indigenous offshore oil supply industries*

Policy	Britain	France	Norway
Assistance with entry	minor	considerable	some
Assisting essential project R&D	minor	considerable	enlarged
National oil company purchasing policies	minor	vital	vital
Full and fair opportunity	vital	redundant	important
Open door to multinationals	vital	restricted	in joint ventures
Discriminatory promotion of indigenous firms	minor[a]	vital	important

Source: Cook and Surrey, 1983.
[a] Platform construction by British firms has been the subject of government promotional policies.

protectionism in other countries, one can only be pessimistic about the longer-term export prospects of these countries. It would appear that successive British governments have failed to take into account global dynamics, barriers to entry and foreign protectionism, leaving British companies largely confined as providers of locationally determined inputs into the oil-gathering industry.

Norway and France
Under the British policy of 'full and fair opportunity', oil company purchasers were merely expected *not* to discriminate against British suppliers, and the policy fell well short of one of positive discrimination in favour of the British supply industry. In this respect British policy was quite different from that of Norway and France. These two countries adopted procurement and other rules aimed at promoting indigenous suppliers and/or used their national oil companies' purchasing policies to the same end. This observation is brought out in Table 11.1, which compares British, Norwegian and French government policies towards their offshore oil supply industries.

There are several methods that governments may and have used to discriminate in favour of indigenous companies with the objective of building a domestic production and export capability:

● *Legislation:* the basic petroleum laws can in principle contain clauses on mandatory joint ventures, technology transfer and petroleum engineering and management training programmes for host country personnel. The problem with such an approach is that it is overtly discriminatory and might provoke retaliation (Cameron, 1986, p. 18).

- Use of *national oil companies* (NOCs) which are directed to make purchases from indigenous firms – so providing a secure market for the latter (see, for example, Alleyne, 1980; Sherif, 1980). Norway has been particularly adept in using this device.

- *Production licensing*, which can require the oil companies to discriminate in favour of indigenous sourcing – for example, Norway and China (Mikesell, 1984, and Dabinovic, 1987, discuss the cases of several less developed countries).

- *Import licensing, tariffs and limitation of foreign ownership* as practised by Brazil and Venezuela and some other Latin American countries.

- *Joint ventures*, where foreign suppliers are required to enter into joint ventures with host country indigenous firms.

Norwegian procurement regulations (under the 1972 Decree and 1985 Act of Parliament) place an operator under an obligation to provide Norwegian industry with opportunities to participate in supply and technological development as well as in training Norwegian personnel. Moreover, in the award of service contracts the Ministry of Petroleum and Energy, which receives detailed information about all pending service contracts, favours contract awards to, in order of priority, wholly owned Norwegian companies, joint venture companies, a foreign affiliate located in Norway and, as a last resort, foreign exporters. Foreign company entrants to Norway are also strongly encouraged by regulations to enter into joint ventures, thus affording technology transfer to the Norwegian partner.

Norway's national oil company, Statoil, has also played an important role in the 'Norwegianization' of Norway's offshore supplies industry. It was granted by law an automatic 50 per cent share in all licence awards and has used this position to direct supply contracts to Norwegian suppliers. In an interesting development, Statoil has acquired exploration rights in other countries and 'it would be unrealistic not to expect an international Statoil to function *vis à vis* the Norwegian supply industry in the same way as Elf and Total function *vis à vis* the French supply industry' (Cameron, 1986, p. 86).

The French, in fact, have been particularly assiduous in creating an environment suitable for the development of indigenous French companies in the offshore oil supply industry. The national oil company has discriminated strongly in favour of a 'buy French' policy; competition by foreign multinational corporations in France has been restricted; money has been made available for research and development by French companies; and individual companies have been promoted on a selective basis. Norwegian government policy has also discriminated in favour of indigenous firms, with, in particular, the joint venture and national oil company purchasing policies being strongly favoured. Indeed, the French and Norwegian governments have clashed over the matter of the protection of their offshore supplies industries. In the mid-1980s the Norwegians wished to develop the giant Troll and Sleipner offshore natural gas fields at a capital cost of $8 billion. This cost included building a 682 mile pipeline to move gas to the markets of West Germany, Belgium, Holland and France. However, the French pointed to the negative effect that their gas purchases from Norway would have on their balance of payments with Norway and insisted upon a countervailing trade flow. The French wanted this countervailing trade flow to take the form of the reservation for French offshore supply companies of construction and other supply contracts that would be needed on the offshore gas project as well as some other trade concessions from the Norwegians. The Norwegians rebuffed the French demands and drew up new plans to develop a smaller offshore gas project leaving the French market out of consideration (*Wall Street Journal*, 2 December 1986).

Some other countries
Considering other examples of government policy by host governments, Randall (1987) describes Venezuela as an example of a country that has promoted an indigenous oil supplies industry through a comprehensive policy of import substitution. In 1977, foreign direct investment was allowed only in the form of joint ventures and a 1979 tax law provided for heavier taxation of technical services than technical assistance. In 1981, new procurement standards made it easier to prohibit the contracting of foreign consultancy services when an indigenous alternative could be used. Import tariffs of 30 per cent for non-consultancy services were introduced in 1982. As a result of these protectionist measures, Venezuelan enterprise increased its share of procurement contracts won. However, the failure of Venezuelan enterprise to penetrate certain sectors of the oil supplies industry (e.g. the collection and interpretation of seismic data, production of oil field equipment and machinery, and exploration and well-production services) led to the authorization of direct foreign investment by American offshore oil supply multinationals. In other words, despite the introduction of strong protectionist measures over a period approaching ten years, Venezuela's reliance upon the multinational offshore oil supply firms was still clearly evident. It was also true that the relative cost of the indigenously produced Venezuelan equipment and services remained high relative to what could be obtained from the foreign companies (Randall, 1987).

Surrey (1986, 1987) has described how the 'impressive' development of Brazil's offshore oil supply industry was used as a component of that country's import substitution-based industrialization effort. The national oil company, Petrobras, was given wide powers over the oil sector and used these powers to direct procurement towards Brazilian suppliers. By 1985, Brazilian firms (including foreign affiliates in Brazil) received as much as 93 per cent of procurement expenditures and had established themselves in virtually all subsectors except those of the highest technology – again, especially those sectors where the multinational offshore supply companies dominate. Surrey, however, warned that the protected growth of indigenous supply industry capacity might have compromised economic efficiency. But it is also true that Braspetro, Petrobras's export subsidiary, has won export orders for oil exploration and development projects in a number of Latin American, African and Middle Eastern countries. These, though, have been under managed trade agreements rather than competitive tender.

Several studies have appeared recently on China's oil industry, its relationship to Chinese industrialization, the foreign oil companies and the offshore multinational oil industry supplies companies (Cameron, 1986; Fridley and Christoffersen, 1987; Kaempfer and Min, 1986; Oldham et al., 1987). What is particularly interesting in this is that China had for twenty years or so excluded foreign enterprise and built a 'comprehensive' onshore oil industry. Moreover, by the early 1970s China had begun to produce some oil offshore. In other words, the Chinese, working upon a base of Soviet petroleum technology (acquired in the 1950s), had built up an indigenous technology and oil production capability.

However, if this technology had been of comparable efficiency, China would have had no need to turn to the international oil industry. But, beginning in the late 1970s, China did indeed turn to the international oil industry. The reason is readily apparent: China's indigenous oil technology was inferior to that which could be purchased from the international oil industry. So inferior in fact that offshore oil gathering in deeper waters could not be tackled. Chinese technology was also backward in the more technologically advanced area of secondary recovery.

Thus, while Venezuela and Brazil were making strenuous efforts to limit the scope of the international oil industry, with relatively little success in the technologically advanced areas of the industry, China was welcoming in these companies. In both cases, the presence of the international oil industry was based upon its competitive advantages (with an outright advantage when indigenous companies in a given technological area did not even exist).

Even when indigenous oil supplies firms do exist, usually with some degree of protection, Chevalier (1987) has pointed out that they often do not operate projects efficiently through the comprehensive phases of design, construction and operation. We may say that government support tends to distort incentives to transactional efficiency. Chevalier comments:

> Financial devices such as joint ventures appear clearly as an interesting means of transferring technologies and providing guarantees that the project will be well operated. For developing countries, it is probably the best way to build up local expertise. Moreover, it is also an opportunity to put the international companies in a position of qualitative competition. For a given project, the country may organize a tender offer which is not only in terms of price but also takes into account the type of training and transfer of technology which might be proposed by the bidders. Transfer of technology becomes a challenge for competitiveness in the long run. (Chevalier, 1987, p. 230)

Technology transfer

Technology transfer to indigenous companies is perhaps the single most urgent matter for the strength of a nation's oil supplies industry. Technology is known to be an important contributory factor to a nation's economic growth but, as implied above, it can matter whether that technology is owned locally or by foreign entities, a point that has been made in connection with the wider Scottish economy (Forsyth, 1972), Latin American economic performance (Barnet and Muller, 1974; Seidman, 1975), and American dominance of Canadian industry. This situation is especially true with the oil supply industry, because its intermediate inputs in any single oil province are required for a finite period of time – the expected life of that oil province. Nor are the inputs of all supply industry subsectors needed in large quantities over the entire life of an offshore oil province. Construction of offshore structures (e.g. rigs, platforms and undersea pipelines) is needed mainly in the earlier stages of the life of an oil province. The demand for all inputs will vary as an oil province passes through its several exploration, development, production and final close-down phases.

In the short term, tapping of foreign-owned technology through the conduit of the multinational corporation does enable a country quickly to exploit an oil province. In the long term, sometime in the early part of the next century in the case of Britain's North Sea oil, when these multinational firms close their Scottish affiliates little is likely to be left behind unless indigenous firms are able to supply foreign markets from an established Scottish base. For that base to be created, indigenous firms must develop firm-specific advantages of their own so that they may compete with their foreign rivals. This longer-term problem is especially acute in an oil-producing country such as Venezuela (Anez, 1978), which lacks a well-developed manufacturing sector that could respond competitively to the opportunities provided by the large offshore and onshore oil supplies market located within its national borders. What is more surprising, perhaps, is that Britain, a country that is both industrialized and has long experience in the international oil industry, has also found difficulty in creating a competitive presence in the internationally mobile technological 'core' sectors of the offshore oil supply industry.

Furthermore, the arrival of the oil industry also has had some negative consequences for the 'traditional' industries in Britain's main offshore service base (Aberdeen, in north-east Scotland), i.e. agriculture, fishing, textiles and paper. Problems have arisen because the oil industry's strong demand for labour and for property has created external pecuniary diseconomies for the traditional industries, which have increased their costs of production and reduced their competitiveness. It has been estimated that for every 100 oil-related jobs that have been created, eight jobs in the non-oil sector have been lost (Harris *et al.*, 1987). Accordingly, shorn of much of the employment provided by its traditional sectors, eventual exit by the offshore supply industry will shock the local economy and return the locality to its historical position of high unemployment and outward labour migration. In such circumstances, whether off-the-shelf utilization of foreign technology can be regarded as wholly beneficial depends largely upon one's rate of time preference. Certainly, some local politicians in Aberdeen city do worry about the long-term prospect (Bonney, 1986).

A picture of dependency

With over 1,000 oil-related companies located in the Aberdeen area, it might seem churlish to challenge the view that Aberdeen is the 'oil capital of Europe'. However, the results of the sample survey reported in Chapter 6 do cast strong doubt on this grand characterization.

A capital should be composed of head offices, and impulses should spread out from the centre across its domain. But the offshore oil supply industry in Aberdeen, Britain's main service base and easily the largest in Europe, is not like this. Rather, it is composed mainly of affiliates of parent companies located elsewhere in the world. The impulses overwhelmingly flow into rather than out of that oil service base, and its domain is primarily restricted to the British sector of the North Sea oil province.

The predominance of affiliates with their limited horizons points to the idea that Aberdeen is not so much an 'oil capital' as an 'oil satellite'. That is, impulses for decision-making on matters such as capital investment, research and development expenditure and the definition of market horizons come from outside the local area. We will not repeat here the discussion in Chapter 6 of these descriptive characteristics of the offshore oil supply industry in the Aberdeen area, but for the continuity of this chapter it is worthwhile to pick out two of the more important highlights. First, 90 per cent of affiliates were set up by their parents especially to service North Sea oil activity (rather, to service the offshore oil supply industry over a broader horizon). But while 98 per cent of these affiliates had some decision power within the local area, only 18 per cent of wholly oil-related affiliates had decision-making powers that extended overseas and most of these were just across the North Sea in Norway, and, therefore, dependent upon essentially the same oil province. Secondly, Aberdeen-based affiliates were relatively unimportant within their ownership group as measured by the affiliates' share of group employment or sales (Hallwood, 1986). For example, 30 per cent of affiliates account for less than 1 per cent of group employment, while 31 per cent of affiliates accounted for less than 1 per cent of group sales. Strikingly, two-thirds of affiliates in Aberdeen accounted for only 10 per cent or less of their respective group's total employment, while 55 per cent of affiliates accounted for just 10 per cent or less of their groups' worldwide sales. Put another way, only 18 per cent of affiliates accounted for over half of their group's employment and even fewer, 15 per cent, for their group's sales.

Ownership of Scottish industry by foreign companies has been viewed as creating a dependent economy with undesirable economic consequences (e.g. Firn, 1975; Forsyth, 1972; Hood and Young, 1976; McDermott, 1979). These consequences are said to include control over subsidiaries that transcends national authority, weak linkage(s) with the local economy, the creation of a minimum skilled and relatively homogeneous labour force, and absorption of local enterprise. Yet this judgement is overly one-dimensional. The internationalized industry's peculiar dynamic spatial organization and industrial organization structure ought to be considered. These organizational matters, while related, are distinct from ownership. Their effects may be to reduce the beneficial effects that might otherwise be gained from an increased level of local ownership. Little local benefit is gained from owning a plant that will shortly lose its local market and be relocated, perhaps thousands of miles away, so as to be able to exploit some other local market.

This argument is especially appropriate in the case of the offshore oil supply industry. As has been shown, its spatial organization is broadly governed by the relocational decisions of international oil companies and its industrial organization structure has been largely created in a foreign country (the USA). The firms supply markets whose global spread is vast and is continuing to grow over time, but the size of these markets is markedly time-variant in any individual location and the markets are cut off from one another by high transport costs. Accordingly, local ownership in one of the offshore oil supply industry's less-than-permanent locations will not necessarily raise the level of regional autonomy. Local prosperity will remain conditioned by outside forces, in this case by both geological imperatives (as oil and gas begin to run out or can be gathered only at higher cost) and the retention of ownership in foreign hands of the crucial internationally mobile sectors of the industry.

The prosperity of a locally owned supply industry in a given location may be extended beyond this geologically circumscribed time horizon if a presence in export markets can be created. The qualification 'may' is important. Local manufacturing capacity is sustainable if export sales can be made to flourish, but provision of service inputs to customers in foreign markets by locally owned firms by no means guarantees strong linkage(s) with the local economy. Generally, in the oil-gathering business, services have to be applied on-site and/or the oil companies require that service input facilities be located close to their own on-land facilities in each offshore oil province.

Thus, matters of ownership, industrial organization and global relocation must all be taken into consideration when assessing the long-run prospects for the host region. The progress that has been revealed in Aberdeen and surrounding areas, at least up to 1984, is not at all encouraging. First, what local ownership has been established in the offshore oil supply industry is mainly in the production of locationally determined inputs, so that penetration of export markets on a large scale is unlikely. Secondly, eventual global relocation by the oil companies will penalize locally owned suppliers, which will have to face increased transport costs and local competition. Third, even though the ownership structure of the offshore oil supply industry favours penetration by local firms, barriers to entry to the geographically mobile sectors do exist.

British government policy towards the oil companies and their suppliers, as we have seen, has been largely restricted to two areas: disseminating information to British industry on the existence of domestic multi-billion pound markets in the oil-gathering business and ensuring that British suppliers are able to compete on a 'level playing field'. The latter aspect is concerned with the non-discriminatory operation of the invited tender-bidding auction system universally adopted by the oil companies for procurement purposes. Some leverage is applied by the British government through the OSO and by leaseblock ·

licensing policy. But British policy falls a good deal short of the discriminatory policies that have been adopted by other countries.

Whether the British government's hands-off or other governments' hands-on policy will be the more successful in the longer run remains open to question. A hands-on policy may create jobs in the short run but leave an over-expanded sector as local oil production declines and American multinational corporations continue to retain dominance of the technological core. The British policy at least has the short-term benefit of tapping competitive sources of offshore oil-gathering technology and avoids overinvestment in indigenous firms that are bound to find long-run survival most problematic.

Notes

1   Indigenous companies' sales share (I) depends upon UK-located companies' sales share (L), the foreign share of employment (E) and the foreign companies' productivity advantage (V), viz:

$$I = L[1 - (E)(V)],$$

with $L = 0.74$, $E = 0.47$, and V guessed to be 1.1.

12

Conclusions: on choosing a market in the offshore oil-gathering business

---

The main purpose of this monograph is to discover whether organizational-arrangements found in the offshore oil gathering business align with predictions derived from the transaction cost paradigm. The matching of predictions with arrangements is taken as being a satisfactory case study test of that paradigm. The main hypothesis is that transaction cost enconomizing explains choices that transactors make between institutional organizational-forms. In fact, two separate branches of transaction cost theory have been developed – the measurement cost and the rent appropriation (Williamson, 1985, and Alchian and Woodward, 1988) – and both are needed to explain the complex institutional-arrangements found in offshore oil gathering.

In order to draw conclusions together this final chapter is divided into seven main parts. The first lists some stylized facts about the offshore oil gathering business as well as the main organizational arrangements found in the industry. It is the latter that are to be explained. After outlining the main features of the transaction cost paradigm it is then used systematically to explain such features as the internationalization of offshore service-companies; the use of the invited tender-bid auction through which oil companies procure many of the intermediate inputs used in offshore oil gathering; the reasons as to why oil platforms but usually *not* drilling rigs are vertically integrated by oil companies, the importance of idiosyncrasy – of product or *process* – in the choice of organizational arrangements; and, finally, why auctions are often preferred by transactors when product idiosyncrasy is a transactional feature.

Stylized facts

The main stylized facts described in earlier chapters were as follows: first, the international offshore oil supply industry is made up of two quite distinct groups of firms – the oil companies and the multinational offshore oil supply firms. The oil companies create 'pools' of demand in geographically wide-spread offshore oil provinces and the multinational suppliers supply these markets, almost always through affiliates that they establish for this purpose. The dynamics of this internationalization process belongs largely to the theory of the multinational corporation (described in Chapter 5).

Secondly, the operational focus of offshore oil production is the oil production platform with its associated topside and seabed fixed structures. An oil company will own (often in a consortium) the production platform and its fixtures – but it will have had other companies complete the work of design and construction.[1]

Thirdly, another large expense is use of an offshore drilling rig. Unlike the production platform, an oil company will usually *not* own the rigs which it uses preferring to hire on a time-contract basis the services of specialist offshore drilling companies. There are many other service-inputs into offshore oil gathering and it is a striking fact that the oil companies also usually purchase these on a time-contract basis.

Evidence on the degree of oil company vertical *dis*-integration from upstream-ownership of firms supplying service-inputs is shown in Table 3.4 on page 38. Three features in particular stand out: (a) the high overall degree of vertical disintegration – with over 91 per cent of inputs into offshore oil gathering being procured through the market; (b) the relatively high degree of vertical integration in two sectors-reservoir engineering and production engineering consultancy; and (c) the consistency of these patterns across the ten oil companies listed.[2] An obvious task is to explain this preference for a high degree of vertical disintegration in offshore oil gathering. The explanation given is shown to accord with the economics of governance structures as hypothesized in the transaction cost paradigm.

Fourthly, many of the services that are used in offshore oil gathering are specific to that industry but are transferable within it – either intra- or inter-service-base. Examples of services of this type include mud engineering and logging, well site geology, core analysis, electrical logging services, wireline services, workover services, reservoir engineering and production engineering.[3] Geophysical and geological services, while not entirely specific to the oil industry, do require a large industry-specific body of knowledge. Many types of equipment are also specific to – but mobile within – the oil industry: drill rods, downhole tools and many other types of tools are examples. But some structures, once installed, have zero (or scrap) value in transfer e.g. the platforms themselves, downhole casings, topside modules and various other structures. We have assessed whether these asset specificity features line up with the organizational-arrangements that are predicted by the transaction cost paradigm.

Fifth, many inputs into offshore oil fathering are idiosyncratic i.e. non-standardized and complex. An idiosyncratic good is multi-attribute and probably variable in these attributes. A production platform is an example as there are many design possibilities and no two are identical; also many service inputs are idiosyncratic as the skill level and experience of personnel are variable, different technologies or techniques can be used and the intensity of the work effort may vary.

Sixth, close proximity of suppliers' facilities to oil company production-bases is considered by the oil companies to be essential in many cases. Examples are either operational in character (drilling services, mud supply, wireline services, and workover services), or are closely connected with data-collection (well-site geology, drilling control, mud logging, electrical logging and well testing).[4]

The juxtaposition of close proximity and vertical *dis*integration is, in the view of the transaction cost paradigm, somewhat surprising and needs to be explained. Clearly, site specificity is not sufficient to induce vertical integration.

Finally, in the many subsectors of offshore oil gathering, the number of suppliers varies from just a few to very many.[5] In the technological core of the industry, however, just a few suppliers dominate many markets.[6] In fact, the oil companies tend to trade with the same few multinational offshore oil supply firms in many separate locations. But fewness of numbers can lead to small numbers bargaining problems with the allocation of rents between transactors being indeterminate.[7] How the oil companies cope with this potential for rent appropriation is most interesting: they have done so by choosing a market-arrangement – the invited tender-bid auction – which induces competition between potential suppliers (discussed in Chapters 7–10).

Indeed, several interesting organizational features are found in the offshore oil-gathering business. These are: (a) the prevalence of multinational corporations at the technological core of the industry; (b) procurement by invited tender-bid auction; (c) surveillance of potential bidders by oil companies; (d) limited use of processes of market search for 'best prices'; (e) quasi-vertical integration; and (f) tapered integration. We have seen whether the transaction cost paradigm can explain these organizational features.

Some theory

The transaction cost paradigm, originating in the seminal work of Coase (1937), is concerned with choice between comparative organizational arrangements. Coase's insight was that cost-economizing motivates the choice of organizational arrangements. Distinct costs – communication, or, more generally, transaction costs, are incurred in running organizations – in particular the costs of price-discovery and price-enforcement. Two separate versions of the transaction cost paradigm have been developed – the 'measurement cost' and the 'rent appropriation' and both are needed to explain the organizational arrangements found in offshore oil gathering.

The *measurement cost* version emphasizes the costs of measuring or valuing the component parts of a product that is to be exchanged, or, to use McManus's (1975) terminology, 'enforcing' the terms of a contract. Many goods or services, even when standardized, are not entirely identical and transactors are aware that they can appropriate more value from a transaction by incurring measurement costs. For example, buyers will sort in a barrel of oranges to find the highest quality. Sellers too have incentives to incur sorting costs if they can sell the higher quality oranges at a premium great enough to cover the sorting costs (this example is due to Barzel 1982). Measurement cost economizing can explain the existence of trade-marking and product warranties as these have the effect of reducing measurement costs and increasing the attractiveness of purchases.[8]

Casson (1982a), quite independently, saw that the desire to reduce measurement costs (or 'monitoring' costs in his terminology) helps to explain the existence of multinational service companies such as hotel chains. In this view the brand-name of an international hotel chain has a measurement cost advantage over local hotels. Provided that the customers themselves are internationally mobile, repetition of trades at one location gives the brand-name company a measurement cost advantage over local-based rivals.

In Williamson's 'heuristic' *rent appropriation* model of comparative governance (1985, pp. 90–5) it is the degree of asset specificity that explains the choice of organizational arrangements.[9] In the most extreme case, a specific asset is committed to just one transaction, or, with relational contracting, one sequence of transactions. Such an asset has zero (or scrap) value transfer earnings; the degree of asset specificity declines as trading opportunities to earn positive transfer earnings increase.

Williamson's transaction cost model rests on two main propositions: (a) the high powered incentives of markets lead to greater cost efficiency than do internal cost control regimes so there is a presumption that, but for transaction costs, market exchange has a cost advantage; but, (b) the cost of using markets rises relative to internal governance as asset specificity increases. This follows because an opportunistic trading partner may attempt to appropriate the rent earned by a specific asset – so expensive safeguards are needed (e.g. as embodied in legal contracts, or a productive asset may be designed in some way so as to reduce its specificity). It is asset specificity which is at the root of the small numbers bargaining problem: transfer prices may become irrelevant in the determination of prices. The same may also be said of small numbers bargaining due to high concentration ratios where prices are determined strategically rather than by the 'automatic' forces of competitive markets.[10]

Internationalization

The dominant theory of the multinational corporation derives from the rent appropriation version of the transaction cost paradigm: market failures mitigate in favour of the internalization of markets. Buckley and Casson (1976) originated this well known view and Rugman (1981 and 1982) formalized it as a 'general' theory of the multinational corporation.

However, just as rent appropriation does not constitute the whole of the transaction cost paradigm, rent appropriation fails as a complete theory of the multinational corporation. Measurement cost economizing is needed to explain the existence of some multinational corporations. As already noted, Casson (1982a) explicitly admitted measurement costs to the theory of the multinational corporation. By now, measurement costs have been applied to explain the internationalization of several industries in what are known as 'follow-the-customer' models.

In fact, the explanation of the internationalized component of the offshore oil supply industry (mainly American multinational corporations such as Baker International, Combustion Engineering, Dresser Industries, Halliburton and Santa Fe) requires the utilization of both versions of the transaction cost paradigm. Market failure, due to fears of rent appropriation (including external diseconomies emanating from an incompetent licenser), partly explains why the American multinationals prefer not to licence their technology to host country companies. It is also true that in some oil service-bases, at least in the early days, indigenous companies with the requisite skills simply did not exist.[11]

However, the novel insight developed in Chapter 5 stresses motives of measurement cost economizing: the multinational offshore service companies came into existence – say at the Scottish offshore service-base in Aberdeen – in order to enhance the efficacy of arm's length markets not, as the rent appropriation version asserts, to internalize them. What, in fact, is observed in a service-base is not an absence of markets – with production being organized in a few giant vertically integrated oil companies, rather, highly active arm's length markets are found with vertical *dis*integration predominating.

The existence of active markets between two sets of multinational corporations derives from the motive of measurement cost economizing. The leading offshore oil supply firms, through repeated trades with oil companies at other locations (initially in their home country, the USA) have created favourable reputations for themselves – a 'brand image' similar in kind to that of the international hotels. Note too that in both the offshore oil service and international hotel businesses the customers are internationally mobile and can be expected to be measurement cost economizers. Moreover, it was argued at length that the question of measurement cost economizing can be taken a stage further by considering the question of which types of arm's length market-arrangement best serves to minimize measurement costs.

Thus, when a new service-base is established, the oil companies know from prior successful repetition of trades that they can rely upon the multinational service companies for high-quality intermediate inputs into oil gathering. The multinational service companies, therefore, have a measurement cost advantage over potential host country rivals. But, measurement costs are not the only barrier to entry faced by indigenous enterprises: the established multinationals often have an absolute advantage over potential rivals in their knowledge of oil industry technology, sources of skilled labour and of how the relevant markets operate. Indeed, Demsetz (1982) is of the opinion that knowledge monopolies are the chief barrier to entry and we may add measurement costs advantages as one such knowledge monopoly.

The invited tender-bid auction

In the stylized facts listed above, asset specificity was listed as a feature of the oil-gathering industry. Asset specificity may be dealt with through internalization of the market – the 'classic' response according to the transaction cost paradigm – but its effects may also be coped with through selection of a suitable variety of market arrangement. Joskow (1987) has described the use of long term contracts as a means of dissipating rent appropriation problems. Perhaps surprisingly, the oil companies cope by using spot market contracting – by means of a competitive auction – to determine terms and conditions for time-related service-contracts.

It is particularly interesting that *market* organizational arrangements can be adapted to cope with potential rent appropriation. Oligopoly theory has been preoccupied with the determination of posted-prices.

This is true of conjectural-pricing and price-leadership models as well as many game-theoretic models. In such imperfect markets strategic attempts at rent appropriation or appropriation of consumers' surpluses is entirely conceivable. Demsetz (1968a), however, suggested a highly inventive scheme to introduce competitive price-bidding into a situation of small numbers bargaining. Potential suppliers should be required to compete through a procurement auction for the right to supply. Such a system benefits the purchaser by affecting a carryover of pre-contract award price-competition into the contract execution period.[12] It has been argued here that the economics of the invited tender bid auction used by oil companies squares with this insight.

This market-arrangement is a variety of first-price sealed bid procurement auction that, but for the fact that bidders are individually *invited* to bid, is similar to contracting processes common in the construction industry. It was also argued (in Chapter 9) that the 'invited' component is an element deriving from the peculiar internationalization of the offshore oil gathering business.

In fact, the rent appropriation characteristics of different types of auction markets are not identical – a matter that has not yet been investigated in great detail in the transaction cost literature. In this literature, rent appropriation occurs primarily in the context of relational contracting, where transactors enter into repeated transactions. The auction is most often associated with classical contracting, where a transaction between two parties is on a spot market and is not repeated (e.g. the auction of an old master or an old chair). Demsetz's suggestion to use the auction in the relational context is, therefore, somewhat unusual. In practice though auctions are used by transactors to perform repeated exchanges: for instance when fish dealers daily buy fish from the same group of fishermen, or oil companies procure services from the same set of contractors.

In most types of auction there is one seller (or one buyer in a procurement auction) and only a few buyers (sellers), so perfect competition does not exist – and the latter is indeed the case in offshore oil gathering given its asset specificity and market concentration features. Indeed, in a monopoly-monopsony or oligopsony situation the price-outcome is indeterminate. However, by committing itself to the rules of an auction the seller can induce the buyers to act competitively: that is, bidding up to their individual private valuations is the only means of obtaining the item sold. The rules of the auction, therefore, induce price competition.

Surveillance   Surveillance is not so much an organizational-arrangement but is an adjunct to the invited tender-bid auction. It increases the latter's efficacy by effecting measurement cost economizing. An oil company faces the problem of which firms to invite to bid from the set of potential suppliers located in a service-base. Most often it will not invite all potential suppliers to bid because this would be too expensive: in fact there will be an optimal number of bidders. An oil company will have knowledge of individual suppliers based upon previous experience of working with them. But this information will become dated, so the oil companies also collect files of information on individual supply firm capabilities – from newspaper reports, trade conferences, trade fairs and trade magazines. The cost of this information is a measurement cost of using the market. Optimal expenditure on surveillance occurs when its marginal cost equals the marginal expected benefit derived from identifying lower cost suppliers.

Search-shopping   Surveillance is not the same thing as the better known concept of search-shopping. In the latter case, a transactor is assumed to know the probability distribution of prices – and these prices are always posted prices. Neither of these two assumptions are true in the case of surveillance as prices are set sequentially by auction and, because they do not yet exist, their probability distribution cannot be known. A similarity in the concepts is that expenditures are incurred on obtaining information prior to purchases being made. The oil companies do practice a small amount of search-shopping type behaviour – mainly for inexpensive items for which it is not worth incurring the cost of running an auction.

An over-riding asset specificity problem

Compare now the case of an oil company wanting to obtain the separate intermediate services inputs of an oil production platform and of an offshore drilling rig. Either could be vertically integrated or acquired through a market. So a decision has to be made between vertical integration and market procurement. Following the rent appropriation version of the transaction cost paradigm, it is predicted that if asset specificity features predominate the oil company will choose vertical integration.

In fact, oil companies chose to own oil production platforms but they usually do *not* own drilling rigs. These comparative organizational-arrangements are consistent with the transaction cost paradigm because asset specificity is high in the case of a platform but much lower in the case of a rig. The latter is not site-specific and, at contract renewal, its services can be contracted to another user. Moreover, it appears that the market for drilling rigs is competitive given the large number of rig companies working in the UK continental shelf.[13] The market for rigs in a given oil province may also be described as being 'contestable' as rigs can quite inexpensively be transferred between provinces.

A production platform, in contrast, is a highly specific asset: both of site and of physical capital. An arm's length market would surely suffer from small number bargaining problems. Neither an independent platform-owner – should one exist – nor the oil company which hired platform services (but retained ownership-rights to the oil through the license agreement) could be satisfied with a market-arrangement. Both the 'upstream' platform-owner and the 'downstream' oil company would be aware that the other party could act opportunistically at contract renewal. One possible scenario is that a geographically diversified oil company, with many of its own sources of crude oil (as well as the markets for crude oil), would have the greater potentiality for opportunism as it could hold out longer in a bargaining dispute. Thus, with obvious risks of rent appropriation, it would be unlikely that investment in platforms would be forthcoming, much less optimal, and oil companies would have to invest in their own platforms.

Related to the question of platform-ownership is the concept *quasi-vertical integration*. This is understood to be the ownership by a firm located at one stage of a vertical production chain of some, but not all, inputs used at another stage of that chain. Thus a downstream firm may provide certain inputs – such as asset specific capital equipment – to an upstream supplier of an intermediate input. Monteverde and Teece (1982) pointed out that quasi-vertical integration will be prevalent when bargaining power between vertically linked, but independent, companies is asymmetric.

Several examples of quasi-vertical integration were found between the oil companies and their suppliers. The oil companies often provide contractors working on offshore platforms with drilling equipment, lifting gear, kitchens and wireline and logging equipment. The appropriable quasi-rents hypothesis is a good explanation of why this should be so. For example, if a crane operating company had also to provide the lifting equipment it might fear that the quasi-rent would be appropriated: the specialized offshore lifting gear perhaps having no readily found alternative use in the locality. With a possible threat of under-investment the solution is for the oil company to own the capital assets (the cranes) and for the crane-operating companies to supply the specialized personnel.

Tapered integration   In several sub-sectors of the offshore oil supply industry the oil companies combine 'inhouse' production with procurement from arm's length suppliers. This is tapered integration following Porter's (1980) definition. One reason for tapered integration relates to the economics of the multi-plant firm (Hirshleifer 1956): inhouse marginal cost is less than market price for only a fraction of the firm's requirements. However, it is doubtful that this is the main reason for tapered integration by oil companies in two important consultancy subsectors – reservoir engineering and production engineering. Information gathered in these activities may be very valuable to rival suppliers and is best protected through vertical integration.

There are other examples of tapered integration by the oil companies, in particular, in the sub-sectors drilling services, drilling control and mud logging services and workover services. Secrecy here is not so much of a problem (but it can be) and an oil company maintains a small inhouse production capability so as to facilitate its ability to direct and to cooperate with contractors.

Product idiosyncrasy and choice of organizational-arrangements

In his influential book of 1985 Williamson does not stress differences between product idiosyncrasy and asset specificity as separate determinants in the choice of organizational-arrangements. The effect on organizational-arrangements of asset specificity and product complexity are treated as being indistinguishable.[14] In a similar vein, Joskow (1988, p. 101) posits a direct association between product complexity and the cost of drawing up contracts – implying that increasing product complexity, like asset specificity, mitigates in favour of vertical integration. But what is found in the oil gathering business is an association of product complexity and vertical disintegration. Why should this be so?

It is not always the true that asset specificity and product idiosyncrasy are closely related. It is quite easy to find idiosyncratic goods being produced by standardized productive assets and standardized goods by specialized productive assets. There are three types of asset specificity: site, physical asset, and human capital.[15] Quite obviously there is no reason to suppose that a specific site must always be used to produce an idiosyncratic good. For example, coal, bauxite or copper concentrates may be produced from specific sites for the needs of an electric utility, an aluminium smelter and a copper smelter respectively, but these intermediate inputs need not be idiosyncratic, indeed, they can be traded as standardized commodities. A specific physical asset such as a carbody press may also produce standardized outputs (thousands of identical car bodies), and specific human capital may also produce a standardized output, for example, a heart surgeon fitting heart pacemakers.

Consider the case where asset specificity is high and idiosyncrasy varies from low to high. Should equal propensities for vertical integration be expected even as product idiosyncrasy varies? It is hypothesized that, for a given high level of asset specificity (and given scale economy characteristic), the market solution will be more frequently chosen as product idiosyncrasy increases. This is because increasing product idiosyncrasy has the effect of raising the cost of vertical integration compared with the use of the market – i.e. the reverse of the Williamson-Joskow argument. This relative cost increase may occur in both 'traditional' production costs and in transaction costs.

An advantage of standardization is that production-runs may be relatively long so economies of scale may be achieved. By contrast, idiosyncratic goods tend to have shorter production runs because of the fragmentation of demand. As mentioned earlier, oil companies are reluctant to purchase intermediate services from one another because valuable geologic information could be let out. This can be to the advantage of the oil company gaining the information as it may be able to place better informed bids when bidding for licenses on adjacent leaseblocks. Indeed, Mead (1986) has shown that superior information is helpful in winning licenses. However, an independent firm may aggregate demand for idiosyncratic products and still achieve economies of scale. So, for example, oil companies usually hire the services of paleontologists from independent suppliers, rather than produce the service inhouse. The geology-service company, in turn aggregates the market demand of several oil companies in a service-base.

Long production runs, or, rather the sales generated therefrom, may also serve efficiently to amortize the extra sunk costs incurred in organizing the production of idiosyncratic goods: instead of one good of a standard design, several different, though similar, goods have to be produced, and this may absorb managerial capacity. Also, when a good is multi-attribute and the attribute set is varied frequently, expense will be incurred in doing so. Product redesign and re-tooling costs are not necessarily trivial matters. Hence, it is predicted, given that it would be difficult to sell surplus output to other oil companies, idiosyncratic products are more likely to be procured through the market.

The argument that product idiosyncrasy has a bearing on the choice between the market and vertical integration is well explained using Williamson's 'heuristic model of comparative governance'. In Figure 12.1 production costs is a function of asset specificity (K). The ΔC function shows the comparative pecuniary advantage of the market over vertical integration as a negative function of K. We retain the argument that the relative production cost advantage of the market due to economies of scale is greatest when asset specificity is low. The ΔG function shows the relative transaction cost advantage of the market declining as K increases. In Figure 12.1 the overall relative advantage of 'the market' is given by the sum of the two cost advantages ($\Delta C + \Delta G$), and the switch-over point from using the market to vertical integration occurs at $\hat{K}$.

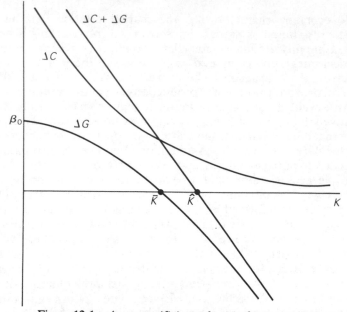

Figure 12.1   *Asset specificity and vertical integration*
Source: Williamson, 1985, Figure 4.2, p. 93.

Now, it is argued that the more idiosyncratic is an intermediate good or service the greater will be the propensity to use the market. This is easily shown in Figure 12.1. First, when a good is idiosyncratic and produced under conditions of economies of scale, the relative production cost advantage of market aggregation by an independent supply firm is increased: the ΔC function is shifted to the right as idiosyncrasy increases. Secondly, the unit transaction cost of organizing the 'inhouse' production of idiosyncratic goods is relatively high: the ΔG function is also shifted to the right as idiosyncrasy increases. As a result, the switch-over $\hat{K}$ becomes higher as idiosyncrasy rises, which implies that product idiosyncrasy favours market procurement.

This is not to argue that we expect to find firms producing inhouse only standardized products while procuring through the market idiosyncratic goods. That would be very strange. First, as just demonstrated, the effect of idiosyncrasy on market procurement operates only at the margin.

Secondly, new products, whose processes of production outside firms are unfamiliar, are likely to be produced inhouse. This is the conclusion drawn by Langlois and Robertson (1989) from their study of the American automobile industry. Thus, to this point it has been (implicitly) assumed that outside suppliers are familiar with the production processes of idiosyncratic products. But, change this assumption, and the bias turns back in favour of vertical integration. Thus, we recognize that familiarity with production processes, as well as the nature of an intermediate product, is relevant to the vertical integration decision. We could characterize 'familiarity with process' as 'dynamic idiosyncrasy'. Langlois (1988) considers relationships between economic change and vertical integration and concludes that asset specificity is but one of several determinants of the degree of vertical integration. In support of this, Armour and Teece (1980) find that the extent of vertical integration relates directly to the scale of a company's research and development effort – R&D effort here acting as an index of a company's dynamism. Moreover, Demsetz (1988) argued that it is often wrong to assume that production costs are identical between firms: 'the production costs of other firms might simply be too high' (p. 147). Indeed, Demsetz is critical of much of the transaction cost literature for assuming, usually implicitly, that firms have identical knowledge of production processes. He argues that it is through this assumption that the choice of organizational arrangement is reduced to one of comparative transaction costs. But, as a matter of fact, knowledge of production processes is not evenly distributed – a view which entirely concurs with his earlier view (Demsetz, 1982) that knowledge monopolies are the major barrier to entry.

Thirdly, suppliers will drive for the standardization of idiosyncratic goods in order to reap any scale economy and sales-amortization benefits that may exist. So idiosyncratic products are apt to go through a process of standardization.

Auctions and product idiosyncrasy

But, when products are idiosyncratic, why is the auction market preferable to either posted-pricing or pricing on a commodity exchange? One reason was mentioned earlier: auctions can defuse the rent appropriation properties inherent in imperfect markets. Secondly, when a product is traded infrequently transactors have no ready reference price with which to gauge the correct price on the next trade. Perhaps the product is so idiosyncratic that no previous trade of the product has ever occurred (for example, when a newly designed oil platform or rig is sold).

Thirdly, there is a cost associated with affixing prices to the quantities to be exchanged: the services of cost accountants, quantity surveyors and marketing specialists have to be employed. Call this a 'price-definition cost'. Posted-pricing of all combinations of a multi-attribute good prior to a buyer stating its requirements – which is normal for a

standardized good like washing powder, chocolate bars and TV sets –
could become very expensive. Better then to wait for the buyer to define
what is wanted and, in the oil-gathering business, state a single price at
the auction. Buyers can also expect to gain by using the auction method
rather than shopping (i.e. comparing posted-prices) because part of the
cost of price-setting will probably be incident upon them.

The auction has another advantage in the context of the oil-gathering
business. An offshore leaseblock concession is often leased to several
concessionaires. This helps to diversify risk and so is beneficial to the
industry. One of the joint concessionaires becomes the lead company
taking over the whole business of organizing oil exploration and,
subsequently, development and production on the leaseblock. Problems might arise if the lead company were vertically integrated because
the joint concessionaires would find it difficult to verify costs. An
advantage of using markets, in this case the auction, is that separate
input prices are verifiable.[16]

Verification also gives the auction a transaction cost advantage over
negotiation-haggling organizational-forms. These latter generally pre-
clude verification of the competitiveness of prices paid and so give
procurement personnel scope to accept bribes (Frihagen 1983).

Conclusions

This monograph has attempted to explain the main organizational-
arrangements found in the offshore oil-gathering industry using the
economic theories of the transaction cost paradigm. Its findings may
also be regarded as a case study test of that paradigm. It turned out that
several organizational features were indeed aligned with predictions
derived from this body of theory. These were: (a) that high levels of
asset specificity were associated with vertical integration and quasi-
vertical integration; (b) that a suitable market-arrangement – the
invited tender-bid auction – was selected by the oil companies on the
basis of both its rent-appropriation and measurement cost economizing
properties and that its use was predictably accompanied by investment
by the oil companies in market surveillance; (c) that measurement cost
economizing is important in the internationalization of the offshore oil
gathering industry – explanations based only on rent appropriation
economizing would be incomplete; (d) that idiosyncrasy-complexity –
either of product or process can play an independent explanatory role
in the choice of organizational-arrangements; and (e) the auction is a
favourable market-device for exchanging idiosyncratic products.

Notes

1 In the case of the Brent field on the UK continental shelf five separate companies were contracted by the operator (Shell) to design topside structures and twenty-two different fabricating companies were also used. Another sixty companies were contracted to make the platform operational: e.g. fitting of many types of electronic devices, generators, pumps, valves, lifting gear.

2 Less systematic information suggests that these features are typical in other offshore supply-bases.

3 Descriptions of the details of the myriad technical inputs used in offshore oil gathering can be found in glossaries published by the oil companies e.g. Phillips Petroleum, *Glossary*, 1980.

4 It was not necessary that firms engaged in data analysis, tools manufacture or structures construction be in close proximity to the oil company purchasers.

5 For example, in Scotland in the mid-1980s there were only four suppliers of seismic equipment used in exploration, five companies specializing in installation of subsea structures and five well completion contractors. However, in certain other subsectors much larger numbers of suppliers compete: e.g. suppliers of valves and fittings (60), rig equipment suppliers (58) and diving equipment suppliers (49) (*Noroil Contacts*, Summer 1984).

6 World market four-firm concentration ratios are often high: drill bits 93 per cent; pressure pumps 92 per cent; wireline services 83 per cent; and drilling fluids 55 per cent. In the newer computer applications there are only a handful of suppliers: five companies in measurement while drilling and also in seismic services. Enhanced recovery and subsea well head production equipment manufacture are similarly dominated by just a few firms (UNCTAD 1982 and Standard and Poors 1986).

7 Williamson (1985) claims the same for situations of small numbers bargaining caused by asset specificity.

8 Both Barzel and Cheung (1983) also explain that when measurement costs are irreducibly high, vertical integration may be preferred to market procurement because inhouse production yields better knowledge of, and quality control over, a product.

9 The term 'rent appropriation' is, in fact, due to Klein, Crawford and Alchian 1978.

10 While high transaction costs favour vertical integration, in certain circumstances, economies of scale may mitigate in favour of market-exchange: the market aggregating the demands of many buyers so compensating, up to a point, for transactional inefficiency due to asset specificity.

11 For example see Special Committee (1976) for a description of the development of oil gathering in Latin America in the early years of this century.

12 Demsetz argued in connection with public utility regulation and implied that costs of running regulatory arrangements could be avoided by running a one-time procurement auction. Williamson (1976) and Goldberg (1977) pointed out that Demsetz had overlooked certain transaction costs, such as the cost of a post-contract disputes machinery, which could turn the argument back in favour of regulation. But that point need not detain us here.

13 In the northern North Sea 22 such companies were operating 72 drilling rigs in the mid-1980s (Scottish Petroleum Annual, 1987).

14 In the theoretical analysis of the determinants of vertical integration Williamson wrote 'as goods and services become very close to *unique* (K is high) . . . aggregation economies of outside supply can no longer be realized' (emphasis added, 1985, p. 92). Here 'K' is the degree of asset specificity. It is apparent that product uniqueness (or idiosyncrasy) and asset specificity are not distinguished as independent arguments.

15 Williamson (1983) points to a fourth type of specific asset: dedicated assets. These do not necessarily have low transfer earnings but have been committed to supplying the needs of a particular customer.

16 Cheung (1983) pointed out that vertical integration has the advantage for buyers of allowing them to observe only the price of the final good and avoiding having to know the prices of individual inputs. But, in the case under consideration, the very opposite is true: buyers (say of oil exploration services) need to have prices of each intermediate input verified so as to be sure that rent shifting has not occurred.

Bibliography

Adelman, M. A. (1955), 'Concepts and statistical measurement of vertical integration' (Princeton, NJ: National Bureau of Economic Research, Princeton University).

Adelman, M. A. (1972), *The World Oil Market* (Baltimore, Md: Resources for the Future).

Alchian, A. A. (1977), 'Electrical equipment collusion: why and how', in A. Alchian (ed.), *Economic Forces at Work* (Indianapolis: Liberty), pp. 259–72.

Alchian, A. A. and Demsetz, H. (1972), 'Production, information costs and economic organization', *American Economic Review*, vol. 62, pp. 777–95.

Alchian, A. A. and Woodward, S. (1988), 'The firm is dead; long live the firm, a review of Oliver E. Williamson's *The Economic Institutions of Capitalism*', *Journal of Economic Literature*, vol. XXVI, March, pp. 65–79.

Alleyne, D. H. N. (1980), 'State petroleum enterprise and the transfer of technology', in United Nations (1980), pp. 109–22.

Amihud, Y. (ed.) (1976), *Bidding and Auctioning for Procurement and Allocation* (New York: New York University Press).

Anderson, E. and Schmittlein, D. (1984), 'Integration of the sales force: an empirical examination', *Rand Journal of Economics*, vol. 15, pp. 385–95.

Anderson, M. H. (1984), *Madison Avenue in Asia* (New Jersey: Associated University Press).

Anez, C. M. (1978), 'International transfer of technology for oil and gas exploration with special reference to the Venezuelan oil industry' (PhD, University of Sussex).

Armour, H. O. and Teece, D. J. (1980), 'Vertical integration and technological innovation', *Review of Economics and Statistics*, vol. LXII, pp. 470–4.

Bain, J. S. (1968), *Industrial Organization*, 2nd edn (New York: Wiley).

Bain, J. S. (1970), 'The comparative stability of market structures', in J. Markham and G. F. Papanek, *Industrial Organization and Economic Development: Essays in Honor of Professor Edward S. Mason* (New York: Houghton Mifflin).

Ball, C. and Tschoegl. A. (1982), 'The decision to establish a foreign bank branch or subsidiary: an application of binary classification procedures', *Journal of Financial and Quantitative Analysis*, September, pp. 411–24.

Barnes, I. R. (1955), 'Comment', *National Bureau of Economic Research* (Princeton, NJ: Princeton University).

Barnet, R. J. and Muller, R. E. (1974), *Global Reach: The Power of the Multinational Corporation* (New York: Simon and Schuster).

Barzel, Y. (1982), 'Measurement costs and the organization of markets', *Journal of Law and Economics*, vol. 25(1), April, pp. 27–48.

Blois, J. (1972), 'Vertical quasi-integration', *Journal of Industrial Economics*, vol. 4, pp. 253–72.

Boddewyn, J. J., Halbrich, M. B. and Perry, A. C. (1986), 'Service multinationals: conceptualization, measurement and theory', *Journal of International Business Studies*, Fall, pp. 41–57.

Bonney, N. (1986), 'Local economic development: perspectives from Scotland's northeast', Paper presented to the Regional Studies Association (Scottish branch), Aberdeen University.

Brimmer, A. and Dahl, F. (1975), 'Growth of American international banking: implications for public policy', *Journal of Finance*, vol. 30, May, pp. 341–63.

Broemser, G. M. (1968), 'Competitive bidding in the construction industry', PhD dissertation, Stanford University, California.

Buckley, P. and Casson, M. (1976), *The Future of the Multinational Enterprise* (London: Macmillan).

Cameron, P. (1986), *The Oil Supplies Industry* (London: Financial Times Business Information Ltd).

Casson, M. C. (1981), 'Forword', in Rugman (1981).

Casson, M. C. (1982a), 'Transaction costs and the theory of the multinational enterprise', in A. M. Rugman (ed.), *New Theories of the Multinational Enterprise* (New York: St Martins Press), pp. 24–43.

Casson, M. C. (1982b), *The Entrepreneur* (Totowa, NJ: Barnes and Noble Books).

Casson, M. C. (1986), *Multinationals and World Trade: Vertical Integration and the Division of Labour in World Industries* (London: Allen & Unwin).

Casson, M. C. (1987), *The Firm and the Market* (Oxford: Basil Blackwell).

Caves, R. E. (1971), 'International corporations: the industrial economics of foreign investment', *Economica*, vol. 38, February, pp. 1–27.

Caves, R. E. (1974), 'Causes of direct investment: foreign firms' shares in Canadian and United Kingdom manufacturing industries', *Review of Economic Statistics*, vol. 56, August, pp. 279–93.

Caves, R. E. (1982), *Multinational Enterprise and Economic Analysis* (Cambridge: Cambridge University Press).

Cheung, S. N. S. (1983), 'The contractual nature of the firm', *Journal of Law and Economics*, vol. XXVI, April, pp. 1–21.

Chevalier, J.-M. (1987), 'Technology renting or transfer of technology: issues and options for the developing countries', in Khan (1987).

Clark, R. and McGuinness, A. (1987), *The Economics of the Firm* (Oxford: Basil Blackwell).

Coase, R. H. (1937), 'The nature of the firm', *Economica*, N.S., vol. 4, pp. 386–405.

Cohen, K. J., Maier, S. F., Schwartz, R. A., and Whitcombe, D. K. (1986), *The Microstructure of Securities Markets* (Englewood Cliffs, NJ: Prentice Hall).

Cook, L. and Surrey, J. (1983), *Government Policy for the Offshore Supplies Industry: Britain Compared with Norway and France*, SPRU Occasional Paper 21.

Cusumano, M. (1985), *The Japanese Automobile Industry* (Cambridge, MA: Harvard University Press).

Dabinovic, T. E. J. P. (1987), 'Petroleum service contracts in Argentina, Brazil and Colombia: issues arising from their legal nature', *Journal of Energy and Natural Resources Law*, vol. 5(1), pp. 15–30.

Densetz, H. (1968a), 'Why regulate utilities?', *Journal of Law and Economics*, vol. 7(1), April, pp. 55–66.

Demsetz, H. (1968b), 'The cost of transacting', *Quarterly Journal of Economics*, vol. 82, February, pp. 33–53.

Demsetz, H. (1982), 'Barriers to entry', *American Economic Review*, vol. 72(1), March, pp. 47–57.

Demsetz, H. (1988), 'The theory of the firm revisited', *Journal of Law, Economics, and Organization*, vol. 4(1), Spring, pp. 141–61.

Department of Commerce (1942), Bureau of the Census, *Census of Manufacturing*, vol. 1, Washington DC: US Government Printing Office.

Department of Commerce (1981), Bureau of the Census, *Census of Manufacturing*, vol. 1, Washington DC: US Government Printing Office.

Department of Commerce (1982), Bureau of the Census, *Census of Manufactures*.

Department of Commerce (1985), *A Competitive Assessment of the US Oil Field Equipment Industry* (Washington DC: International Trade Administration).

Doheny, E. L. (1921), 'Pioneering in Mexico', address before the American Petroleum Institute; in Special Committee (1976).

Dunning, J. H. (1973), 'The determinants of international production', *Oxford Economic Papers*, November, pp. 289–336.

Dunning, J. H. (1977), 'Trade, location of economic activity and the multinational enterprise: a search for an eclectic approach', in B. Ohlin, P. O. Hesselborn and P. M. Wijkman (eds), *The International Allocation of Economic Activity* (London: Macmillan).

Dunning, J. H. (1981), *International Production and the Multinational Enterprize* (London: Allen & Unwin).

Dunning, J. H. (1987), 'Multinational enterprises and the growth of services: some conceptual and theoretical issues', University of Reading, *Discussion Papers in International Investment and Business Studies*, No. 114, December.

Dunning, J. H. (1988), 'The eclectic paradigm of international production: a restatement and some possible extensions', *Journal of International Business Studies*, Spring, pp. 1–31.

Dunning, J. H. and Norman, G. (1987), 'The location of offices of international companies', *Environment and Planning A*, vol. 19, pp. 613–31.

Edwards, R. and Hallwood, C. P. (1980), 'The determination of optimum buffer stock intervention rules', *Quarterly Journaly of Economics*, vol. 94, February, pp. 151–66.

Engelbrecht-Wiggans, R. (1980), 'Auctions and bidding models: a survey', *Management Science*, vol. 26, no. 2, pp. 119–42.

Ferguson, J. M. (1974), *Advertising and Competition: Theory, Measurement, Fact* (Cambridge, MA: Ballinger).

Firn, J. R. (1975), 'External control and regional development: the case of West Central Scotland', *Environment and Planning*, vol. 8, pp. 685–705.

Forsyth, D. J. C. (1972), *US Investment in Scotland* (New York: Praeger).
Fraas, A. G. and Greer, D. F. (1977), 'Market structure and price collusion', *Journal of Industrial Economics*, vol. 26(1), pp. 21–44.
French, K. R. and McCormick, R. E. (1984), 'Sealed bids, sunk costs, and the process of competition', *Journal of Business*, vol. 57(4), pp. 417–41.
Fridley, D. and Christoffersen, G. (1987), 'Self-reliant petroleum development: the China model', in Khan (1987).
Friedman, L. (1956), 'A competitive bidding strategy', *Operations Research*, vol. 4, pp. 104–12.
Frihagen, A. (1983), *Offshore Tender Bidding* (Bergen, Oslo, Stavanger, Tromso: Universitetsforlaget).

Gallick, E. C. (1984), 'Exclusive dealing and vertical integration: the efficiency of contracts in the tuna industry', *Bureau of Economics Staff Report*, US Federal Trade Commission.
Gaskin, M. and MacKay, D. I. (1978), *The Economic Impact of North Sea Oil on Scotland* (London: HMSO).
Goldberg, L. and Saunders, A. (1980), 'The causes of US bank expansion overseas', *Journal of Money Credit and Banking*, November, pp. 630–43.
Goldberg, V. P. (1977), 'Competitive bidding and the production of pre-contract information', *Bell Journal of Economics*, vol. 8(1), Spring, pp. 250–61.
Goldberg, V. P. and Erickson, J. R. (1987), 'Quantity and price adjustment in long term contracts: a case study of petroleum coke', *Journal of Law and Economics*, vol. 30(2), October, pp. 369–98.
Grossman, S. J. and Hart, O. (1986), 'The costs and benefits of ownership: a theory of vertical integration', *Journal of Political Economy*, vol. 36.
Grubel, H. (1977), 'A theory of multinational banking', *Banca Nazionale del Lavoro, Quarterly Review*, no. 123, December, pp. 349–64.

Hallwood, C. P. (1986), *The Offshore Oil Supply Industry in Aberdeen: the Affiliates – their Characteristics and Importance*, North Sea Occasional Paper 23, Department of Political Economy, Aberdeen University.
Harris, A. H. *et al.* (1987), 'Incoming industry and structural change: oil and the Aberdeen economy', *Scottish Journal of Political Economy*, vol. 34(1), February, pp. 69–90.
Hart, O. (1988), 'Incomplete contracts and the theory of the firm', *Journal of Law, Economics, and Organization*, vol. 4.
Hennart, J. F. (1982), *A Theory of the Multinational Enterprise* (Ann Arbor: University of Michigan Press).
Hey, J. D. (1979), *Uncertainty in Microeconomics* (New York: New York University Press).
Hirshleifer, J. (1956), 'On the economics of transfer pricing', *Journal of Business*, July.
Holt, A. (1979), 'Uncertainty and the bidding for incentive contracts', *American Economic Review*, vol. 69(4), September, pp. 697–705.
Hood, N. and Young, S. (1976), 'US investment in Scotland – aspects of the branch factory syndrome', *Scottish Journal of Political Economy*, vol. 23(3), pp. 276–94.

Horst, T. (1972a), 'Firm and industry determinants of the decision to invest abroad: an empirical study', *Review of Economics and Statistics*, vol. 54, August, pp. 258–66.

Horst, T. (1972b), 'The industrial composition of US exports and subsidiary sales to the Canadian market', *American Economic Review*, vol. 62, March, pp. 37–45.

Hymer, S. H. (1976), *The International Operations of National Firms: A Study of Direct Foreign Investment* (Cambridge, MA: MIT Press).

Industrial Marketing Research Association (1975), *Profit Opportunities Arising from North Sea Oil – Finding and Using the Facts*, Litchfield, Staffordshire.

International Management and Engineering Group (1972), *Study of the Potential Benefits to British Industry from Offshore Oil and Gas Developments* (London: HMSO).

Isaac, R. M. and Walker, J. M. (1985), 'Information and conspiracy in sealed bid auctions', *Journal of Economic Behavior and Organization*, vol. 6, pp. 139–59.

Jacoby, N. H. (1974), *Multinational Oil: A Study in Industrial Dynamics* (New York: Macmillan).

Johnson, H. G. (1970), 'The efficiency and welfare implications of the multinational enterprise', in C. P. Kindleberger, *The International Corporation: A Symposium* (Cambridge, MA: MIT Press).

Joskow, P. L. (1985), 'Vertical integration and long term contracts: the case of coal burning electric generating plants', *Journal of Law, Economics, and Organization*, vol. 1, pp. 33–80.

Joskow, P. L. (1987), 'Contracts duration and transaction specific investment: empirical evidence from the coal markets', *American Economic Review*, vol. 77.

Joskow, P. L. (1988), 'Asset specificity and the structure of vertical relationships: empirical evidence', *Journal of Law, Economics, and Organization*, vol. 4(1), Spring, pp. 95–117.

Kaempfer, W. H. and Min, H. M. (1986), 'The role of oil in China's economic development, growth and internationalization', *Journal of Energy and Development*, vol. 11(1), pp. 13–26.

Kay, N. M. (1983), 'Optimal size of firm as a problem in transaction costs and property rights', *Journal of Economic Studies*, vol. 10(2), pp. 29–41.

Kemp, A. G. and Rose, D. (1982), 'The effects of taxation of petroleum exploration: a comparative study', *North Sea Study Occasional Paper*, No. 17, Department of Political Economy, University of Aberdeen.

Kemp, A. G. and Rose, D. (1985), 'Fiscal aspects of field abandonment in the UKCS', *North Sea Study Occasional Paper*, No. 22, Department of Political Economy, University of Aberdeen.

Khan, K. I. F. (ed.) (1987), *Petroleum Resources and Development: Economic, Legal and Policy Issues for Developing Countries* (London and New York: Belhaven Press).

Kindleberger, C. P. (1969), *American Business Abroad: Six Lectures on Direct Investment* (New Haven, Conn.: Yale University Press).

Klein, B. R., Crawford, R. A. and Alchian, A. A. (1978) 'Vertical integration, appropriable rents, and the competitive contracting process', *Journal of Law and Economics*, vol. 21, October, pp. 297–326.

Knickerbocker, F. T. (1973), *Oligopolistic Reaction and Multinational Enterprise* (Cambridge, MA: Harvard University Press).

Knight, F. H. (1957), *Risk, Uncertainty and Profit* (New York: Kelley & Millman).

Langlois, R. N. (1986), *Economics as a Process: Essays on the New Institutional Economics* (Cambridge: Cambridge University Press).

Langlois, R. N. (1988), 'Economic change and boundaries of the firm', *Journal of Institutional and Theoretical Economics*, vol. 4, pp. 635–57.

Langlois, R. N. and Robertson, P. L. (1989), 'Explaining vertical integration: lessons from the American automobile industry', *Journal of Economic History*, vol. XLIX(2), June, pp. 361–75.

Levitt, T. (1985), *The Marketing Imagination* (New York: Free Press).

Levy, D. T. (1985), 'The transaction cost approach to vertical integration: an empirical examination', *Review of Economics and Statistics*, vol. LXVII(3), pp. 438–45.

Loasby, B. J. (1986a), 'Organization, competition and growth of knowledge', in Langlois (1986).

Loasby, B. J. (1986b), 'Competition and imperfect knowledge: the contributions of G. B. Richardson', *Scottish Journal of Political Economy*, vol. 33(2), pp. 145–58.

McAfee, R. P. and McMillan, J. (1987), 'Auctions and bidding', *Journal of Economic Literature*, vol. XXV(2), pp. 699–738.

McDermott, P. (1979), 'Multinational manufacturing firms and regional development: external control in the Scottish electronics industry', *Scottish Journal of Political Economy*, vol. 26(3), pp. 287–306.

MacDonald, J. M. (1985), 'Market exchange or vertical integration: an empirical analysis', *Review of Economics and Statistics*, vol. LXVII(2), May, pp. 327–31.

McManus, J. C. (1972), 'The theory of the international firm', in G. Paquaet (ed.), *The Multinational Firm and the Nation State* (Toronto: Collier-Macmillan).

McManus, J. C. (1975), 'The cost of alternative economic organizations', *Canadian Journal of Economics*, vol. VIII, pp. 334–50,

Magee, S. (1976), 'Information and multinational corporations: an appropriability theory of direct foreign investment', in J. Bhagwati (ed.), *The International Economic Order* (Cambridge, MA: MIT Press).

Mancke, R. B. (1976), 'Competition in the oil industry', in Mitchell (1976).

March, J. G. and Simon, H. A. (1958), *Organizations* (New York: Wiley).

Maskin, E. and Riley, J. (1984), 'Optimal auctions with risk averse buyers', *Econometrica*, vol. 52(6), November, pp. 1473–518.

Mason, E. S. (1939), 'Prices and production policies of large-scale enterprise', *American Economic Review*, vol. XXXIX, Supplement, March, pp. 61–74.
Masten, S. (1984), 'The organization of production: evidence from the aerospace industry', *Journal of Law and Economics*, vol. 27, pp. 403–18.
Mead, D. E. (1978), 'The effect of vertical integration on risk in the petroleum industry', *Quarterly Review of Economics and Business*, vol. 18(1), pp. 83–90.
Mead, W. J. (1986), 'Competition in outer shelf oil and gas lease auctions: a statistical analysis', *Natural Resources Journal*, vol. 26, Winter, pp. 95–111.
Mikesell, R. F. (1984), *Petroleum Company Operations and Agreements in the Developing Countries* (Washington DC: Resources for the Future).
Milgrom, P. R. (1989), 'Auctions and bidding: a primer', *Journal of Economic Perspectives*, vol. 3(3), Summer, pp. 3–22.
Milgrom, P. R. and Weber, R. J. (1982), 'A theory of auctions and competitive bidding', *Econometrica*, vol. 50(5), September, pp. 1089–122.
Mitchell, E. J. (ed.) (1976), *Vertical Integration in the Oil Industry* (Washington DC: American Enterprise Institute).
Monteverde, K. and Teece, D. J. (1982), 'Appropriable rents and quasi-vertical integration', *Journal of Law and Economics*, vol. 25(2), October, pp. 321–8.
Mulhern, J. H. (1986), 'Complexity in long-term contracts: an analysis of natural gas contract provisos', *Journal of Law, Economics and Organization*, vol. 2.
Myerson, R. B. (1981), 'Optimal auction design', *Mathematical Operations Research*, vol. 6(1), February, pp. 58–73.

National Register Publishing Company (1987), *International Directory of Corporate Affiliations: 1987–88* (Wilmette, Il.: Macmillan Directory Division).
Nigh, D., Cho, K. R. and Krishnan, S. (1986), 'The role of location related factors in US banking involvement abroad: an empirical examination', *Journal of International Business Studies*, Fall, pp. 59–86.
Noroil Contacts (1984), Summer.

O'Driscoll, G. P. (1986), 'Competition as a process: a law and economics perspective', in Langlois (1986).
Offshore Supplies Office (1987), *Information Offshore*, Glasgow.
Ohmae, K. (1985), *Triad Power* (New York: Free Press).
Okun, A. M. (1981), *Prices and Quantities: A Macroeconomic Analysis* (Washington DC: Brookings Institute).
Oldham, G. *et al.* (1987), *Technology Transfer to the Chinese Offshore Oil Supply Industry*, Occasional Paper 27, Science Policy Research Unit, University of Sussex, England.
Ouchi, W. G. (1980), 'Markets, bureaucracies and clans', *Administrative Science Quarterly*, vol. 25, March, pp. 120–42.

Palay, T. (1984), 'Comparative institutional economics: the governance of rail freight contracting', *Journal of Legal Studies*, vol. 13, June, pp. 265–88.
Penrose, E. T. (1968), *The Large International Firm in Developing Countries: The International Petroleum Industry* (London: Allen & Unwin).

Penrose, E. T. (1971), *The Growth of the Firm: Middle East Oil and Other Essays* (London: Cass).
Perry, M. K. (1980), 'Forward integration by Alcoa: 1888–1930', *Journal of Industrial Economics*, vol. 29(3), pp. 37–53.
Phillips Petroleum (1980), *Glossary*, Phillips Petroleum Company.
Porter, M. (1980), *Competitive Strategy* (New York: Free Press).

Randall, L. (1987), *The Political Economy of Venezuelan Oil* (New York: Praeger).
Rees, G. L. (1972), *Britain's Commodity Markets* (London: Paul Elek Books).
Richardson, G. B. (1959), 'Equilibrium, expectation and information', *Economic Journal*, vol. 69(2), pp. 223–37.
Richardson, G. B. (1960), *Information and Investment* (Oxford: Oxford University Press).
Riley, J. G. and Samuelson, W. F. (1981), 'Optimal auctions', *American Economic Review*, vol. 71(3), June, pp. 381–92.
Robinson, M. C. (1985), 'Collusion and the choice of auction', *Rand Journal of Economics*, vol. 16(1), Spring, pp. 141–5.
Rugman, A. M. (1981), *Inside the Multinationals: the Economics of Internal Markets* (New York: Columbia University Press).
Rugman, A. M. (ed.) (1982), *New Theories of the Multinational Enterprise* (London: Croom Helm).
Rugman, A. M. (1985), 'Internalization is still a general theory of foreign direct investment', *Weltwirtschaftliches Archiv*.
Rugman, A. M. (1986), 'New theories of the multinational enterprise: an assessment of internalization theory', *Bulletin of Economic Research*, vol. 38(2), pp. 101–17.

Sabi, M. (1988), 'An application of the theory of foreign direct investment to multinational banking in LDCs', *Journal of International Business Studies*, Fall, pp. 433–47.
Schelling, T. C. (1956), 'An essay on bargaining', *American Economic Review*, vol. 46, June, pp. 281–306.
Schelling, T. C. (1960), *The Strategy of Conflict* (Cambridge, MA: Harvard University Press).
Scottish Petroleum Annual (1987), Aberdeen Petroleum Publishing Company.
Seidman, A. (1975), *Natural Resources and National Welfare: The Case of Copper* (New York: Praeger).
Sherif, S. (1980), 'Activities and capabilities of state petroleum enterprises', in United Nations (1980), pp. 48–58.
Shubick, M. (1970), 'On different methods for allocating resources', *Kyklos*, vol. 23, Fasc. 1, pp. 332–7.
Simon, H. A. (1957), *Models of Man* (New York: Wiley).
Smith, V. L. (1976), 'Bidding and auctioning institutions: experimental results', in Amihud (1976).
Smith, V. L., Williams, A. W., Bratton, W. K. and Vannoni, M. G. (1982), 'Competitive market institutions: double auctions versus sealed bid-offer auctions', *American Economic Review*, vol. 72(1), March, pp. 58–77.

Sofianos, G. (1988), 'A comparison of market making structures', Federal Reserve Bank of New York, *Research Paper*, No. 8821, September.

Special Committee Investigating Petroleum Resources (1976), *America's Petroleum Interests in Foreign Countries* (New York: Arno Press, the New York Times Company).

Standard and Poor's (1986), *Industry Surveys: Oil and Gas: Section II*, 20 March.

Stark, R. M. and Rothkopf, M. H. (1979), 'Competitive bidding: a comprehensive bibliography', *Operations Research*, vol. 27(4), March/April, pp. 364–90.

Stigler, G. J. (1951), 'The division of labour is limited by the extent of the market', *Journal of Political Economy*, vol. 59, pp. 185–93.

Stigler, G. J. (1961), 'The economics of information', *Journal of Political Economy*, vol. 69, pp. 213–25.

Stigler, G. J. (1964), 'A theory of oligopoly', *Journal of Political Economy*, vol. 72(1), pp. 44–61.

Stigler, G. J. (1968), *The Organization of Industry* (Illinois: Irwin).

Stuckley, J. (1983), *Vertical Integration and Joint Ventures in the Aluminum Industry* (Cambridge, MA: Harvard University Press).

Surrey, J. (1986), 'Oil and industrialization in Brazil', *European Network Energy Economics Research*, no. 2, pp. 77–83.

Surrey, J. (1987), 'Petroleum development in Brazil', *Energy Policy*, February, pp. 7–21.

Teece, D. J. (1976), *Vertical Integration and Divestiture in the US Oil Industry* (Stanford: Institute for Energy Studies, Stanford University).

Teece, D. J. (1982), 'Towards an economic theory of the multiproduct firm', *Journal of Economic Behavior and Organization*, vol. 3, March, pp. 39–64.

Teece, D. J. (1985), 'Multinational enterprise, internal governance, and industrial organization', *American Economic Review*, vol. 75, pp. 233–8.

Teece, D. J. (1986), 'Transaction cost economics and the multinational enterprise', *Journal of Economic Behavior and Organization*, vol. 7, pp. 21–45.

Terpstra, V and Chwo-Ming Yu (1988), 'Determinants of foreign investment of US advertising agencies', *Journal of International Business Studies*, Spring, pp. 33–46.

UNCTAD (1982), 'Conditions for accelerating the transfer of oil exploration technology to developing countries', in *Petroleum Exploration and Strategies in Developing Countries*, UK (Natural Resources Division).

United Nations Centre for Natural Resources, Energy and Transport (1980), *State Petroleum Enterprises in Developing Countries* (New York: Pergamon Press).

Uniworld Publishing Inc. (1984), *Directory of Foreign Firms in Foreign Countries*, 10th edn, New York.

Value Line (various), *Investment Report*.

Vernon, R. (1966), 'International investment and international trade in the product cycle', *Quarterly Journal of Economics*, vol. 30, May, pp. 190–207.

Vernon, R. (1971), *Sovereignty at Bay: the Multinational Spread of United States Enterprises* (New York: Basic Books).
Vernon, R. (1979), 'The product cycle hypothesis in a new environment', *Oxford Bulletin of Economics and Statistics*, vol. 41, November, pp. 255–67.
Vickrey, W. (1976), 'Auctions, markets and optimal allocation', in Amihud (1976).

Weinstein, A. K. (1977), 'Foreign investment by service firms: the case of the multinational advertising agencies', *Journal of International Business Studies*, Spring–Summer, pp. 83–93.
Williamson, O. E. (1971), 'The vertical integration of production: market failure considerations', *American Economic Review*, vol. 61, May, pp. 112–23.
Williamson, O. E. (1975), *Markets and Hierarchies: Analysis and Anti-Trust Implications* (New York: Free Press).
Williamson, O. E. (1976), 'Franchise bidding for natural monopolies – in general and with respect to CATV', *Bell Journal of Economics*, vol. 7(1), Spring, pp. 73–104.
Williamson, O. E. (1981), 'The modern corporation: origins, evolution, attributes', *Journal of Economic Literature*, vol. XIX, December, pp. 1537–68.
Williamson, O. E. (1983), 'Credible commitments: using hostages to support exchange', *American Economic Review*, vol. 73.
Williamson, O. E. (1985), *The Economic Institutions of Capitalism: Firms, Markets, Relational Contracting* (New York: The Free Press).
Williamson, O. E. (1988), 'The logic of economic organization', *Journal of Law, Economics, and Organization*, vol. 14(1), pp. 65–93.
Wall Street Journal (1978), 'McDermott, Brown and Root said by industry sources to "squeeze" competition', 15 December, p. 1.

Yamane, T. (1970), *Statistics an Introductory Analysis*, 2nd edn (New York: Harper & Row).

Index

Numbers in italics refer to figures in text